A Theology of Community Organizing

The rising importance of community organizing in the US and more recently in Britain has coincided with the developing significance of social movements and identity politics, debates about citizenship, social capital, civil society, and religion in the public sphere. At a time when participation in the formal political process and membership of faith groups have both declined dramatically, community organizing has provided a new opportunity for small community groups, marginalized urban communities, and people of faith to engage in effective political action through the development of inter-faith and cross-cultural coalitions of groups. In spite of this, little critical attention has been paid to community organizing.

This book places community organizing within debates about the role of religion in the public sphere and the rise of public theology in recent years. The book explores the history, methodology, and achievements of community organizing, engaging in a series of conversations with key community organizers in the US and Britain. This volume breaks new ground by beginning to articulate a cross-cultural and inter-faith 'Theology for Community Organizing' that arises from fresh readings of Liberation Theology.

Chris Shannahan is a Lecturer in Religion and Theology at the University of Manchester and was previously a Research Fellow in Urban Theology at the University of Birmingham and Director of the University's Urban Religion Community Education Programme. He worked as an inner city Methodist Minister for sixteen years. He is actively involved in a range of community development projects in Birmingham. He has spoken at conferences held by the Iona Community, the Progressive Christianity Network, the American Academy of Religion, the British Sociological Association and the Association of American Geographers. He recently launched a Metropolitan Religion Study group at the University of Birmingham aimed at graduates in the West Midlands and a community centred Urban Theology Forum. His first book, *Voices from the Borderland* (2010), provided a critical exploration of contemporary urban theologies and called for the development of a new inter-disciplinary and cross-cultural pattern of urban theology that is more attuned to the complex and interrelated fluid urban world of the twenty-first century.

Routledge Studies in Religion

1 **Judaism and Collective Life**
Self and Community in the
Religious Kibbutz
Aryei Fishman

2 **Foucault, Christianity and
Interfaith Dialogue**
Henrique Pinto

3 **Religious Conversion and Identity**
The Semiotic Analysis of Texts
Massimo Leone

4 **Language, Desire, and Theology**
A Genealogy of the Will to Speak
Noëlle Vahanian

5 **Metaphysics and Transcendence**
Arthur Gibson

6 **Sufism and Deconstruction**
A Comparative Study of Derrida
and Ibn 'Arabi
Ian Almond

7 **Christianity, Tolerance and
Pluralism**
A Theological Engagement with
Isaiah Berlin's Social Theory
Michael Jinkins

8 **Negative Theology and Modern
French Philosophy**
Arthur Bradley

9 **Law and Religion**
*Edited by Peter Radan, Denise
Meyerson and Rosalind F.
Atherton*

10 **Religion, Language, and Power**
*Edited by Nile Green and Mary
Searle-Chatterjee*

11 **Shared Idioms, Sacred Symbols,
and the Articulation of Identities
in South Asia**
*Edited by Kelly Pemberton &
Michael Nijhawan*

12 **Theology, Creation, and
Environmental Ethics**
From Creatio Ex Nihilo to Terra
Nullius
Whitney Bauman

13 **Material Religion and Popular
Culture**
E. Frances King

14 **Adam Smith as Theologian**
Edited by Paul Oslington

15 **The Entangled God**
Divine Relationality and Quantum
Physics
By Kirk Wegter-McNelly

16 **Aquinas and Radical Orthodoxy**
A Critical Inquiry
Paul J. DeHart

17 **Animal Ethics and Theology**
The Lens of the Good Samaritan
Daniel K. Miller

18 **The Origin of Heresy**
A History of Discourse in Second
Temple Judaism and Early
Christianity
Robert M. Royalty, Jr.

19 **Buddhism and Violence**
Militarism and Buddhism in
Modern Asia
*Edited by Vladimir Tikhonov and
Torkel Brekke*

20 **Popular Music in Evangelical Youth Culture**
Stella Sai-Chun Lau

21 **Theology and the Science of Moral Action**
Virtue Ethics, Exemplarity, and Cognitive Neuroscience
Edited by James A. Van Slyke, Gregory R. Peterson, Kevin S. Reimer, Michael L. Spezio and Warren S. Brown

22 **Abrogation in the Qur'an and Islamic Law**
By Louay Fatoohi

23 **A New Science of Religion**
Edited by Gregory W. Dawes and James Maclaurin

24 **Making Sense of the Secular**
Critical Perspectives from Europe to Asia
Edited by Ranjan Ghosh

25 **The Rise of Modern Jewish Politics**
Extraordinary Movement
C.S. Monaco

26 **Gender and Power in Contemporary Spirituality**
Ethnographic Approaches
Anna Fedele and Kim E. Knibbe

27 **Religions in Movement**
The Local and the Global in Contemporary Faith Traditions
Robert W. Hefner, John Hutchinson, Sara Mels and Christiane Timmerman

28 **William James's Hidden Religious Imagination**
A Universe of Relations
Jeremy Carrette

29 **Theology and the Arts**
Engaging Faith
Ruth Illman and W. Alan Smith

30 **Religion, Gender, and the Public Sphere**
Edited by Niamh Reilly and Stacey Scriver

31 **An Introduction to Jacob Boehme**
Four Centuries of Thought and Reception
Edited by Ariel Hessayon and Sarah Apetrei

32 **Globalization and Orthodox Christianity**
The Transformations of a Religious Tradition
Victor Roudometof

33 **Contemporary Jewish Writing**
Austria after Waldheim
Andrea Reiter

34 **Religious Ethics and Migration**
Doing Justice to Undocumented Workers
Ilsup Ahn

35 **A Theology of Community Organizing**
Power to the People
Chris Shannahan

A Theology of Community Organizing

Power to the People

By Chris Shannahan

Routledge
Taylor & Francis Group

LONDON AND NEW YORK

First published 2014 by Routledge

2 Park Square, Milton Park, Abingdon, Oxfordshire OX14 4RN
711 Third Avenue, New York, NY 10017

*Routledge is an imprint of the Taylor & Francis Group,
an informa business*

First issued in paperback 2018

Library of Congress Cataloging-in-Publication Data

Shannahan, Chris.
    A theology of community organizing : power to the people /
by Chris Shannahan. — 1 [edition].
        pages cm. — (Routledge studies in religion ; 35)
    Includes bibliographical references and index.
  1. Religion and sociology.   2. Communities—Religious aspects.
  3. Community organization.   4. Community power.   I. Title.
    BL60.S52845 2013
    201'.76—dc23
    2013023604

ISBN: 978-0-415-89093-9 (hbk)
ISBN: 978-1-138-54884-8 (pbk)

Typeset in Sabon
by Apex CoVantage, LLC

Contents

List of Figures   ix
Dedication   xi
Acknowledgements   xiii

Introduction   1

PART I
Experience

1 What Is Community Organizing?   9

2 Reweaving the Fabric of Society: Community Organizing in
   Britain   33

PART II
Analysis

3 Part of a 'New Politics'   63

4 Enrichment and Challenge: Lessons from Social Theory   86

PART III
Reflection

5 Finding the Faith to Organize   115

6 A Theology of Community Organizing: Becoming Yeast
   in the City   139

PART IV
Action

Conclusion   167

Notes   171
Bibliography   197
Index   207

Figures

1.1   The PICO Learning Cycle   21
2.1   The Values Base of Citizens UK   46
2.2   The Organizational Structure of Citizens UK   47
2.3   London Citizens' Main Campaigns, 1996–2010   49
2.4   London Citizens' Living Wage Actions, 2001–2010   52
3.1   Political Process Theory   70
3.2   The 'Life Cycle' of Social Movements   79
4.1   Lefebvre's Social Space Triad   87
6.1   Prioritizing Insignificance and Liberative Reversals   141
7.1   The Theology of Community Organizing Cycle   168

Dedication

This book is dedicated with love to my family—
To Mary, Bethany and Jonathan—
Only believe and anything is possible.
Walk through the open door and seize the day.

Acknowledgements

I am grateful to all of the people who have encouraged, advised and put up with me over the last three years as I have been writing this book. Without their help I would not have been able to complete the journey. In particular I want to thank my family—Mary, Bethany and Jonathan (and Scamp too)—for their constant support and love and for giving me the space to write. Moving further afield I would like to thank former colleagues in the Theology and Religion Department at the University of Birmingham for their advice and friends within the community organizing family in the United Kingdom for their encouragement long before this book even began to form itself as an idea. Lastly I am grateful to the editorial team at Routledge—in particular, Lauren Verity, Laura Stearns, Katie Laurentiev and Stacy Noto—for their guidance and encouragement as this book has taken shape. Without the support of you all, this book could not have been written. Thank you.

Introduction

The dawning of the twenty-first century was marked by three major cultural shifts. First, the fall of the Berlin Wall in 1989 and the ending of the Cold War stimulated a shift away from ideological politics and a political turn towards civil society, particularly in European liberal democracies. Second, in spite of the continued numerical decline of many religious institutions, faith groups in the United Kingdom and the United States assumed a renewed significance within social movement politics and were increasingly embraced as critical partners by government as a result of their ongoing grass-roots social capital. Third, the veracity of the secularization thesis that had its roots in the work of Max Weber assuming an almost unquestioned status, particularly in Western Europe, began to fray at the edges. Whereas the levels of regular attendance at worship and the membership of many formal religious institutions continued to decline, former advocates of the secularization thesis such as Peter Berger acknowledged the ongoing sociological significance of faith as a primary factor in civic engagement.[1] As the new millennium began, therefore, we witnessed the tentative emergence of a complex new social landscape characterized by a postsecular civil society politics on which the grass-roots social capital of faith groups (particularly in urban contexts) provided increasingly significant resources for activism in a plural public sphere.

Luke Bretherton suggests that 'we are currently going through a period of de-construction and re-construction in which perennial questions about the relationship between religious and political authority are being asked again'.[2] What role then might faith-based activism play in the superdiverse context of the twenty-first century? Is the role for faith groups that of consensual conduits of the common good, caring without critically questioning, or of agitating activists engaging in radical models of activism premised on an affirmation of the divine bias to the oppressed? An either-or answer to this provocative question would be misleadingly simplistic, for complex community relationships are not that straightforward. That said, the question remains a pertinent one. Bretherton suggests that on this new cultural landscape faith groups face three temptations in relation to their civic engagement. The first temptation is that of being co-opted by government. The second temptation is that of a communalism which can either pit different faith groups against each other as enemies to be 'defeated of defended from' or smooth away the distinctness of diverse religious traditions in the name of community cohesion. The third temptation is that of commodification. Religious faith is reduced to just another commodity that can be bought or sold within the marketplace of a consumerist society.[3] Writing of the political engagement of the Black Church in urban communities in the United Kingdom, Robert Beckford echoes Bretherton's point in sharp terms. Beckford argues that churches can turn away from political engagement because they have 'sold out' (to a consumerism driven faith), been 'bought out' (giving up on prophetic activism in exchange for grants to support their community development work) or 'scared out' to the suburbs as a result of their fear of political engagement.[4] How then can faith groups respond to this dilemma and on what values should their activism be based?

I will suggest throughout this book that a critical embrace of broad-based community organizing offers faith groups an answer to this question. On the uncertain cultural landscape I have sketched out, community organizing has made widespread advances in recent decades, not only in its North American heartland but also in Europe. It represents an effective expression of what we could call postsecular social movement politics. Community organizing has increasingly provided faith groups with an effective model of relational and networked grass-roots activism for a globalized age and a clear means of translating a theological commitment to the common good into action. It has made its way from Saul Alinsky's 'Back of the Yards' campaign in Chicago in 1938–1939 to the twenty-first-century White House of Barack Obama and from the backstreets of the East End of London in the 1990s to the social policy arena of 10 Downing Street and David Cameron's 'big society' agenda following the 2010 UK General Election. This book was born amidst the creative uncertainty that arose from these major cultural shifts and the challenge of faith-based political activism on such a landscape and will:

1. Explore the sociopolitical impact of broad based community organizing in the United States and the United Kingdom
2. Analyze the involvement of faith groups within broad-based community organizations and the theological significance of community organizing within a superdiverse society
3. Develop a liberative theology of community organizing that has the capacity to critique and resource the activism of faith-based community organizers

NONE OF US ARE 'NEUTRAL'

The philosopher Michel Foucault argues that 'knowledge is . . . defined by the possibilities . . . offered by discourse'.[5] In other words, what we know is not the autonomous articulation of our inner life but an expression of the social relationships in which we share and the cultural, political and economic forces which shape the communities to which we belong. Stephen Pattison affirms the tenor of Foucault's assertion and argues that theological reflection should be seen as an experience-centered and contextualized form of discourse, 'since all theology is human discourse, and all human discourse is conditioned by the socio-political nature of reality, all theology must be regarded as biased'.[6] As the pioneer of Latin American liberation theology Gustavo Gutiérrez suggests, 'Theology follows. It is the second step.'[7] Theology is inherently contextual and inevitably biased.

With this in mind, it is important to make my own standpoint clear from the outset. Whereas this book arose from the creative uncertainty borne of the cultural shifts to which I referred previously, it emerged much more specifically from my own longstanding engagement with community organizing in the United Kingdom—it is an example of contextual political theology. I am not a disengaged observer but a critical friend of community organizing. I am involved in community organizing because I believe it to be the most effective means of translating a divine bias to the oppressed into credible political activism in the twenty-first century. Therefore this book represents a personal search for a rigorous but liberative theology of community organizing which can resource the activism of faith-based organizers in a superdiverse era. It is my hope that the chapters that follow might play a small part in enabling faith-based community organizing to fulfill its potential as a theology of liberation for a superdiverse century.

GEOGRAPHY MATTERS—BUT HOW MUCH?

Whereas, as I show in chapter 3, social movement politics and models of activism shaped by essentialist identity politics have worldwide significance, the practice of community organizing has largely been focused in the United States and, more recently, the United Kingdom. It is with this in mind that I have chosen to focus my discussions in these two distinct but comparable societies. I will frame my detailed examination of community organizing in the United Kingdom as a case study which, whereas unique in some respects, can inform wider debate in our translocal globalized century for four reasons. First, the geographically concentrated and politically centralized nature of the United Kingdom makes it more possible to consider the political impact of community organizing on national politics than the far larger and politically decentralized United States. Second, the processes of secularization are more obviously advanced in the United Kingdom than in the United States, and therefore it becomes more possible to map out the terrain of a postsecular civil society politics. Third, due to the overwhelmingly urban focus of community organizing in the United Kingdom, it has animated a more diverse faith base than most community organizing in the United States, resting on the activism not only of Christians, Jews and

Muslims but also of Sikhs, Hindus and Buddhists. In an era of normative ethnic and religious diversity and resurgent critiques of multiculturalism, UK-based community organizing offers us a snapshot of faith-based activism in a superdiverse society, thereby providing resources for community organizers in superdiverse US cities such as New York, Los Angeles and Chicago. Fourth, culturally the United Kingdom sits between continental Europe and the United States, offering us a window onto faith-based activism in an economically neoliberal society with a social democratic political heritage that is currently in flux. An engagement with the UK context (implicitly and explicitly) can therefore offer insights that can be critically drawn upon in both continental Europe where nascent expressions of community organizing have begun to emerge and in the United States.

AN INTERDISCIPLINARY APPROACH

It is fashionable to proclaim the importance of interdisciplinary research, although such proclamations can sometimes appear little more than skin deep when we move past a book's introduction. As I have argued elsewhere, a theoretically credible contextual theology must move beyond superficialities to embrace a thoroughly interdisciplinary approach.[8] Consequently, within the chapters that follow I engage in depth with theoretical debates within political and social theory, urban studies, social movement theories, studies of multiculturalism and superdiversity and third-space thinking in order to lay the groundwork for a convincing contextual theology of community organizing.

A THEOLOGICAL COMPASS

As I suggested previously, this book should be seen as an example of contextual political theology. I have also intimated my own alignment with the broad thrust of liberation theology. Given that a key aim of this book is to resource ongoing faith-based community organizing, it is important to be clear. I am interested in the capacity of theology to stimulate progressive and liberative social change. The British urban theologian Kenneth Leech makes my point with clarity: 'The only theology to which I am committed is one which is part of the current of liberation'.[9] Consequently, my critical engagement with contemporary grass-roots politics, my dialogue with current social theory and my exploration of the resources that can be used to fashion a theology of community organizing will be set against the twin foundational assertions of liberation theology—in an unjust society a loving God necessarily has a bias to the oppressed, and as a result, all people of faith are required to embrace a preferential option for the oppressed. It is against these plumb lines that my engagement with community organizing practice, political movements, social theory and the resulting theology of community organizing should be measured.

PLOTTING THE WAY AHEAD

This book is divided into four parts, each one resembling a step within the pastoral cycle as it is used within contextual theologies:

- Part I (chapters 1 and 2) revolves around experience. Within these chapters I chart the development of community organizing in the United States and the United Kingdom, outlining the values and methodology upon which it is based and exploring the nature, scope and social impact of key campaigns.
- Part II (chapters 3 and 4) revolves around analysis. Within these chapters I consider expressions of extra-institutional politics, what I will refer to as the 'new politics'. In particular I engage with debates on social movements, essentialist identity politics and the cultural politics of difference. I establish a dialogue throughout between such models of activism and community organizing and demonstrate the ways in which such expressions of the 'new politics' can critique, inform and enrich broad-based community organizations.
- Part III (chapters 5 and 6) revolves around reflection. Within these chapters I draw on experience and analysis in order to forge a liberative theology of community organizing. In chapter 5, I explore the foundations of such a theology and engage in a critical dialogue with the work of Robert Schreiter, Luke Bretherton and Chris Baker in order to hammer out its shape, approach and key themes. In chapter 6 I draw my analysis in previous chapters together as I articulate the broad outline of a liberative theology or community organizing, a model for inter-faith reflection groups akin to base ecclesial communities and a spirituality of community organizing that is capable of energizing burnt-out community organizers.
- Part IV (the conclusion) revolves around action and response. In line with the pastoral cycle which guides contextual theologies, I conclude the book by outlining a 'Theological Charter for Community Organizing' which raises key questions for faith groups and faith-based community organizers as they explore the ways in which they can translate theological and ethical values into liberative political action.

Part I

Experience

1   What Is Community Organizing?

INTRODUCTION

Broad-based community organizing represents a powerful movement for social change in the fluid world of the twenty-first century. Since Barack Obama took office as the forty-fourth President of the United States in 2009, it has attracted widespread media attention, but contemporary community organizing actually points to an ancient phenomenon. It is part of a heritage of organized civic engagement that stretches back many centuries, perhaps even to the Peasants' Revolt in fourteenth-century England. Over the intervening centuries, the activism of the Levellers and the Diggers in seventeenth-century England, the labor organizing of early nineteenth-century trades unionists like the Tolpuddle Martyrs in Britain, the grassroots democracy in early nineteenth-century America that enthralled Alexis de Tocqueville, the civil rights movement in the United States and the Indian movement for independence inspired by the nonviolent philosophy of Mahatma Gandhi prefigured the activism that characterizes community organizing today.[1] This rich backstory provides the often-unacknowledged ground on which broad-based community organizing began to build in the early 1940s in the United States. It is a story that underpins this book.

    The fact that community organizing has taken on the mantle fashioned by earlier traditions of civic activism does not minimize its importance as a model of civil society politics, a generator of bridging and linking social capital and a vehicle used by marginalized communities working for social justice. Its relational methodology is well suited to the networked societies of the twenty-first century and has enabled it to fashion a model of intra-cultural and translocal civic activism that challenges those narrowly framed models of identity politics characterized by the introverted resistance identities explored by Manuel Castells and the ethnic absolutism described by Paul Gilroy.[2] In chapter 3, I ask if community organizing is sufficiently open to critical dialogue with other models of civic activism. At this point, however, it is important to reflect briefly on some comparable models of organized civic activism and the ways in which they are similar to and different from Alinsky-inspired organizing before turning to the story of broad-based community organizing in its US home. Since the late 1960s, such civic activism has included the development of feminist and womanist movements, the struggles for gay rights, the antiapartheid struggle and environmental activism.[3] Here, however, I highlight just the patterns of organized civic activism that bear the closest resemblance to the methodology of community organizing.

CIVIC ACTIVISM: THREE EXAMPLES

Debates about civil society stretch back as far as Aristotle's reflections on the nature of citizenship in ancient Greece. However, as Michael Edwards notes, its emphasis on the sociological potential of loose associational life has gained powerful currency in a post-Cold War world where established models of civil society have been increasingly questioned.[4] Whilst Edwards is right to note that the idea of civil society as a metaphor for an inclusive society strikes a particular chord in the translocal world of the twenty-first century, the relational model of political life to which he points is one that has shaped patterns of networked civic activism for much of the past century. Three examples of such activism highlight the line of tradition within community organizing stands: the civil rights, antiwar and drop-the-debt social movements.

The development of the postwar civil rights movement in the United States can be symbolized by two distinct moments, one signifying legal struggle and the other nonviolent direct action. In 1954 the National Association for the Advancement of Colored People took the case of *Brown v. The Board of Education of Topeka* in Kansas to the US Supreme Court to prove that it was unconstitutional to maintain schools that were segregated on the basis of ethnicity. A year later, in December 1955, Rosa Parks refused to give up her seat in the White section of a local bus in Montgomery, Alabama, and was forced off the bus by the driver. Her moment of resistance gave rise to the Montgomery bus boycott which was led by the young Baptist pastor Rev. Martin Luther King Jr. and supported by the Black churches of the town. Throughout the following decade, the organized activism of the civil rights movement revolved to a large degree around Gandhian principles of strategic nonviolent direct action.[5] In his 1963 'Letter from Birmingham City Jail' Martin Luther King Jr. spoke of the central importance of carefully organized nonviolent direct action, echoing strands of the methodology of Saul Alinsky's community organizing. However, alongside research, negotiation and direct action, King added another key element, that of 'self-purification'.[6] For King, unlike Alinsky, a firm ethical foundation for activism was vital if it was to be sustained. King suggested in his 1961 address 'Love, Law and Civil Disobedience' that this foundation was provided by 'an overflowing love which seeks nothing in return'.[7] For Alinsky and for many who built upon his community-organizing legacy, it was not selfless love but the identification of mutual self-interest that provided community organizations with direction and potency. It is true that the nonviolent civic organizing that characterized the civil rights movement under King was increasingly replaced with the 'by any means necessary' Black Power movement after his murder in 1968.[8] However the continued importance of King's 'love ethic' shaped the presidential campaigns of Jesse Jackson during the 1980s and his ongoing work within the Rainbow/PUSH coalition. It underpins the radically inclusive activism of Glide Memorial United Methodist Church in San Francisco and has found an online twenty-first century life in Civic Frame, a US-based network that draws on popular culture to forge liberative educational actions and civic engagement largely within the African-American community.[9] The love or self-interest debate is one to which I will return in depth in chapter 5.

A second example of civic activism dates from the early 1960s to the present day. The antiwar movement that arose during the 1960s in protest about US involvement in the Vietnam War drew upon the model of mobilization embodied by the civil rights movement, particularly in relation to student opposition to the military draft. The antiwar movement in the United States drew together disparate political, religious, civil rights and students groups around a set of focused aims, much like broad-based community organizations. The generalized problem of opposition to the war was turned into a set of specific issues, enabling effective mobilization and targeted activism. Since the beginning of the US- and UK-led War on Terror arising from the 2001 terrorist attacks in New York and Washington, DC, a similar model of organized antiwar activism has arisen in the United Kingdom through the emergence of the Stop the War coalition, which has drawn not only on socialist groupings but on a wide range of faith communities.[10]

A third example of organized civic activism relates to the emergence during the late 1990s of an international movement that called for the cancellation of unpayable debt in the global south by the year 2000. The beginning of a new millennium was to be a year of jubilee—a new start free from debt. Whilst this social movement embraced a diverse range of faith-based and political organizations the premise upon which it was built was found in the Hebrew Scriptures. Leviticus 25:10 commands the people of Israel to 'consecrate the fiftieth year and proclaim liberty throughout the land to all its inhabitants'. In this year, all debts were to be cancelled and property was to be returned to its original owners. In 1997 growing concern about international debt led to the founding of Jubilee 2000, which was backed by trades unions, refugee groups, aid agencies and faith communities. As a result of its broad base, Jubilee 2000 was able to mobilize over seventy thousand people in protest at the 1998 G8 summit in Birmingham, UK, to put pressure on the leaders of the world's richest nations to cancel the debt owed by the world's poorest countries. This campaign utilized the networks provided by faith communities to engage in a targeted campaign of letter writing to world leaders, turning a generalized problem into a specific issue around which strategic action could be planned. The social movement originally animated by Jubilee 2000 led to the emergence of Make Poverty History and the involvement of global pop stars at the Live 8 concerts ahead of the 2005 G8 summit in Scotland.[11] Moreover, it has since stimulated the development of the broader based Jubilee Debt Coalition and, in 2013, the Enough Food IF alliance.[12]

In later chapters, I consider two questions: First, does broad-based community organizing subsume other single-issue social movements within its multi-issue and long-term agenda? Second, has community organizing neglected the added value that a loose alliance with alternative modes of civic activism might add and thereby marginalized itself from other patterns of progressive action for social justice? However, in this chapter, as a prelude to these questions, I focus specifically on the historical development of the community organizing first articulated by Saul Alinsky in the Back of the Yards neighbourhood in Chicago, for it is his ideas and activism that stimulated the growth of contemporary community organizing in the United States and the United Kingdom. I will examine the methodology of the community organizing stimulated by Alinsky and the relationship between community organizations and faith groups. The pattern of community organizing that shaped the political philosophy of Barack Obama and directly influenced his first presidential campaign during 2008 connects directly with this Alinkskyite tradition. Consequently, exploration of this heritage is an important precondition for any critical understanding of contemporary community organizing and its relationship with models of progressive faith and political leadership in the twenty-first century.

THE LEGACY OF SAUL ALINSKY

Paul Henderson and Harry Salmon suggest that 'through his beliefs, thoughts and actions [Alinsky] . . . gave Community Organising an identity which it has retained, with only slight modifications, for more than 50 years'.[13] Born in 1909 into an Orthodox Jewish family in Chicago, Alinsky worked for the Institute of Juvenile Research as a prison sociologist after leaving university before becoming a community organizer and researcher in the impoverished South Side Back of the Yards neighbourhood in Chicago amongst labourers in the meat-packing industry in 1938. His initial aim was limited to the establishment of a neighbourhood committee that would campaign for the recognition of a meat-packer's trades union. The first public meeting of the network in 1939 drew over three hundred people from 109 local organizations. Alinsky sought to connect representatives of the nascent meat-packers trades union together with faith groups and community projects in the neighbourhood. It was at this meeting that the Back of the Yards Neighbourhood Council was established and contemporary community organizing was born. Buoyed by the success of such organized collective action and the recognition that it depended on the ongoing engagement of organizations rather than individuals, Alinsky, with the support of the Roman Catholic Archdiocese of Chicago, established the Industrial Areas Foundation in 1940, which became the hub of his community organizing for the rest of his life.

During his lifetime, Alinsky was a divisive figure, as Sanford Horwitt and also Jenifer Frost illustrate with reference to his tense relationship during the mid 1960s with the Students for a Democratic Society's Economic Research and Action Project and the broader civil rights movement.[14] Was Alinsky a radical prophet committed to the struggle for social justice or an amoral pragmatist for whom almost any means justified the end? Alinsky himself wrote relatively little, but what he did write does not offer a clear answer to this question. In *Reveille for Radicals,* he argued that true radicalism is founded on a deep and active commitment to the equality of all people and a willingness to engage in struggle wherever such equality is denied. In the same book, however, Alinsky also affirmed the central importance of self-interest and strategic conflict with other progressive activists who did not align themselves with the methodology he propounded and was dismissive of the practical value of any engagement with social theory: 'The word "academic" is a synonym for irrelevant'.[15] Such an approach continues to characterize much community organizing as I show in later chapters. Towards the end of his life, the same tension can be found in Alinsky's *Rules for Radicals,* where he argues that the purpose of community organizing is to give power to those who are disempowered, 'to realize the democratic dream of equality', whilst seemingly exhibiting a moral relativism in his assertion that the end of social justice justifies almost any means: 'in war the end justifies almost any means.'[16] Within *Rules for Radicals* Alinsky laid out a model of pragmatic radicalism. Almost forty years later such pithy assertions as 'Power is not only what you have but what the enemy thinks you have' or 'Pick the target, freeze it, personalize it and polarize it' remain central to the methodology of much community organizing.[17] In spite of such ambiguity, it is on the pragmatic radicalism of Alinsky and his understanding that effective activism depends on the building of a permanent people's organization characterized by organized people, organized power and organized money that most contemporary community organizing rests. For Alinsky, activism almost inevitably dissolved into impotent idealism or single-issue social movements when such a permanent people's organization was not present as a guiding force. It is on this foundation that key broad community organizations in the United States such as the Industrial Areas Foundation, ACORN, the Gamaliel Foundation, Pico National Network and the Direct Action and Research Training Centre (DART) have built since Alinsky's death in 1972.

The story of community organizing in the United States revolves around the development of these organizations and their relationship with the Alinsky legacy, and so it is to them that I now turn. However, before I focus on this story, I want to sharpen my description of community organizing by outlining in brief what it is not. These are characteristics that I return to in my discussion of the 'new politics' in chapter 3. First, Alinskyite community organizing is not short-lived or spontaneous activism but is focused on long-term strategic change. Second, community organizing is not reducible to the mobilization of people around single issues because of its multi-issue agenda. Third, community organizing is not the same as advocacy because its aim is to empower people to speak and act for themselves (often described as the 'iron rule' of organizing). Fourth, strategic community organizations insist that they should not be equated with social movements because, it is argued, such movements have a tendency to be short term and single issue, whereas community organizations aim to build permanent networks of action. Fifth, whereas community organizations may agitate for more equal access to welfare, they are not service agencies. Sixth, community organizations rely on the deliberate development of tension as a tool for social change. Aware of the distinctiveness of community organizing, I now turn to the story of its growth in the United States, its methodology, its ongoing values and its engagement with faith groups.

THE INDUSTRIAL AREAS FOUNDATION

Following its establishment in 1940, the Industrial Areas Foundation (IAF) developed its base in Chicago and, through the work of Edward Chambers and Tom Gaudette, focused on the strategic development of powerful and stable grass-roots community organizations that had the capacity to empower marginalized communities as a means of bringing about long-lasting social change.[18] Influenced by Alinsky, the IAF still emphasizes the centrality of the self-interest of individuals and organizations in effective community organizing and the development of sufficient power to bring about lasting social change.[19] Consequently, in its development of sixty-three affiliated community organizations (at May 2013) in the United States, Canada, Germany and the United Kingdom, the IAF has emphasized the importance of the training of local leadership. This focus on training led Alinsky to establish the IAF organizer-training programme in 1969. Over forty years later the training of local leaders remains at the heart of community organizing in both the United States and the United Kingdom. Following the death of Alinsky, his successor as executive director, Edward Chambers, began to focus far more strategically than Alinsky on the development of community organizing within faith communities. Part of the current mission statement of the IAF makes this clear: 'The work of the Industrial Areas Foundation flows directly from a commitment to Judeo Christian and democratic values. This angle of vision has led to the development of organizational relationships that grow the voices of families and communities that have little power over decisions that impact their own lives'.[20] In 2013 the work of the IAF focused on ten key issues:

1. Monitoring criminal justice (Iowa)
2. Education (Texas, Arizona, Maryland, California and New York City)
3. The environment (New Jersey and Washington, DC)
4. Financial reform (Wisconsin and Boston)
5. Health care (California and Massachusetts)
6. Housing (Chicago, Baltimore, New York City, Alabama and Washington, DC)
7. Immigration and migrant workers rights (California, Arizona, Nebraska and Maryland)
8. Employment, training and the living wage (Louisiana, Texas and Iowa)
9. Neighbourhood development (Texas; Washington, DC; Maryland and Alabama)
10. The rights of seniors and pensioners (Maryland and Alabama)

Jay Macleod suggests that the proactive embrace of faith groups represented an implicit shift away from Alinsky's strong emphasis on self-interest and the fostering of confrontation as the foundation of successful organizing, which was anathema to many faith communities.[21] Macleod notes that this change in approach followed the lead taken in the late 1950s by the civil rights movement in the southern states of the United States and goes on to argue that the growing relationship with faith groups led to a new emphasis: 'Self-interest has yielded to values of justice, concern for the poor, the dignity of the person, participation and respect for diversity as motivation for involvement'.[22] Macleod's point is well made but underplays the extent to which self-interest continues to play a central role in the self-understanding of community organizing. Whereas, due in large part to its establishment by Alinsky, the IAF is arguably the most widely known example of community organizing, a number of other key organizations have emerged since the 1960s, often drawing much more directly on an explicit faith foundation.

THE GAMALIEL FOUNDATION

The Chicago-based Gamaliel Foundation was established at the height of the civil rights struggle in 1968 to support the Contract Buyers' League, which was an organization on the West Side of the city that sought to protect African-American homeowners from loan sharks. The foundation takes its name from the Pharisee Gamaliel who the Acts of the Apostles (Acts 5:33–40 and 22:3) suggests taught the apostle Paul. The organization has, since its inception, affirmed a clear faith-based philosophy as seen in its vision statement: 'The Gamaliel Foundation is a community of people living out our faith and values to collectively transform our society and bring about justice locally, nationally and globally'.[23] Whereas the IAF has developed congregational organizing for largely pragmatic reasons, the Gamaliel Foundation is a clear example of explicitly faith-based community organizing as its self-description makes clear: 'Gamaliel's organizing work draws on struggles for justice by people of faith stretching back thousands of years and spanning many nations, faiths, and cultures. Our work draws on Biblical scripture, Christ's life and teaching, the Torah, the Qur'an, Catholic social teaching, the founding principles of American democracy [and] the U.S. civil rights movement'.[24] The foundation incorporates sixty-one affiliated grass-roots community organizations. It is active in seventeen states in the United States, in the United Kingdom (including a partnership with the national campaigning organization Church Action on Poverty) and South Africa.

Whereas the Gamaliel Foundation emerged in the late 1960s as a localized advocacy agency from the mid-1980s, it began to develop a more strategic focus as a training institute that saw its role to be that of empowering grass-roots community organizations, although in 2006 the foundation reaffirmed its focus on enabling grass-roots campaigns for social justice.[25] It was on such a neighbourhood-based organizing project in a largely African-American community on the South Side of Chicago that Barack Obama worked from 1985 to 1988 organizing around concerns over unemployment, education, economic underinvestment and political disenfranchisement.[26] Stimulated by his experience of community organizing, Obama later became a civil rights lawyer, and it was community-organizing methodology that animated his presidential campaign during 2008 and the initiation of his Organizing for America network during the first year of his presidency.[27]

Under the direction of Barack Obama's former Chicago mentor Greg Galluzzo, who led the Gamaliel Foundation from 1986 to 2010, the organization placed a stronger emphasis on regional and national campaigns which have included a focus on health care reform, public transport, housing policy and immigration reform, as seen in its 2010 'Faith and Democracy Platform' paper.[28] The foundation increasingly provides a linking and training role as a 'national organisation [that] gives purpose, direction and energy to creating and maintaining local organizations'.[29]

THE PICO NATIONAL NETWORK

The Pacific Institute for Community Organisation (PICO) in Oakland, California, was established in 1972 by the Jesuit priest John Bauman. From the outset PICO was, like the Gamaliel Foundation, an explicitly faith-based community organization, although initially its work was largely focused on local neighbourhoods in Oakland. In the face of social upheaval and deindustrialization during the early 1980s PICO refocused on a model of organizing specifically with faith groups which, as a result of their localized social capital, provided a more solid base from which to operate than that offered by fragile and fluid neighbourhood networks. This shift stimulated a reframing of organizing, leading to an emphasis on the primacy of faith-based values, rather than localized issues, as the key motivating factor in PICO's activism: 'Rather than bringing people together simply based on common issues like housing or education, the faith-based . . . organizing model makes values and relationships the glue that holds organizations together'.[30] This emphasis is evidenced in PICO's statement of values, which expresses the potential of faith to bring about social transformation, the unifying potential of religion as a motivator of common civic activism and the enriching nature of religious diversity.[31]

In the early years of the twenty-first century, PICO began to extend its base eastwards from California and in 2004 was renamed People Improving Communities through Organizing and, a year later, the PICO National Network. PICO-affiliated community organizations have focused organizing around low pay, neighbourhood safety, preventing the repossession of homes from low-income families, immigration policy reform, work with public schools and equal access to health care for poor or uninsured Americans.[32] Since the election of Barack Obama as US president in 2008, PICO has placed a strong emphasis on the campaign to grant citizenship to the up to eleven million undocumented migrant workers in the United States as seen in its Campaign for Citizenship. A key element of this campaign has been the development of prayer vigil networks alongside direct action and the lobbying of political leaders. A second recent emphasis has been placed on campaigning around gun violence, exemplified by the multifaceted Lifelines to Healing campaign.[33] Third, in its recent Bringing Health Reform Home campaign, PICO has placed a strong emphasis on actions intended to solidify the federal healthcare reforms of the Obama administration and to ensure equal access, irrespective of income.[34] In 2013 there were fifty-six local and regional PICO-affiliated groups in eighteen US states, as well as emergent organizations in Central America and Rwanda.

Unlike either the Gamaliel Foundation or the IAF, PICO has developed a clear engagement with contemporary social theory. A particular focus has been placed on the relationship between ideas about social capital and community organizing. PICO claims that community organizing 'builds the social fabric of communities' and resources the development of bridging social capital'.[35] A partnership with the political scientist Paul Speer has recently analyzed patterns of civic engagement, and a further relationship was forged at the beginning of the new millennium with the sociologist Richard L. Wood to explore the relationship between faith-based organizing in poor neighbourhoods and democratic participation.[36]

ACORN

In 1970, Wade Rathke began work as a National Welfare Rights community organizer in Arkansas, working specifically with people trapped on social welfare. It was out of this early campaigning that Rathke and Gary Delgado established Arkansas Community Organizations for Reform Now

(ACORN). Whereas the IAF, the Gamaliel Foundation and PICO retained a strong ethic of political independence, ACORN was, from the start, fully involved in advocacy within the Democratic Party alongside its more traditional community organizing, and as early as 1974 almost two hundred ACORN members won seats in the local legislature of Pulaski County in Arkansas. This early political campaigning continued as ACORN developed its membership base to over five hundred thousand members in more than one hundred US cities, as well as developing organizing in Peru, Argentina, Mexico, India and Canada. In the early 1980s ACORN not only led protests in Washington, DC, against Ronald Reagan's welfare and housing policies but offered direct support for the Democratic presidential candidate, the Rev. Jesse Jackson, in the 1984 presidential campaign and in the 1988 election provided thirty of Jackson's delegates at the Democratic Convention through its political action committees.

From 2008 to 2010, ACORN was accused of claiming political impartiality whilst providing 'get out the vote' support for Barack Obama during his 2008 campaign to become the Democratic nominee for US president. People within the organization were accused of financial irregularities, and attempts were made during 2009 to block further federal grant aid to ACORN, although this was ruled unconstitutional later in the same year in a judgment that suggested that ACORN had been unfairly singled out because of its liberal political agenda.[37] In spite of this, ACORN filed for liquidation in November 2010, effectively drawing to a close its forty-year history of community organizing and political advocacy.[38]

In the light of this controversy, it would be possible to neglect ACORN's long-standing activism. ACORN describes its mission in the following terms: 'The members of ACORN take on issues of relevance to their communities, whether those issues are discrimination, affordable housing, a quality education or better public services'.[39] The key issues that ACORN organized around between 1970 and 2010 were the targeting of low-income families by loan companies for high-interest loans, the repossession of the homes of low-income families unable to meet large mortgage repayments, regional and national campaigning for health care reform, campaigns to regularize the legal status of undocumented immigrants, the institution of a living wage to replace a minimum wage, voter registration campaigns, action to prevent utilities companies from cutting off low-income families and the Gulf Coast Recovery campaign in New Orleans following Hurricane Katrina in August 2005.

The activism and history, and the rise and demise of ACORN illustrate not only the potential of community organizing as a powerful model of political activism but also the possible pitfalls and fragility of such civil society politics. Robert Fisher's *The People Shall Rule* (2009) and *Seeds of Change* (2010) by John Atlas chronicle the ACORN story.[40]

DART

The Direct Action and Research Training Center (DART) is the youngest and smallest of the major strategic broad-based community organizations in the United States. It was founded in Miami, Florida, in 1982 following five years preparatory organizing by the Rev. Herb White of the United Church of Christ. Like PICO and the Gamaliel Foundation, DART exemplifies faith-based community organizing as its mission statement clearly reveals: 'Scripture describes the vision of society where justice prevails and where God's bounty is fairly shared by all . . . As people of faith, God requires us to "do justice" '.[41] From 1982 to 1990 the organization solidified its base in Florida. From 1990 to 2000 DART expanded its work to Ohio, Michigan and Kentucky and, more recently, to Indiana and Virginia. In 2001 DART followed the lead of the IAF and the Gamaliel Foundation by launching its own DART Organizer's Institute to provide training for potential community organizers.[42]

By 2013 DART employed thirty-five professional community organizers and drew upon 450 volunteer organizers across nineteen affiliated local community organizations in five states (Florida, Indiana, Kentucky, Ohio and Virginia) in the east and the south-eastern United States. DART, like other strategic broad-based community organizations, has sought to marry its idealism with a pragmatic approach to organizing around issues where there is a realistic chance of bringing about measurable change. Over the last twenty years, DART has developed campaigns in relation to literacy classes in public schools, preschool provision for children in 'at risk' families, affordable housing, the retention of banks in marginalized communities, community policing, health care reform, employment training for the recently unemployed, policy in relation to recent immigrants and neighbourhood campaigns in relation to drugs counselling and crime reduction.

PUTTING PRINCIPLES INTO PRACTICE—COMMUNITY ORGANIZING METHODOLOGY

In *Rules for Radicals* Alinsky speaks about the training of community organizers and outlines an idealized list of qualities they need to develop. First, Alinsky suggests, the education of a community organizer begins with the development of the ability to critically reflect on experience. Second, the organizer must be able to communicate in a manner that connects deeply with the experience of the communities alongside which she or he is working. Such engaged communication rests, says Alinsky, on an ability to listen to and reflect upon the experience and self-interest of local people without falsely pretending to be part of the community. Third, the community organizer needs to develop an ability to challenge unreflective received wisdom and the skill of asking disruptive questions to those with power and those who are powerless about 'the world as it is' whilst also inviting reflections on 'the world as it should be'. Fourth, Alinsky insists that a commitment to creative social change gives life to the organizer, as well as enables her or him to develop innovative actions that surprise those with power and force them to react. Fifth, Alinsky insists that in order to survive defeat the organizer must have the capacity to see beyond the short term and recognize that they are part of a larger struggle for social justice. Finally, Alinsky suggests that the successful organizer is one who understands that social justice always emerges from conflict.[43] How might the reflections of the pioneer of community organizing impact its approach today?

The IAF has engaged with faith communities for largely pragmatic reasons whereas PICO, DART and the Gamaliel Foundation are explicitly faith-based community organizations. In spite of this distinction, the methodology they all adopt is broadly similar. In order to understand the success of community organizing in the United States, it is important to get to grips with its methodology to civil society politics. The methodological approach that unites all broad-based community organizations is exemplified by the PICO community organizing model that follows. Community organizing methodology reflects an ongoing process that can be compared to the use of the pastoral cycle within contextual theologies and the hermeneutical circle within theologies of liberation, as the work of Laurie Green within urban theology and the liberation theologian Juan Luis Segundo attest.[44] The methodological approach of broad-based community organizations finds another echo in the action-research methodology used by sociologists and educationalists which Peter Reason and Hilary Bradbury suggest 'bring[s] together action and reflection . . . in the pursuit of practical solutions to issues of pressing concern to people'.[45] Methodology, therefore, serves practice.

The PICO organizing cycle which I discuss next indicates the communal nature of community organizing but neglects the key role played by the community organizer who guides this reflexive process. In his examination of global contextual theologies, Robert Schreiter speaks of the trained theologian as an animator, somebody who brings specific skills to the fashioning of local theologies by indigenous communities.[46] In the same vein the community organizer brings particular training to the act of organizing but is the enabler and not the author of action—almost a midwife. However, it is important to recognize two factors that impact the enabling role of the organizer. First, such a person by virtue of their lead role in community organizations is imbued with power and status. In marginalized communities where the perception of professionals may be a negative one, it can be difficult for local people to challenge the views of the trained community organizer. Second, as I noted in the introduction, we should ask if it is ever possible for anybody to bracket out personal values and biases because all human reflection arises from the context which shapes us and our own subjectivity. In

Figure 1.1 The PICO Learning Cycle

Source: http://www.piconetwork.org, accessed 27 January 2010.

spite of their best intentions, is it, therefore, ever possible for a community organizer to approach an issue in the community in a neutral manner in order to allow people the reflective freedom to arrive at their own conclusions? Aware of these reflections on the work of the community organizer, I now turn to the methodology of community organizing as expressed in the PICO organizing model.

There are four stages within the PICO cycle. First, there is the building of relationships which involves one-to-one conversations, listening campaigns and consultation in the neighbourhood. This initial stage can be compared with the use of experience as the foundational stage of theological reflection within contextual theologies. The Gamaliel Foundation faith-based organizer Dennis Jacobsen suggests that 'the one-on-one interview is the primary tool of organizing'.[47] This intimate personal conversation is in essence a strategic discussion aimed at developing a relationship, identifying an individual's specific commitments and their willingness to become involved in specific organizing actions. It is worth considering how natural such a conversation can be and how much it expresses a genuine interest in the individual when, as Jacobsen acknowledges, it is, in essence a strategic interview. A key emphasis within community organizing is the assertion that it is vital to identify a person's self-interest in the one-to-one because, it is argued, organizing is most successful when it relates to those issues that most clearly benefit individuals or institutions. This elevation of self-interest is defended by Jacobsen who seeks to uncouple it from selfishness and to align its identification with the path of self-becoming amongst people of faith.[48] Whilst it remains central to Alinskyite organizing, the emergence of faith-based community organizations and the growing reliance of net-works like the IAF on the social capital of faith groups raise questions about the centrality of self-interest rather than ethical values as the key driver of community organizing. The foundational importance of a values base to organizing is exemplified by the PICO statement of values and the Gama-liel Foundation's summary of its philosophy.[49] A second strand within this initial methodological stage is the use of 'listening campaigns' whereby the full-time organizer and volunteers consult with faith groups or community organizations about their concerns and the issues they feel need address-ing in their neighbourhood. The third element of this initial stage broadens listening beyond member groups to the people who live in the neighbour-hood where an action may take place. This process of 'door-knocking' and neighbourhood meetings is intended to supplement the questions raised in one-to-ones and listening campaigns and to sharpen specific issues around which organizing might successfully be developed. The purpose of this first methodological stage is to clearly identify problems about which local faith and community groups feel strongly and around which organizing cam-paigns can be structured.

The second stage in the methodological cycle aims to turn problems which people may feel powerless to address into issues with specific characteristics that can be analyzed and around which strategic and measurable actions can be mounted. Like the pastoral cycle within contextual theologies, this stage revolves around careful research into the specific characteristics of the issue and its causes. The work of the Indianapolis Neighbourhood Resource Center (established 1994) offers a good example of the importance of this step in the methodology of community organizing. As part of their online *Organizer's Workbook*, the centre suggests that it is out of this period of research that an informed strategy for action can be developed which ad-dresses the nature of power in a situation and outlines the ways in which the issue impacts on different groups within the community. Social analysis helps to identify potential allies in any future action, the goals of such an action and the tactics that are most likely to enable real change in relation to the issue identified.[50]

The third stage in the community organizing cycle is strategically directed campaigning and is comparable to the action phase in the pastoral cycle. Typically, community organizers and activists will seek to mobilize large numbers of people to pressurize key officials who have the power to ad-dress the issue at hand. This action stage may include public assemblies, the nonviolent picketing of the offices of public officials or the use of press conferences to raise wider public consciousness. A key element in this stage is the ability of community organizations to demonstrate their power to bring about effective pressure for action and change—organized people as an equal to organized power. In an American context it was because the IAF believed that faith groups could effectively mobilize large numbers of people that they moved after Alinsky's death to a congregational model of community organizing. Whereas such a pragmatic approach perhaps makes tactical sense in a US context, Henderson and Salmon ask if such a reliance on strong faith communities is feasible in the more secularized context of the United Kingdom.[51]

The final stage in the community organizing cycle is the critical evaluation of the success of an action which enables the development of more effective future campaigns. A key challenge in this evaluation stage is the encouragement of constructive critique rather than effusive praise. In the context of community organizing alongside marginalized groups this raises important questions about power relations in community organizations. Where these are relatively egalitarian and based on strong relationships the critique of a paid and often professional organizer is possible. However, where a culture of deference towards the organizer may have evolved the constructive benefit of such evaluation is perhaps questionable. A central methodological emphasis within community organizing since the 1960s has been the provision of leadership training for groups that are part of community organizations. Such training, which is normally led by community organizers, has become a key plank of the work of all strategic community organizations and will often be spread over a whole week. This training focuses on the principles and practice of community organizing and, in the case of the Gamaliel Foundation, is offered to specifically faith-based audiences. A focal point for such training in the United States is the Midwest Academy in Chicago, although COMM-ORG possibly offers a more critical engagement with the possibilities and problems, successes and failures of community organizing.[52]

COMM-ORG is an Internet-based forum that was established by the sociologist Randy Stoeker through the University of Illinois in 1994 to facilitate both the development of community organizing practice and critical debate about the insights that contemporary social and political theory can offer to practitioners. The forum uses papers by organizers and academics to develop a critical model of community organizing and offers an Internet-based syllabus for community-organizing training. Such an online initiative stands in contrast with less dialogical and, arguably, utilitarian community-organizing training. This virtual network claims to connect with over one thousand practitioners and academics in the United States, Asia, Australia, Germany, India, New Zealand, Pakistan Russia and the United Kingdom, suggesting that 'community organizers and academics can both benefit by exchanging information and resources. The COMM-ORG membership is composed of about half academics and half practitioners (including some government officials and funders).[53] COMM-ORG is not obviously aligned with any specific broad-based community-organizing network. This apparent independence gives rise to a wide range of approaches and analyses of community organizing. It is, however, difficult to establish how influential COMM-ORG is within wider community-organizing networks.[54]

FAITH AND THE PUBLIC SPHERE

Community organizing is not inherently faith based as the engagement in both the United States and the United Kingdom with trades unions, neighbourhood associations, students and community groups demonstrates. In both the case of the IAF in the United States and Citizens UK, whereas some organizers have been personally motivated by their own religious faith, the increasing reliance on faith communities has been shaped by pragmatism rather than principle. It is important to ask therefore what difference, if any, faith makes. Are there specific characteristics of faith-based community organizing that alter the model of community organizing that was first honed by Alinsky? What are the key values that shape faith-based organizing and how are these embodied in broad-based community organizations? In plural and increasingly secular societies, the role of faith groups in the public realm is a contentious one. On what basis do faith communities step into the public realm and engage in community organizing?

In later chapters I examine how debates about the evolving nature of the contested and plural public sphere in contemporary Euro-American societies can enrich community organizing through the development of a more critical and holistic understanding of the public realm. At this point, however, I simply want to view the public sphere in the terms employed by Jurgen Habermas as a discursive public space that is shaped by a wide range of contested cultural, political, ideological and spiritual narratives.[55] In marginalized neighbourhoods in both the United States and the United Kingdom, it is often the case that local faith groups are the only remaining social institutions generating social capital and giving voice to people who may feel that statutory bodies fail to listen to their concerns, as Chris Baker and Hannah Skinner point out with reference to the United Kingdom.[56] As Adam Dinham, Robert Furbey and Vivien Lowndes note following the election of the Blair government in Britain in 1997, Labour government ministers increasingly emphasized the key role of faith communities in relation to grass-roots service provision, social cohesion and civic participation.[57] If only for pragmatic reasons faith groups continue to play a key role in civil society politics.

There are, however, other arguments made by faith-based community organizations for their civic activism that arise from core theological values. This perspective is summarized in the Gamaliel Foundation vision statement: 'People with faith in a good and just God and people who share these values will organize through Gamaliel to bring about shared abundance, sacred community, unrelenting hope, equal opportunity and justice within our communities and throughout the world.'[58] This engagement within the public sphere as a core expression of religious faith is commented upon by the pioneer of Black British liberation theology, Robert Beckford, who argues that 'action is integral to theology . . . because it ensures that doing theology is synonymous with social change; we explore the meaning of God in the world in order to set about changing the way things are'.[59] Writing out of his experience as the director of the Gamaliel National Clergy Caucus, the Lutheran pastor Jacobsen also argues that progressive activism in the public sphere is a foundational expression of Christian faith: 'The church enters the public arena in order to be the church, in order to be true to itself, in order to be faithful to its Lord', not to fill the church on Sunday mornings but to put into practice the ethical demands of Jesus.[60] Jim Wallis, the founder of the Sojourners Community, affirms Jacobsen's view, suggesting that 'the Bible reveals a very public God. But in an age of private spiritualties, the voice of a public God can scarcely be heard'.[61] Wallis argues that since the early 1980s the political right in the United States has engaged powerful conservative evangelical churches in the public sphere but largely only in relation to issues of sexuality.[62] For Wallis there is a need to reclaim the public articulation of Christian faith from the political right and from the privatization of what should be a personal but public faith because, he argues, 'we meet the personal God in the public arena and are invited to take our relationship to that God right into the struggle for justice'.[63] Beckford suggests that the kind of engagement espoused by both Jacobsen and Wallis returns us to the model of activist faith articulated by the Hebrew prophets, which is characterized by holistic prophetic direct action that recognizes the complexity of urban injustice and is motivated by a clear bias to the oppressed.[64]

WHAT DIFFERENCE DOES FAITH MAKE?

It is in light of the arguments noted above that the key strategic faith-based community organizations in the United States have developed their engagement in the public sphere. Whilst Jacobsen strives to defend the Alinskyite identification of self-interest as the key motivator for community organizing, none of the faith-based community organizations directly refer to its relevance in relation to their work or the commitment of faith groups that are part of the networks they represent. Instead they speak of seven faith-based principles that stimulate their community organizing.

First, as the Gamaliel Foundation make plain in their Faith and Democracy Platform, faith-based organizing affirms the interconnectedness of humanity and the central importance of the communal nature of faith as a foundational principle of faith-based organizing: 'We hold that all people are part of a sacred community, intended by God to realize their own dignity, worth, power and voice.'[65] Implicit in this faith statement is an affirmation of the Judaeo-Christian doctrine of creation wherein all people are made in the image of God and the Christian understanding of incarnation whereby the divine word becomes flesh and draws people into a relationship of solidarity with each other and with God. Religious faith, according to the Gamaliel Foundation, is an inherently social activity. Second, the PICO network suggests that its community organizing is founded on a belief in the potential for transformation in relation to individuals, faith groups and society. The organizing of PICO, DART and the Gamaliel Foundation rests on a confidence that the liberating God who intervenes in history can make it possible for the 'world as it is' to be transformed into the 'world as it should be'. The Gamaliel Foundation vision statement insists that such transformation enables the empowerment of marginalized people and is always intimately related to the transformation of injustice into justice. Third, whereas the Gamaliel Foundation recognizes that religion has been used in the United States to divide people and bolster injustice, they insist that faith can 'unite all people through hope, acceptance and a deep desire for justice'.[66] Fourth, faith-based organizing in the United States is inherently and consciously inclusive as the PICO statement of values exemplifies: 'PICO values the racial, ethnic, religious and regional diversity that has shaped America.'[67] Such faith-based community organizing is premised on equality and a celebration of plurality as a gift from God and therefore resists all forms of racism and religious exclusivity. Fifth, the DART coalition suggests that the world envisioned by the Bible is one where 'God's bounty is shared by all'.[68] Moreover faith-based community organizing is rooted in a liberative reading of Jesus' call to preach a gospel of release to the poor and the captive (Luke 4:16–21). Sixth, as the Gamaliel Foundation's Faith and Democracy Platform makes plain, such a mandate compels people of faith to work to ensure equal participation in communal life because 'participation is a deeply theological concern . . . A community, in which full and fair participation is denied to anyone, is a community living outside God's intentions for the created order.'[69] Seventh, such a mandate implies a liberative approach to the Biblical theme of hope, whereby the promise of liberation is not confined to a distant hereafter but is a transformative force in the 'world as it is'.

A further use of Biblical resources within faith-based community organizing in the United States draws upon scriptural figures as exemplars of community organizing praxis and the potential of hesitant people to become key leaders in community organizations. The patriarch Moses is used as a template of such leadership. In Exodus 3–4 Moses encounters God and is challenged to travel to Egypt to lead the Israelites out of slavery. Moses is reluctant to respond, suggesting that he is 'slow of speech and slow of tongue' (Exodus 4:10). However God empowers Moses, giving him a wooden staff as a sign of his authority. It is this snapshot from Moses' life that faith-based community organizing draws upon as a parable of empowerment in 'leadership training'. Gregory Pierce summarizes: 'Yahweh chose a man with a speech impediment to lead the Israelites out of Egypt. Jesus chose an uneducated, head-strong fisherman . . . to build his Church.'[70] The story sheds light on the fundamental importance that faith-based organizing in the United States has placed on the significance of leadership, inclusivity and the human capacity for transformation.

Furthermore, in a reflection on faith-based community organizing for the PICO National Clergy Caucus, Kendall Baker draws explicitly on Jesus' calling of the seventy in Luke 10 as a model for the building of broad-based community organizations.[71] Baker argues that Jesus' calling of the seventy demonstrates his understanding of a simple equation: 'Mission = Creative Vision + Social Program.'[72] He suggests that Luke 10 can act as a template for faith-based organizing because Jesus recognizes the necessity of combining idealistic vision with organized activism. The seventy become leaders, the foundation of a broad-based organization for mission, avoiding an over-reliance on a single charismatic leader. Baker also views this Gospel passage as a meditation on power and resistance. People's existential longing is turned into a focused issue upon which the seventy have the power to act. In Luke 10:9 Jesus sets a specific agenda for the seventy: 'cure the sick who are there and say to them, the kingdom of God has come near to you.' Baker argues that in this passage Jesus identifies the three-pronged agenda that guides faith-based community organizing: building relationships (eating in people's homes), the response to self-interest (curing the sick) and making hope real (announcing the presence of the kingdom of God).[73] The marriage of vision and pragmatism becomes critical.

Baker's use of Luke 10 as a template for the building of broad-based community organizations finds echoes in Jacobsen's theological reflection on faith-based organizing and in particular his argument that the Bible can act as a powerful resource in the sustenance of community organizations. For Jacobsen the 'Logos' or 'Word of God' through which creation is shaped and ordered becomes a key organizing principle within God's relationship with humanity. The vision that the writers of Proverbs 29:18 insist enables the life of God's people is rooted in social realities through the sustaining power of the incarnate 'Logos'.[74]

The growth of faith-based community organizations in the United States has provided organizing with a solid mobilizing base in communities. Furthermore, the theological resources upon which networks like PICO, DART and the Gamaliel Foundation draw have provided previously pragmatic community organizing with a far clearer reflective base. Faith-based organizing draws upon the conviction that all people are created in the divine image to resource the building of interconnected, cross-cultural and interfaith organizing, and its identification of the incarnation as a radical expression of solidarity can animate egalitarian organizing. Faith-based community organizations in the United States build upon this foundation in their insistence that the God revealed in the Biblical narrative is one who identifies with those who are oppressed and that the struggle for inclusive social justice is not a political tactic but a core expression of discipleship. Civic engagement becomes more than activism—it is participation in the ongoing liberative work of God. Such a focus presents Alinsky's juxtaposition of 'the world as it is' and 'the world as it should be' in a new and broader light.

RIGHT UP TO DATE: A COMMUNITY ORGANIZER
IN THE WHITE HOUSE

The 2008 US presidential campaign was historic in two key respects. First and foremost, it led to the election of the first African-American as the forty-fourth president of the United States of America, and second, it placed a former community organizer in the White House. At the 2008 Republican Convention during the presidential campaign, prominent Republicans such as Rudy Guiliani and Sarah Palin, the Republican nominee for vice president, sought to use Barack Obama's background as a community organizer to belittle his leadership experience.[75] Their comments stimulated a debate far beyond the Republican Party Convention. In an article on the *Time* magazine blog, the journalist Joe Klein typified the critique of Guiliani and Palin's dismissal of community organizing: 'So here is what Guiliani and Palin didn't know—Obama was working for a group of churches that were concerned about their parishioners, many of whom had been laid off when the steel mills closed on the south side of Chicago.'[76]

In spite of Republican criticism, Obama drew upon the models of mobilization utilized by the civil rights movement and the tactical skills that he had honed as a community organizer with the Gamaliel Foundation during the 1980s as the centrepiece of his election campaign. The Obama team employed a large number of organizers who drew upon the methodology of community organizing to fashion one of the most effective political campaigns in US history. A broad coalition of grass-roots groups was built through the use of door-knocking in local neighbourhoods, 'listening campaigns', 'one-to-ones' and small house meetings which focused on people's shared values and self-interest. Even the central slogans of the Obama campaign echoed the pragmatic radicalism of community organizing: 'Yes we can' and 'Change we can believe in.' When complemented by an unprecedented use of the Internet, social networking websites such as Facebook and the online Obama for America campaign, these core community-organizing tactics, as well as a grounding in the philosophy of the civil rights movement, enabled the Obama campaign to facilitate a massive level of enthusiasm and voter turnout, as Peter Dreier comments.[77] Within the campaign Obama also displayed his awareness of the social capital of faith communities, many of whom had been aligned with the political right since the presidency of Ronald Reagan during the 1980s, as his appearance at the televised Saddleback Church's Civil Forum in August 2008 and, in particular, his quotation of Jesus' parable in Matthew 25:45—'Truly I tell you, just as you did to one of the least of these . . . you did it to me'—demonstrated.[78] Barack Obama's election as US president in November 2008 shone a bright light on community organizing. During his first presidential term from 2009 to 2012, his translation of the campaigning Obama for America network into Organizing for America, his development of the Faith Based Initiatives programme of George W. Bush into the White House Office for Faith

Based and Neighbourhood Partnerships, his use of small-scale organizing collectives and communities and the capacity of social media such as Facebook offered echoes of the same methodology in government. In spite of Obama's election to a second presidential term in 2012, it is perhaps still too early to tell whether the model of organized civic activism first forged by Saul Alinsky in the late 1930s has, with a community organizer in the White House, reinvented politics in the United States. What has become clear is that community organizing has reinvigorated progressive religious life and civil society politics in a manner not seen since the heady days of the civil rights movement.

ASSESSMENT: CHALLENGES AND QUESTIONS

Whilst, as I suggested at the beginning of this chapter, organized civic activism is not new, the broad-based community organizing initiated by Alinsky was most likely to emerge in an American context for three reasons.

First, Alinsky was able to draw upon an American philosophical tradition that can be traced back over two hundred years to the principles articulated in the American Constitution and, more specifically, the *Federalist Papers* published by Alexander Hamilton, James Madison and John Jay in the New York newspapers, *The Independent Journal, The New York Packet* and *The Daily Advertiser* between 1787 and 1789.[79] In these eighty-five articles, Hamilton, Madison and Jay reflect not only on the Constitution itself but on the relationship between individual and state, neighbourhood and nation. The *Federalist Papers* explore how it might be possible to fashion a Union that could unite and respect diverse and plural communities and build an inclusive and peaceful civil society whilst respecting traditions of self-sufficiency and individualism. Such a perspective and its legacy contrast with a tradition of more centralized government in the United Kingdom. A second expression of the philosophical tradition that enabled the initial development of community organizing in the United States is found in the work of the nineteenth-century political writer Alexis de Tocqueville whose 1831 journey from France to America led to the seminal text *Democracy in America*. Harvey Mitchell reasonably points to Tocqueville's neglect of the endemic injustice and inequality rooted in the enslavement of African-Americans, his unsubstantiated suggestion that the American Revolution had created a large measure of equality of opportunity and his generalized faith in the civic power of local associations.[80] However, in spite of Mitchell's critique, Edwards suggests that a 'neo-Tocquevillian tradition is particularly strong in the USA, where it dovetails naturally with pre-existing traditions of self-governance . . . and is closely linked to other schools of thought such as communitarianism.'[81] Tocqueville's exploration of the democratic impulse in post-revolution America, his reflections on liberty and the empowering potential of associational life stand as markers in the communitarian tradition that gave rise to Alinsky's early organizing in Chicago, the development of community organizing over the last sixty years and the methodology adopted by Obama during the 2008 presidential campaign.

Luke Bretherton is one of the handful of political theologians to have engaged in critical depth with community organizing.[82] In his recent work, Bretherton argues that community organizing has implicitly drawn on the heritage of the nineteenth-century American populism evidenced in the ultimately abortive Peoples Party of the 1890s. As Bretherton notes it is difficult to offer a single definition of populism. It can be anti-political advocating, 'direct forms of democracy in order to circumvent the need for deliberative processes and the representation of multiple interests in the formation of political judgments. The leader rules by direct consent without the hindrance of democratic checks and balances or the representation of different interests.'[83] Bretherton persuasively points to elements of Alinskyite organizing that are reminiscent of 'anti-political' populism, such as a focus on strong leadership, 'the dichotomisation and simplification of issues', 'a localism that distrusts universalist ideologies', a 'distrust of party politics' and a 'suspicion of theory'. Bretherton, however, usefully points to an alternative model of populism which he describes as 'political' that has echoes within community organizing. Such populism, he suggests, is characterized by 'forging a political space, not limiting, subverting or closing it down', developing 'a broad-base of local leaders rather than relying on one charismatic leader'.[84] Bretherton argues that the community organizing that began with work of Alinsky in Chicago is a contemporary expression of such 'political populism' in that it 'seeks to generate a politics of the common good as against a politics dominated by the interests of the one, the few or the many'.[85] Bretherton's characterization of community organizing represents an insightful analysis of the ideals that motivate community organizers. However, his assessment needs to be tested against the practice of community organizing. Is this commitment to the forging of a common-good politics translated into practice? This is a question to which I return in succeeding chapters.

Second, early community organizing in the United States was able to draw on a long-standing American tradition of voluntary civic engagement. As Alinsky himself writes, 'Citizen participation is the animating spirit and force in a society predicated on voluntarism.'[86] In his influential examination of what he sees as the dramatic decline in communal life in postwar America, Robert Putnam highlights the historic struggle between the demands of the community and the individual since the Pilgrims aboard the *Mayflower* landed in Virginia almost four centuries ago. He notes a concern about the disintegration of associational life but also points to an ongoing tradition of voluntarism and involvement with civic or charitable organizations which, he argues, provide a powerful source of social capital that has the capacity to reinvigorate a fraying American civil society. I will speak more about social capital and its potential place within a theology of community organizing in later chapters. At this point I simply note his suggestion that the context of the twenty-first century demands new ways of enabling and sustaining inclusive civic life in an increasingly fluid, individualistic and plural America. In words that foreshadowed the thrust of the Obama presidential campaign, Putnam suggests that such a challenge has to revolve around face-to-face personal human relationships because 'in the end . . . institutional reform will not work . . . unless you and I, along with our fellow citizens, resolve to become reconnected with our friends and neighbors'.[87] Within contemporary American life the civic activism exemplified by community organizing represents a powerful example of the informal associational life and social capital to which Putnam refers.

Third, community organizers in the United States have been able to draw upon the enduring importance of faith groups as powerful mobilizing forces, particularly in poor communities in a manner that dwarfs the capacity of faith communities in Britain. The Gallup polling organization suggests that in 2008, 47% of Americans suggested that they attended church on a weekly basis. The more recent Pew Forum on Religion and Public Life report *'Nones' on the Rise* (2012) notes the rapid rise of Americans who, when asked, said that they did not belong to or identify with any religious group or tradition (in 2012 this figure stood at 20%). However, at 50% the level of people claiming to regularly attend a place of worship in the United States in 2012 was three times the figure in the United Kingdom.[88]

Alongside such a statistical distinction between the United States and the United Kingdom a further advantage that American community organizers have been able to draw upon is the enduring cultural significance of faith groups in the United States. I noted previously the dialogue that PICO established at the beginning of the twenty-first century with the sociologist Richard L. Wood. On the basis of his study of PICO's faith-based organizing, Wood notes that it effectively draws on a wide range of theological resources: 'Catholic social teaching, African American social ministry, white Protestant social gospel and Hispanic popular religiosity . . . [and] more recently . . . Jewish social ethics, social evangelicalism, liberation theology [and] Pentecostalism'.[89] Furthermore Wood speaks of the way in the enduring importance of such faith groups in the United States can help to imbue community organizing with a commitment to 'ethical democracy'.[90] Such an ethical underpinning can represent a corrective to a utilitarian model of activism that can appear to instrumentalize or use political or business leaders as nothing more than a means of achieving an organizing goal.

CONCLUSION

In this chapter I have explored the historical development and methodology of community organizing in its US home and sought to align it with a wider and longer tradition of organized civic activism. I have examined the increasing importance and character of faith-based organizing in the United States and highlighted the reflective resources that motivate community organizations like the IAF, PICO, DART and the Gamaliel Foundation. I have suggested that these theological insights have the capacity to resource, enrich and critique an often avowedly pragmatic organizing. In the next chapter I cross the Atlantic and chart the journey of community organizing from its homeland to Britain at the end of the 1980s and ask how the model has evolved in this comparable but significantly different context. The sociologist Grace Davie has suggested that the United Kingdom is increasingly characterized by what she calls 'believing without belonging'.[91] How has this cultural context affected community organizing in Britain and what impact has UK organizing's inherently multifaith character had on its growth since the Citizen Organizing Foundation was established in 1989? This is the question to which I now turn.

SELECTED US COMMUNITY ORGANIZING WEBSITE RESOURCES

ACORN Community Organisation: http://www.acorn.org
Barack Obama and Community Organizing: http://www.barackobama.com
Web-Based Civic Activism: http://www.civicframe.org
COMM-ORG Community Organizing Training: http://www.comm-org.wisc.edu
The Gamaliel Foundation: http://www.gamalielfoundation.org
Indianapolis Neighbourhood Recourse Center: http://www.inrc.org/library
The Midwest Academy: http://www.midwestacademy.com
The PICO Network: http://www.piconetwork.org/about
The Rainbow/PUSH Alliance: http://www.rainbowpush.org
The DART Center: http://www.thedartcenter.org/mission.html

2 Reweaving the Fabric of Society
Community Organizing in Britain

INTRODUCTION

Community organizing was born in Britain just as the Thatcher decade was dying. Half a century after Alinsky established the Industrial Areas Foundation, organizing made the journey across the Atlantic, but the cultural landscape of the United Kingdom was dramatically different from that of the United States as the community organizer Kirk Noden notes.[1] In this chapter, I tell the story of community organizing in the United Kingdom. I explore its strengths and weaknesses and the values that drive it. I consider its distinctness from organizing in the United States and from other forms of civic activism in the United Kingdom. Finally, I assess its growing emergence as a powerful vehicle for the building of social justice and the reinvigoration of civic activism in an era of apparent disengagement from the formal political process.

Before focusing specifically on community organizing in Britain, it is important to recognize the contextual factors that have shaped its development. First, community organizing in the United States has been able to rely on the ability of churches to mobilize large numbers of people to engage in campaigns. In contrast, the dramatic decline in formal church membership and attendance at worship in Britain has severely limited the capacity of the church to provide the same level of numerical support, with the partial exception of the Black Church and the Roman Catholic Church, as Henderson and Salmon, MacLeod and Mark Warren note.[2] Second, because in the United Kingdom community organizing has been developed exclusively in urban centres, it has since its inception been an inherently multifaith model of civic activism. In London the active support of the East London Mosque, for example, has been vital since the mid-1990s and in Birmingham the size and strength of the Sikh community based at the Guru Nanak Nishkam Sewak Jatha has been equally important in terms of its capacity to mount and sustain effective campaigns.[3] This multifaith support base has presented community organizing in the United Kingdom with challenges and opportunities that have been peripheral in the United States, which continues to be largely reliant on the ongoing strength of the Christian community. Third, in contrast to the United States, government in the United Kingdom has historically been largely centralized in Westminster. A lack of meaningful devolved power has meant that UK community organizers have, arguably, needed to be more creative than their US counterparts as they have developed power analyses in relation to specific campaigns.[4] A fourth contrast relates to comparative traditions of voluntarism and civic activism. On the one hand, as Henderson and Salmon note, it could be argued that the effect of the services provided by the welfare state in the United Kingdom has been to militate against civil society politics; however, as MacLeod makes plain, British community organizers began their work in urban centres where the activism of the Labour Party and, in particular, the trades union movement had for a century provided a focus for progressive campaigning for social justice.[5] Fifth, community organizing in the United Kingdom emerged in the face of dramatic economic and political change. Throughout the 1980s, the Conservative government led by Margaret Thatcher adopted a neoliberal economic agenda which transformed the UK economy and appeared to be consciously designed to undermine the organized power of the trades unions as the iconic year-long struggle with the National Union of Mineworkers during 1984 demonstrated. The sixth cultural factor that distinguished early UK community organizing from its US counterpart was its relationship with existing models of community-development work that adopted a different approach and philosophy to that articulated by community organizers. As MacLeod observes, this existing tradition shared with community organizing the aim of empowerment and the practice of long-term engagement. However, Paul Ballard suggests that such community development work, unlike community organizing, was often largely nondirective, uninterested in building permanent power organizations and as interested in the process of change as in measureable results.[6] It is against this cultural backdrop that community organizing in the United Kingdom took its first steps and, as I will show in this chapter, it is with this complex context that it has wrestled as it has grown over the last twenty-five years.

COMMUNITY ORGANIZING IN BRITAIN IS BORN

Community organizing in the United Kingdom is a broad-based model of civic activism rather than a movement that is reliant on any single charismatic individual. In spite of this, the pioneering work of the Quaker former social worker Neil Jameson from the middle of the 1980s has been of pivotal importance as organizing as grown and developed in the United Kingdom. Lina Jamoul and Jane Wills suggest that Jameson had become 'increasingly frustrated about cleaning up after the failures of the state and the corporate sector'.[7] During a trip in the early 1980s to study grass-roots social action in the United States, Jameson visited several Industrial Area

Foundation projects. On his return to the United Kingdom Jameson decided to use the methodology that he had encountered to begin the development of community organizing in Britain. Jamoul and Wills suggest that Jameson was keen to draw upon the heritage of progressive labour organizing and community activism in the East End of London that stretched from the struggles of the Matchgirls strike in 1888 to the election of a New Labour government in 1997.[8] Because of the early support of the Quaker-influenced Barrow Cadbury Trust and the Anglican Church Urban Fund, Jameson was able to establish the Citizens Organizing Foundation (COF) in 1989.[9] Community organizing in Britain had begun, but as Paul Bunyan implies, it would be a mistake to depict COF as a grass-roots community organization. Its focus from the outset was the strategic promotion of broad-based organizing in communities across the United Kingdom.[10] In a later position paper, COF makes this facilitating role clear when describing itself as 'the national umbrella organization of the broad-based organizing movement in Britain and Ireland'. Central to this task has been an ongoing programme of training focused on teaching 'the art of politics at a neighbourhood level'.[11]

Just a year after the establishment of COF, the United Kingdom's first broad-based community organization Communities Organized for Greater Bristol (COGB) was launched, drawing over thirteen hundred people from twenty-six congregations and community groups to its founding assembly in September 1990. COGB deliberately sought to develop a broad base of support, working alongside Sikh and Hindu communities in the city, although much of its support was drawn from local Anglican parishes, which were being actively encouraged by Peter Frith, the Bishop of Bristol, to respond to the agenda set down just five years earlier by *Faith in the City*. Jameson drew on Alinsky's insistence that successful organizing was rooted in mutual self-interest, developing a range of grass-roots actions relating to community safety, public transport, neglected public parks and industrial noise pollution. Peter Stokes and Barry Knight point to one key area of action developed by COGB, which exemplifies the importance of mass organized action within community organizing. Three hundred COGB members who were savers with the Bristol and West Building Society attended the 1991 annual general meeting after the company's directors refused to put COGB resolutions to the meeting. Local media attention highlighted COGB allegations that the building society was neglecting the housing needs of the poorest section of the community and their presence at the annual general meeting. Six months after the annual general meeting the Bristol and West established a new community trust and increased its grants to homelessness projects in the city by 700%.[12]

In 1992 the Merseyside Broad-Based Organization (MBO) was established, drawing over two thousand people from more than forty faith and community groups to its founding assembly in Liverpool. During the first year of its life, MBO members began to organize around the illegal dumping of waste on vacant plots of land across inner urban Liverpool. Like its sister organization in Bristol, MBO pursued a series of seemingly fruitless meetings before gathering eight hundred people at an assembly attended by representatives from Liverpool city council, Merseyside police and the Merseyside Waste Disposal Authority. A dossier of evidence of illegal dumping was handed over to public officials, and commitments were made to the assembly to clear all illegal waste sites over a six-month period, to carry out regular spot checks and to hold monthly accountability meetings to continue to monitor the issue.

Following these early successes, COF quickly began to develop broad-based organizations in North Wales (Trefnu Cymunedol Cymru) and the Black Country in the West Midlands in 1995 and in Sheffield (Impact) in 1996. It is important to note, however, as Bunyan points out, that many early expressions of UK community organizing have either foundered or disaffiliated from COF to concentrate on local forms of civic activism more akin to the community development tradition. Bunyan suggests that this first chapter of UK organizing created a strong sense of momentum. He also notes, however, that the rapid spread of community organizations in the mid- and late 1990s was initiated before a successfully tested model had been established to act as a prototype for new organizations to draw upon. Bunyan suggests that this contributed to the short-lived activism of many of these early organizations.[13]

Writing just four years after COF was established, MacLeod summarizes five areas of concern in relation to the methodology of community organizing in its early development in the United Kingdom. First, he suggests that 'many community workers . . . accuse organising's practitioners of being "cult-minded" and "scornful of other approaches" and think it essential that broad-based organizing . . . is open enough to be able to work with all those concerned with working out a strategy for community work in the nineties'.[14] Second, with reference to the emergence of organizing in Sheffield, MacLeod suggests that 'people who have been slogging away in the inner city for years are finding it difficult to accept a model imported from the United States, especially when it is promoted by church officials with little previous experience at the grass roots'.[15] Third, he argues that during the early 1990s COF disparaged conferences and detailed critical social research as a distraction from grass-roots activism. Fourth, MacLeod suggests that community development projects and broad-based community organizations appeared to view each other as rivals rather than allies because they exemplified 'fundamentally different approaches to social change'.[16] Fifth, MacLeod suggests that the centrality of self-interest within community organizing as the central dynamic of civic activism is problematic because it is not able to stimulate holistic social change as effectively as the transcendence of self-interest and the assertion of the common good that characterize faith-based traditions of community development work.

COMMUNITY ORGANIZING TAKES SHAPE IN LONDON

Following his early organizing in Bristol, Jameson moved to the East End of London to begin the development of what became The East London Communities Organization (TELCO). Warren suggests that the move to east London was important for strategic and philosophical reasons. From a strategic perspective, he suggests that Jameson felt that it was vital to develop a base in London at the centre of national political and economic power in order to develop the political credibility of COF. Warren suggests that Jameson also wanted to demonstrate COF's commitment to forging cross-cultural and interfaith community organizations.[17] The move to the East End of London placed COF at the heart of one of the most diverse areas of the United Kingdom. The 1,300 people who gathered from thirty faith and community groups at its 1996 founding assembly came from Sikh gurdwaras, Roman Catholic parishes, Hindu temples, Buddhist viharas, Pentecostal churches, mosques, Anglican and Free Churches and local schools. A further reason for COF's move to the East End was the area's long heritage of trades union organizing and Labour party activism that Jameson was keen to utilize in the development of community organizing in London. It is perhaps ironic therefore that during early networking in the mid-1990s Jameson encountered some resistance, not from those on the political right but from activists and faith leaders on the left who, as MacLeod noted in relation to Sheffield, felt as if the value of this long heritage was being implicitly diminished. The claim of Warren that 'TELCO was one of the few groups to be conducting any real grassroots organizing in Britain during the 1990s' also reflected this mistaken perception.[18] COF was clearly developing a new model of civil society politics. However, to imply that it alone was engaged in meaningful grass-roots action for social justice is to neglect the alternative long-standing models of activism with which community organizing has occasionally come into conflict.

A key aspect of Jameson's networking in east London in the mid-1990s was his effort to build relationships with local Muslim leaders and, in particular, the large East London Mosque in Whitechapel.[19] A central part of this relationship building drew upon the mosque's self-interest in relation to its intention to build an extension to its prayer hall on land that Tower Hamlets local borough council had earmarked for housing. Jameson drew upon the infant TELCO to mobilize support for the mosque's planning application and, following a march of three thousand TELCO members, plans were changed and it became possible for the mosque to begin its expansion. Warren notes that this level of commitment persuaded the mosque's committee to join TELCO.[20] Jameson illustrates the close relationship that TELCO had developed with the East London Mosque in his reflection on the Accountability Assembly held ahead of the 2002 London local elections. Speaking of cultural and religious diversity, he observed that 'TELCO teaches that diversity is a political strength . . . We cannot, however, agree on approaches to God or partisan political positions, so the best TELCO leaders avoid these issues and build relationships of mutual respect around an agenda for action we can agree on and fight for together.'[21] Three strands in Jameson's reflection are worth highlighting. First, diversity is not portrayed in moral or theological terms but as a political strength. Second, the proactive embrace of diversity enables the articulation of a shared political agenda. Third, in order to forge a united agenda for action, it is necessary to avoid addressing theological and party political disagreements. I return in later chapters to these questions.

TRAINING AS EMPOWERMENT

Training is a foundational plank of community organizing. London Citizens uses its training to develop 'the skills necessary to be an effective community leader'.[22] Such training is aimed at 'individuals who are interested in thinking deeply about how to improve their own institution or group whilst also strengthening civil society in the twenty-first century so that their values make a real impact in the world'.[23]

The training offered by London Citizens revolves around three key themes. First, it seeks to develop community leadership skills. Second, the training aims to help participants to translate ethical or religious values into organized activism. Third, the training explores the nature and role of hierarchical power in contemporary society and the productive use of relational power within community organizing. In its Leadership in the Real World programme for older high school students, London Citizens sharpens this broad-brush description referring to power analysis, negotiation, the art of persuasion and public speaking, building alliances, mapping communities, one-to-one conversations, listening campaigns, building power and using the media.[24] The former government minister James Purnell who stood down as a Labour Member of Parliament at the 2010 British general election became interested in community organizing after he resigned from Gordon Brown's cabinet in 2009. Purnell, who attended London Citizens training in 2010, pointed to the diversity of those attending.[25] Speaking of this course a London Citizens spokesperson said of Purnell's training, 'He will be in there with asylum seekers, churchgoers and people way outside the political class. They'll do classes on how to speak truth to power, how to negotiate, how to do one-to-ones . . . James will even do one course on how to be a political leader, but he'll be as far away from Westminster as can be.'[26] The training provided by London Citizens seeks to engage a culturally diverse constituency in its training. Warren suggests, with justification, that it has succeeded in its task of empowering new leaders, often from Black and Asian-British communities, as well as those previously marginalized from the political process.[27]

Since its emergence in East London in the mid-1990s, London Citizens has developed a close working relationship with the Geography Department at Queen Mary College, University of London and in particular with Jane Wills. Building on her research into a living wage and her analysis of London Citizens with Lina Jamoul, Wills introduced a Master's degree in community organizing in 2010, the first of its kind in the United Kingdom. She suggests that the degree aims to 'provide an advanced understanding of the theory, history and practice of community organizing in the wider context of contemporary academic debate about social, political and economic change . . . [and] to strengthen the cadre of community organizers being developed in the UK, through an ongoing partnership with Citizens UK'.[28]

BUILDING A 'PEOPLES ORGANIZATION'

The Citizen Organizing Foundation was renamed Citizens UK in 2009. In words that echo Alinsky's stated aim as far back as the Back of the Yards campaign to build a 'people's organization', Citizens UK expresses its desire to 'create a network of competent, informed and organized citizens who act responsibly in the public life of their communities and are able to influence, for the common good, decisions which impact on their communities'.[29] It goes on to suggest that 'Citizens UK is the national home of community organizing—a method that enables ordinary people to bring about change through alliances of institutions acting together for the common good. We train. We assemble. We negotiate. We act.'[30] Although, as I will show, Citizens UK is not the only expression of community organizing in the UK, it remains the only established strategic community-organizing network at the time of writing. Currently Citizens UK works primarily in London where it has established TELCO, South London Citizens, West London Citizens, North London Citizens and Shoreditch Citizens, which together are made up of 250 member groups.[31] An affiliated community organization was established in recent years in Milton Keynes (2007, with fifteen members by 2013), and emergent organizations have been developed in Nottingham and Birmingham with exploratory work being undertaken in Cardiff, Leeds and Glasgow.[32] In 2013, seventeen years after the establishment of London's first broad-based community organization, TELCO, Citizens UK employed thirty-three community organizers and was composed of 265 dues-paying member groups ranging from faith communities, schools and university departments to students unions, trades union branches and voluntary sector community groups. The ongoing recruitment of and relationship with member groups is of fundamental importance within Citizens UK because of the membership-based nature of the 'people's organization' it seeks to build.

In his online COMM-ORG course, Aaron Schutz suggests that although the viability of long-term organizing rests on the success of the broad-based community organization, 'community organizing groups are made up of relationships between individuals'.[33] I suggested in chapter 1 that one-to-ones should be seen as strategic interviews aimed at recruitment rather than the expression of selfless interest in another individual. Fran Monks conversation with Neil Jameson confirms this assessment.[34] Monk writes of Jameson's approach to one-to-ones: ' "Go on Father, you're here to bring about the Kingdom of Heaven, so how's it going?" . . . Neil Jameson . . . admits, "It's a bit embarrassing and often we're thrown out before we get to the cup of tea." But when he finds priests who are willing to step back and grapple with the question of what influence they're really having in their communities, they usually end up signing up for Neil's Citizens Organizing Foundation.'[35] In spite of this apparently confrontational approach, it is important to recognize that the long-term health of a broad-based 'people's organization' like Citizens UK rests on the development of positive, long-lasting and mutually respectful human relationships. Jameson highlights the importance of such mutuality in his conversation with Monks. He suggests that 'people discover how magnificent it is to be in solidarity with others that hitherto they thought were off another planet . . . And then you discover they're worried about their children, like you are, they're mugged by the same muggers and litter is the same problem for them as everyone else.'[36] He goes on to suggest that the trust which results from such a recognition has made it possible to build a 'people's organization' in London where the identification and implementation of campaigns that revolve around mutual self-interest can subvert ideological or religious disagreement. Jameson suggests that 'once you get . . . in a room you don't talk about the ideology . . . You talk about, who can help us, who's an ally . . . what power have we got, what power have they got?'[37]

Although the community organizer stimulates the emergence of broad-based community organizations in the same way that the organic-political intellectual described by Antonio Gramsci, Edward Said and Cornel West articulates the struggles of those alongside whom she or he works, it is the concerns and commitment of member groups that provide the foundation upon which the 'people's organization' is built.[38] Whilst reflecting Alinsky's stress on self-interest, the work of Citizens UK also places an equally clear emphasis on values-led organizing and the translation of political or religious values into effective action as the witness of member groups from South London Citizens illustrates.

- 'I belong to South London Citizens because they are an organization that gets people to use their power, makes sure things happen for the good of everyone and takes on any challenge that betters the lives of the poor.' (Fr. John Clark, Wandsworth)
- 'Being a member allows me to practice my faith as a Muslim in helping to bring about social justice.' (Sarfraz Jeraj, Lambeth)

- 'South London Citizens allows me to sit in a room with people from all faiths, all ages, all racial backgrounds, all walks of life . . . coming together for the good of all.' (Keith Minnott, Lewisham)[39]

REWEAVING THE FABRIC OF SOCIETY: THE PRINCIPLES OF ORGANIZING IN THE UNITED KINGDOM

Neil Jameson speaks with evangelical zeal about community organizing: 'We have found nirvana', he says. 'Community Organizing is the answer to globalization. It is the answer to the collapse of politics.'[40] In the next chapter I consider Jameson's ambitious assertion in greater critical depth as I explore what I call 'the new politics' and the place of community organizing within this broad and still emerging strand of twenty-first-century civil society activism. Here I simply consider one key question: upon what philosophical, ethical and political principles is the community organizing described by Jameson as 'nirvana' built?

Writing of the involvement of the East London Muslim community in the development of TELCO Jameson draws upon two key Islamic concepts to summarize the philosophical thrust of London Citizens. He writes, 'My understanding of Islam is that . . . peace is best achieved through struggle or *jihad*—and that there is no short cut way of achieving it other than through action and reflection whilst trying to bring about a more just world.'[41] Although Jameson does not allude to the contested nature of the term *jihad*, his words provide a useful picture of community-organizing philosophy: a reflective struggle for social justice and harmony.[42] Such a brief summary however does not adequately express the philosophical ground upon which community organizing in the United Kingdom has been built. The 2004 Citizen Organizing Foundation paper 'Reweaving the Fabric of Society' provides greater depth. The paper outlines five 'statements of faith' upon which UK community organizing rests. First, Citizens UK's 'iron rule' exemplifies its commitment to a model of political activism that revolves around empowerment: 'the most valuable and enduring form of development for the human spirit—intellectually, politically and socially—is the development people freely choose to own and act on.' Second, the position paper implicitly adopts a bias towards the oppressed and a commitment to the potential of excluded people to become community leaders through a programme of training. Third, Citizens UK rests upon an action-oriented pedagogy, comparable to that explored by Paulo Freire, which locates the power to bring about social change in the experience of communities rather than existing institutions of power: 'We believe in learning through action or social learning . . . We have to come up with our own solutions for ourselves.' Fourth, Citizens UK relies on the power of intimate human relationships. Contact and mutual respect become the foundation of effective political action and the reinvigoration of civil society. Fifth, Citizens UK exists to build power, to forge a 'peoples' organization' that can become a voice for voiceless communities in the public sphere.[43] Although committed to the forging of the common good, Citizens UK has, since its inception, avoided the articulation of visionary mission statements, preferring instead to deal with the 'world as it is' rather than the 'world as it should be'.[44]

Alongside its position papers, the clearest expression of the values that guide Citizens UK is found on its own website. This is a bottom-up network committed to the pursuit of social justice, which emphasizes mutual self-interest and the capacity of faith and community groups to generate social capital: 'London Citizens is a powerful grassroots charity working with local people for local people. Our goal is social, economic and environmental justice. We meet that goal by training people of all ages, faiths and backgrounds to take action together for change.'[45] Second, this is a political organization that seeks to build the effective political power of grass-roots faith and community groups, 'an experiment in democracy and the exercise of civic power'.[46] The purpose of power for Citizens UK is the building of the 'common good'.[47] Citizens UK describes its mission as the creation of a 'network of competent, informed and organized citizens who act responsibly in the public life of their communities and are able to influence, for the common good, decisions which impact on their communities'.[48] However Citizens UK's ideological pragmatism, emphasis on self-interest and its proactive use of deliberate tension raises questions about its understanding of the 'common good' which I will consider in other chapters. Third, Citizens UK sees itself as the generator of the bridging and linking social capital explored by Putnam in the United States and by Field, Baker and Skinner in the United Kingdom.[49] This emphasis is expressed clearly on the Citizens UK website: 'At the heart of Citizens UK is a very simple idea: our society becomes a better place for everyone when ordinary people work together for change.'[50]

PRAGMATIC MULTICULTURALISM OR FAITH FOUNDATION?

Whereas PICO and the Gamaliel Foundation in the United States embrace their status as specifically faith-based community organizations, community organizing in the United Kingdom has, to date, followed the more pragmatic line adopted by the IAF. The Citizens UK website notes its inherent religious diversity: 'Our leaders are black, brown and white . . . We are Sikh, Hindu, Muslim, Buddhist, Christian and Secular'.[51] However, since its inception Citizens UK has deliberately placed a greater emphasis on the common humanitarian values of dignity, equality and social justice that guide their work than on specific theological themes. Jameson recognizes that for many of the faith groups who are members of Citizens UK, these core values arise from particular religious traditions. However, he argues that in multi-faith cities like London it is necessary to adopt 'the politics of compromise, dialogue and pragmatism' as the most effective means of attaining the 'common good'.[52]

In spite of such self-conscious pragmatism, Citizens UK is, in effect, a de facto faith-based community organization since two-thirds of its member institutions are faith groups. Citizens UK's growing relationships with the East London Contextual Theology Centre, the Leicestershire-based Islamic Foundation and the work of the political theologian Luke Bretherton implicitly recognize the central importance of faith groups within the people's organization it is seeking to forge.[53] All three of these theological centres are strong supporters of the model of community organizing forged by Citizens UK. Bretherton, for example, was one of the key Citizens UK figures to question Conservative Party leader David Cameron (and current UK prime minister) at the May 2010 Citizens UK general election debate.[54] Hence, although Citizens UK adopts a pragmatic faith-based stance, it is important to note that these theological partners are compatriots in the struggle to establish community organizing in the United Kingdom.

Bretherton's analysis of London Citizens' philosophical foundation has particular resonance for people of faith. He argues that community organizing represents a new form of faith-based political activism that should be distinguished from other forms of protest politics. He suggests that it exemplifies a contradictory model of civil society politics: it's 'no' to current injustice is mirrored by a clear 'yes' to an alternative pattern of communal living. Bretherton argues that this perspective finds a strong theological echo in Augustine's use of the term *saeculum,* the flawed earthly city, which can be compared with Alinsky's conception of the 'world as it is'.[55] Bretherton suggests that community organizing offers the Christian community a model of discipleship that reflects the social teaching of the church and challenges the individualization of faith through an invitation to a contradictory model of communal life.

Bretherton goes on to explore the potential connection between community organizing and the Christian Realist tradition most closely connected with Reinhold Niebuhr, pointing to the influence of Niebuhr on politically engaged Protestant Christians.[56] This is a correlation also made in Macleod's theological reflection on early UK community organizing, which suggests that Niebuhr's Christian Realism 'provides a coherent, almost tailor-made, theological underpinning for community organizing' which critiques the political naïveté of religious idealism in favour of a more nuanced realism that balances idealistic vision with pragmatic methodology.[57] Chris Baker does not write specifically about community organizing in his exploration of the possible shape of a public theology suited to the fluid hybridity of an urban 'third space'.[58] However he too argues that Christian Realism and, in particular, the nineteenth-century Social Gospel tradition from which it emerged can provide the tools needed to fashion a prophetic model of discipleship that has the capacity to balance utopian theological liberalism on the one hand and crisis laden religious pessimism on the other.[59] Baker suggests that such a perspective can enable Christian communities to engage creatively with the normative diversity of the urban third space in a critical but provisional manner. So does Christian Realism provide community organizing with its theological base? Bretherton suggests not, in part because it fails to recognize that both Christianity and community organizing represent contradictions of contemporary Western capitalism. For Bretherton, the Christian Realist tradition cannot feed a theology of community organizing because the Christian faith cannot be reduced to the status of the existential handmaiden of progressive liberal democracy. For Bretherton, community organizing offers people of faith a model of communal living that contradicts materialistic capitalism by offering an alternative set of subversive values upon which to build social life.[60] In later chapters, I explore the possibility of developing a convincing liberative theology of community organizing.

SOCIAL MOVEMENT OR PEOPLE'S ORGANIZATION?

In the next chapter, I explore the nature of social-movement politics in depth. At this point, however, it is important to note that like other broad-based community organizations, Citizens UK has largely resisted comparisons with urban social movements for five key reasons. First, Citizens UK views itself as a permanent and structured 'people's organization' rather than a fluid and short-lived social movement. Second, although it has demonstrated a clear commitment to inclusive civil society, Citizens UK is a carefully structured membership-based organization where decisions about campaigns are made solely by member groups. Such an approach inevitably excludes informal community networks or committed individuals who do not belong to any formal institution. Third, while seeking to empower individuals and train community leaders, Citizens UK engages with institutions rather than individuals. Consequently, it is member organizations that vote in strategy teams and assemblies rather than individual people in the hall. This approach relies to a large degree on the ability of leaders within their own institutions to facilitate active involvement in the work of Citizens UK. Fourth, unlike many social movements, Citizens UK works on a multi-issue agenda for civic activism. Priority is given to the health and capacity of the organization rather than the immediacy of any single issue. This multi-issue approach was clearly seen in the Citizens UK 'Peoples Manifesto' presented to the leaders of the Labour Party, the Liberal Democrats and the Conservative Party ahead of the 2010 UK general election.[61] Fifth, unlike many social movements, community organizing is focused around the determination to build ongoing political power as opposed to advocacy or the mobilizing of mass protest. Hence, its activism is pragmatic and focused on the strategic goal of fashioning a new kind of political culture.

Writing in a US context Ellen Ryan argues that community organizing aims to 'build a growing base of people who can deliberate, set goals, and take action together over the long term, reaching out to bring in more people to build deeper and wider organizations as the work unfolds'.[62] Ryan's words pinpoint the distinction between contemporary community organizations and social movements although in the next chapter I will ask if, in fact, the assertion that community organizing is not an example of wider social movement politics is credible. Here I simply introduce the values and structures of Citizens UK in Figure 2.1 below.

VALUES AND STRUCTURES WITHIN CITIZENS UK

Citizens UK's organizational structure arises from the core values previously mentioned and is intended to effectively translate them into practice. The core values that guide the community organizing of Citizens UK might imply a horizontal organizational structure embodying its commitment to equality and social justice. Such an approach would reflect that found in the anti hierarchical social movements that began to emerge during the 1960s, such as the New Left and the environmental, feminist-womanist and antinuclear movements. Jeff Goodwin and James Jasper suggest that such groups sought to 'foster "free spaces" in which creative alternatives to mainstream politics can be imagined, discussed and tried out'.[63] A much older example of such antihierarchical organizations is seen in the early church in Jerusalem as it is depicted in the Acts of the Apostles. According to the author(s) of Acts, this early faith-based social movement combined a focused mission with an egalitarian organizational structure. Acts 4:32ff paints a picture of this social movement: 'the whole group of those who believed were of one heart and soul and no one claimed private ownership of any possessions, but everything they owned was held in common.'

Richard Scott describes such an organizational structure as an 'open system', which emphasizes dialogue and non hierarchical decision-making more than the preservation of organizational structure and boundary-keeping.[64] Alison Gilchrist argues that egalitarian social movements with their horizontal organizational structures resemble networks rather than more formalized and clearly defined organizations. Gilchrist suggests that 'networks operate on the basis of informal connections rather than formal roles, and membership tends to be voluntary and participative'.[65] Gilchrist's conclusions, which are largely drawn from her experience in community development work in the United Kingdom, invite comparisons with Manuel Castells' theoretical argument that the interconnecting facility of overlapping networks has become the dominant political logic of a geographically dispersed

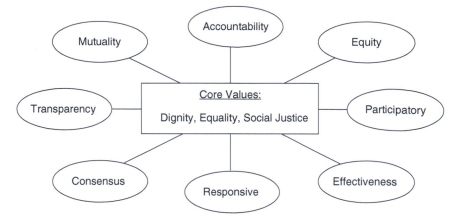

Figure 2.1   The Values Base of Citizens UK

power elite in a globalised century.[66] Furthermore Gilchrist's conclusions affirm Zygmunt Bauman's assessment of late and postmodern societies as increasingly liquid wherein the modernist solidity of membership-based formal organizations has, to a large degree, been supplanted by the more informal and relational politics that Homi Bhabha and Chris Baker suggest arise within the hybrid 'third space' of complex superdiverse societies.[67] The network as described by Gilchrist facilitates the development of informal coalitions and fosters participation. Such an assessment perhaps implies that the network, rather than the formalized organization, is best placed to foster the reinvigoration of an inclusive and dialogical civil society. However, when egalitarian movements grow and become more complex, their 'open system' can be supplanted by a more hierarchical organizational structure which is intended to provide clearer lines of communication, structure and accountability within the expanded organization. Unlike the 'open system', or network, Gilchrist suggests that within hierarchical organizations, roles are clearly delineated and engagement within the group is largely based on formal membership rather than loose affiliation. She argues that in rapidly changing or uncertain contexts, networks can be more effective vehicles of progressive community politics than formalized organizations because they facilitate boundary-hopping, interdependence, the free exchange of ideas and 'opportunities for informal interaction across organizational borders'.[68] This consideration of the liberative potential of social movements, networks and membership-based organizations will form a key part of my analysis of 'the new politics' in chapter 3 and my examination of the insights that contemporary social theory might have to offer community organizing in chapter 4.

A key consideration within Citizens UK has been the development of a decision-making structure that can effectively translate core values into practical action while also facilitating the building of a long-lasting people's organization. Central to this task has been the question of good governance. Although the discussion of what constitutes good governance is by its very nature always provisional, the template offered by Adel Abdellatif of the United Nations Development Programme offers a useful summary of its central characteristics. Abdellatif suggests that good governance has nine characteristics: participation, the rule of law, transparency, responsiveness, consensus orientation, equity, effectiveness, accountability and strategic vision.[69] Below Figure 2.2 depicts the organizational structure of Citizens UK, which resembles a hierarchical membership-based organization rather than an informal and fluid network of association. The organizational form depicted seeks to provide a transparent and accountable framework that is structurally capable of effectively representing the concerns of the faith groups and community organizations that are members of Citizens UK. There is a pyramid of authority, whereby the responsibility for effective community organizing ultimately rests with the director of Citizens UK and its board of trustees, although this authority is ceded to them by the

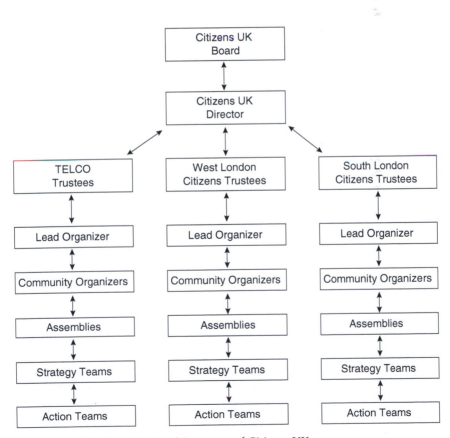

Figure 2.2 The Organizational Structure of Citizens UK

institutions that make up the people's organization. Arguably, this pyramid of authority could be inverted to reflect the fact that the purpose of Citizens UK is to give effective voice and power to the individuals who attend the mosques, churches, gurdwaras, community groups, schools and trades union branches that constitute its membership. The capacity of Citizens UK to organize effective assemblies, strategy groups and the action teams that guide specific campaigns rests with key figures within each member institution in partnership with local professional community organizers. Where key figures within each member institution can mobilize large numbers of people and the community organizer is able to harness, direct and organize this expression of people power, effective campaigns can be mounted and the goals of Citizens UK can be realized. In organizational terms, Citizens UK resembles a fusion of a formalized hierarchy and an open system wherein the community organizer acts as the connector between grass-roots membership and managing trustees. Citizens UK has adopted this decision-making structure as the most effective way of building a long-lasting people's organization capable of forging a new and egalitarian mode of political activism. Two critical questions are implied by my description of the philosophy and the organizational structure of Citizens UK. First, because it relies on the voluntary long-term commitment of large numbers of neighbourhood groups, how effective has Citizens UK been since the emergence of TELCO in 1996 at including, listening to and mounting effective localized grass-roots actions as opposed to strategic national campaigns? Second, in a structure that emphasizes the central importance of the organized mobilization of large numbers of people at assemblies and as part of actions, might it be possible that the voices of larger and more powerful member groups are heard more clearly than the concerns of small and fragile faith groups or community organizations? I consider these questions further towards the end of this chapter.

CITIZENS IN ACTION

Broad-based community organizations exist for a single purpose: to enable people from marginalized communities to build a powerful and long-lasting citizens' coalition for social justice through the effective forging of a new and inclusive model of people's politics.[70] Since its inception it has been this motivation that has driven every campaign that Citizens UK has undertaken. In order to assess the campaigns that it has developed, it is necessary to answer three questions. First, what criteria are used to select campaigns? Second, what kinds of campaigns has Citizens UK mounted over the last ten years? Third, how is the success of these campaigns evaluated? The campaigns that Citizens UK has forged since the establishment of TELCO in 1996 can be divided into three broad categories as shown in Figure 2.3.

Neighbourhood Campaigns	City-wide Campaigns	National Campaigns
Street lighting in Whitechapel	Living Wage campaign	Strangers into Citizens campaign
Waiting times at Newham General Hospital	City Safe Campaign	Citizens for Sanctuary
Community Safety in Newham	Our Homes . . . Our London	Citizens UK General Election Assembly 2010
Retaining local branches of major banks in East London	Citizen Schools	Living Wage campaign
Initial Living Wage Campaign in London Docklands	London Olympics Campaign	
Norlington Boys School in Leyton (Norlington Enquiry into street crime near school)	Governance Campaign	
	Greener Planet Action	

Figure 2.3   London Citizens' Main Campaigns, 1996–2010

There is a clear process by which Citizens UK selects neighbourhood and citywide campaigns that originates with the mutual self-interest of individuals who attend the faith and community groups that are members of the organization. Each member institution is represented on the strategy team that guides the day-to-day work of each of the community organizations that are affiliated to Citizens UK. These representatives bring specific concerns from their own community to the strategy team where they are discussed and then voted upon. Discussion will generally be led by community organizers and will seek to establish the following:

1. Is this a problem that is shared by other member groups?
2. Is it possible to translate the problem highlighted into a specific issue around which a viable strategy can be mounted?
3. Is there a reasonable chance of measureable success in relation to the specific issue?
4. Is there sufficient capacity and commitment to mount a sustained campaign?

Many of Citizens UK citywide actions such as the living wage campaign and the London Olympics campaign emerged as neighbourhood campaigns before being adopted as London-wide actions at accountability assemblies. In order to understand the major campaigns that Citizens UK has undertaken I will use the living wage campaign as a case study for two reasons. First, it exemplifies the core themes that have characterized its work and, second, it is the broad effectiveness of this campaign that has been most widely discussed in the media and in the limited amount of critical analysis of the work of Citizens UK.

A LIVING WAGE

The struggle for a living wage has become an iconic Citizens UK campaign and it's most effective in terms of measureable success. It is a campaign that embodies the core principles that guide its community organizing: human dignity, equality and the building of a people's organization capable of forging an effective model of grass-roots politics committed to the common good. The campaign was initially adopted by TELCO in 2001, two years after New Labour's introduction of a national minimum wage for the United Kingdom in 1999.[71] TELCO's struggle for a living wage drew inspiration from the first modern living wage campaign in Baltimore, Maryland, United States, amongst dockworkers and building labourers during 1994, which was initiated by the IAF-affiliated Baltimoreans United in Leadership Development (B.U.I.L.D.).[72] Margaret Levi, David Olson and Erich Steinman argue that, in the United States, 'living wage campaigns have captured the imagination of organizations that represent low-wage workers . . . The campaigns illuminate the . . . importance of coalitions among the labor movement, community and religious organizations'.[73] The commitment unleashed by this first campaign in Baltimore stimulated numerous other struggles and, by 2013, the introduction of living wage bills in almost 150 cities in the United States from California in the west to Massachusetts in the east. In 2010, Barack Obama commissioned research into the possible introduction of a federal living wage to counter the enduring problem of deep-seated low pay amongst contracted labourers in the United States surviving on federal- or state-based minimum-wage rates.[74] Just a few months before I completed this chapter, Barack Obama included a proposal to increase the federal minimum wage from US$7.25 to US$9.00 per hour in his February 2013 State of the Union speech.[75] However, a bill similar to Obama's proposal was voted down by House Republicans and conservative Democrats when it was put to Congress in March 2013. A federal living wage in the United States, it appears, is still out of reach in 2013.[76]

Jane Wills recognizes that the current London Citizens living wage campaign is part of a far older struggle for a living wage in the UK amongst trades unions and faith groups that stretches back to the nineteenth century.[77] As Wills notes, the argument for a living wage can be traced back to the 1894 treatise of the West Yorkshire Liberal Member of Parliament Mark

Oldroyd, who argued that the payment of a wage that enabled a reasonable standard of living made economic, political and moral sense.[78] Furthermore, as I suggested in chapter 1, the ethical impetus behind London Citizens living wage campaign can be traced back further still to the labour organizing of the Tolpuddle Martyrs in the 1830s and even to the radical egalitarianism of the seventeenth-century Diggers and the assertion by Gerrard Winstanley that the earth should be conceived of as a 'common treasury' to be shared by all.[79]

More specifically, TELCO's adoption of the living wage campaign in 2001 arose from a process of active listening to the concerns of its member organizations. Wills suggests that many people were caught in the seemingly inescapable trap of low pay and devalorised, insecure work that had resulted from the liberalization of the labour market during the 1980s and 1990s, the declining power of trades unions to effectively hold employers to account and the increasing competition from distant low-pay economies that had resulted from the processes of economic globalization.[80] TELCO leaders drew on classic organizing techniques to translate a problem that fostered a sense of impotence into a specific issue that could be systematically addressed. The first step in this process was to raise awareness about the issue in the media and in particular the argument that TELCO was making for a living wage. Writing in *The Guardian* newspaper just as TELCO adopted the living wage campaign, Madeleine Bunting articulated the issue in graphic terms: 'When you arrive in your office this morning, the carpet will have been vacuumed, the bins emptied and the desk cleared of its old polystyrene coffee cups. Do you ever think about the life of the person who clears up your mess . . . They are an invisible workforce . . . In London you occasionally catch glimpses of them . . . as they stand at bus stops at 5am in the morning; they are usually women and often black.'[81]

Second, in an effort to analyze the problem TELCO partnered with the trades union UNISON which represented many low-paid workers, particularly in the National Health Service, commissioning Jane Wills to write the research report *Mapping Low-Pay in East London*.[82] Wills' report provided the resulting living wage campaign with a solid analytical evidence-based foundation. First, Wills charts the endemic problem of low pay and insecure work in East London and suggests that 'East London is . . . emblematic of the social polarization that now blights world cities'.[83] She argues that although the introduction of the UK national minimum wage in 1999 improved the standard of living for over one million workers, especially women, 'it is insufficient to effectively tackle child and adult poverty in London'.[84] Second, the report provided the detailed qualitative and quantitative data in relation to the differing experiences of workers in the private and the public sector that enabled TELCO to target its campaigning on specific employers and issues. Third, Wills' analysis drew on personal stories of individual low-paid workers, providing TELCO with gripping testimonies that humanized an otherwise technical debate. Wills made four telling points: 'People with children are often those who work the longest hours in overtime . . . A number of workers had to do more than one job to survive . . . The majority of low paid workers interviewed were black . . . Workers complained of a lack of respect from managers.'[85] On the basis of such testimony and qualitative analysis Wills' 2001 report effectively made the economic, social and moral case for a living wage. Throughout this long campaign Citizens UK has continued to supplement organized action with its own reports and the academic research of some academics, especially those like Wills who is based at Queen Mary, University of London, in the East End of London. Although it is important to recognize that such research has largely been written by those who are strong supporters of Citizens UK, its veracity cannot reasonably be questioned and it has continued to provide the living wage campaign with a solid analytical foundation upon which its actions have been built.[86]

Third, in light of this initial research, TELCO (and later Citizens UK) adopted a multifaceted pattern of campaigning that modelled the new 'peoples politics' it sought to forge. The breadth of campaigning styles is seen in Figure 2.4.

The research undertaken by Wills enabled Citizens UK to identify specific low-pay employers in a manner reminiscent of Alinsky's advice to early community organizers: 'Pick the target, freeze it, personalize it and polarize it.'[87]

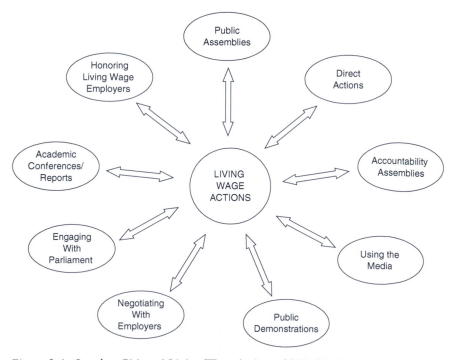

Figure 2.4   London Citizens' Living Wage Actions, 2001–2010

The living wage campaign has targeted specific high-profile employers such as HSBC and Barclays in the banking sector, the Royal London Hospital in the health service, the Hilton Group of hotels and the Greater London Authority in the political sphere, thus generating the maximum publicity for the issues it raises. Early actions, such as the thousand-strong public assembly in 2001 where TELCO members put the case for a living wage to East London MPs, officials from HSBC and John Monks the then General Secretary of the Trades Union Congress, sought to demonstrate Alinksy's assertion that an organized and mobilized people's organization had the power to bring about systemic change. During 2001 and 2002, TELCO members occupied a flagship HSBC branch in London's Oxford Street and others bought shares in HSBC in order to interrupt the annual general meeting and argue the case for the living wage. Such activism exemplified the pragmatic radicalism of Alinskyite organizing through its creative use of deliberately created moments of tension as a stimulus for change, echoing aspects of the direct action that characterized the civil rights movement and Gandhi's campaigning for independence in India. Other early actions during 2002, such as the Parliamentary Hearing for a Living Wage in the House of Commons, the negotiation with National Health Service Trust members at Hackney's Homerton Hospital and the singer-songwriter Billy Bragg's Living Wage Tour, demonstrated an awareness of the need to address complex systems of power in a holistic manner, akin to the methodology adopted by the civil rights movement during the 1960s.[88] Although the aim of Citizens UK continues to be the development of its own power as a distinct people's organization, the living wage campaign illustrates its willingness to develop partnerships with organizations such as trades unions where such relationships strengthen its own work.

The living wage campaign emerged first in east London but its adoption by South London Citizens and West London Citizens in 2004 catapulted it onto a citywide stage. The broad membership base of Citizens UK meant that the campaign could mobilize large numbers of people, and the organization's formalized structure made it possible to maintain effective actions over the extended period necessary to mount sufficient pressure to bring about meaningful change. The communitarian model of political engagement advocated by London Citizens which echoes Alinsky's 'iron rule' of organizing—never do for others what they are capable of doing for themselves—has characterized the living wage campaign. Listening campaigns have been undertaken, actions have been led and assemblies chaired by women, men and young people who belong to the groups that are members of Citizens UK. However, it would be a mistake to imagine that the living wage campaign has represented a spontaneous upsurge of disenfranchised urban Britons. Perhaps the 'iron rule' of empowerment needs to be qualified. Castells, like Gramsci before him, speaks of the motivating and organizational role of political and organic intellectuals who draw on liberative education models to stimulate the critical awareness of marginalized

communities.[89] Bretherton also notes the pivotal role of the community organizer within Alinskyite organizing as one whose role is to agitate, empower, train, organize and articulate the concerns of politically marginalized
people and communities.[90] The Citizens UK living wage campaign is an expression of people's politics but it is important not to romanticize the power
of this people's organization which continues to be facilitated, guided and
structured by its own political and organic intellectuals: professional community organizers.

Over the last decade, a number of milestones have exemplified the wide-
ranging success of Citizens UK's living wage campaign. In 2004 and again
in 2008 mayoral accountability assemblies in London were held where first
Ken Livingstone and then Boris Johnson committed themselves to introducing a living wage within the Greater London Authority. Initially a Living
Wage Unit was established by Mayor Ken Livingstone in 2004, since which
time this initial commitment was reaffirmed by Livingstone's successor, Boris
Johnson. A living wage has been introduced for all direct and contracted
employees and Citizens UK has declared the Greater London Authority to
be a 'Living Wage Employer'.[91] Conservative Mayor Boris Johnson made
it clear that he has accepted the ethical and economic argument for a living wage: 'Paying the London Living Wage is not only morally right, but
it makes good business sense too.'[92] Furthermore living wage agreements
were struck with the London Olympic Committee in 2004 and the Olympic
Delivery Authority in 2007 in relation to the 2012 London Olympics; in the
financial sector with HSBC and Barclays banks in 2006 and 2007; and in the
higher education sector with Queen Mary, University of London, in 2006,
the London School of Economics in 2007 and the School of Oriental and African Studies in 2008. During the 2010 British general election campaign the
Labour Party promised that, if elected, it would introduce a living wage for
up to one hundred thousand low-paid civil servants.[93] In the immediate aftermath of the election, the new Conservative-Liberal Democrat government
explored the possibility of introducing a living wage for all low-paid cleaning and catering staff in Whitehall and across government departments.[94] If
such a policy were instituted it would represent the most high-profile living
wage victory since the campaigns inception in 2001. Although little clear
progress had been made at a national level in the United Kingdom, by 2013
in a speech in April 2013 the leader of the Labour Party, Ed Milliband, committed a future Labour government to introducing a national living wage.[95]

OTHER LIVING WAGE CAMPAIGNS

Although the Citizens UK campaign for a living wage has been widely reported in the British media, it would be a mistake to assume that it has been
the only third-sector agency to embrace the issue. The question of equity,
human dignity and a living wage has deep roots in the Muslim injunction

of *Zakat,* which urges all Muslims to place the struggle for social justice at the heart of their lives as Tariq Ramadan reminds us.[96] Furthermore such a perspective underpins the philosophy of jubilee and the divine bias to the oppressed in the Hebrew and Christian scriptures and its articulation within liberation theology as the work of Jorge Pixley and Clodovis Boff, Gustavo Gutiérrez and R.S. Sugirtharajah demonstrates.[97] The writers of the book of Proverbs 14:31 within the Hebrew Scriptures express such a bias in clear terms: 'Those who oppress the poor insult their Maker, but those who are kind to the needy honor him.' This is a perspective that has also run through the social teaching of the Roman Catholic Church since the publication of the Papal encyclical, *Rerum Novarum,* by Pope Leo XIII in 1891.[98] A clear radical and egalitarian thread can be identified therefore within Jewish and Christian Scripture and tradition. However, it is also important to note the historic incorporation of the Christian Church in Western Europe into the ruling class. Such a close relationship with power has often meant that the clarion call of a preferential option for the poor has been spiritualized, marginalized and neglected.

It is in light of this ambivalent heritage that the UK-based Church Action on Poverty initiated its living wage campaign in 2002 in an effort to challenge the Christian churches to set an example to other employers by providing a living wage for all those employed by the church. In the report that launched its campaign, Church Action on Poverty suggested that in its survey of church employees in the Greater Manchester area in the north of England, 62% were paid less than a living wage.[99] Since the launch of the Church Action on Poverty living wage campaign, many Christian denominations in the United Kingdom have sought, in varying degrees, to respond. In 2006, following the publication of the ecumenical *Faithful Cities* report, the Church of England recommended that Anglican churches should pay all employees a living wage.[100] The following year the British Methodist Conference affirmed the campaign for a living wage but stopped short of compelling churches to pay a living wage, preferring instead to simply recommend that Methodist churches should consider paying employees a living wage rather than the legally required national minimum wage.[101] In a similar vein, the 2008 Assembly of the Baptist Union of Great Britain called for local Baptist churches to consider their employment practice in light of Church Action on Poverty's living wage campaign.[102] The question to be faced by Christian churches in a UK context therefore is whether they are prepared to move beyond principled support for a living wage to the proactive implementation of living wage structures. Citizens UK perhaps needs not only to draw upon the support of faith communities in its own living wage campaign but also to work alongside parallel living wage campaigns such as that mounted by Church Action on Poverty. Such an approach may well lay the ground for a more collective, networked approach to the struggle for dignity at work for those in the United Kingdom who are least able to speak for themselves.

ASSESSING THE LIVING WAGE CAMPAIGN

The living wage campaign represents Citizens UK's longest running, best supported, most widely reported campaign. I have focused in detail upon this campaign because it exemplifies the core values, the methodology, the capacity of the most well-established broad-based community organization in the United Kingdom and the potential of strategic partnership-based social action.

The living wage campaign clearly reflects the core values and aspirations of Citizens UK in a number of ways. First, it arose directly from a process of careful listening to the concerns raised by people who belonged to faith and community groups that were TELCO members. The campaign was not ideologically driven from the top but arose from the experience and testimony of those at the grass roots. Second, as Wills attests, the living wage campaign has exemplified the people's politics that Citizens UK seeks to develop as a vehicle for empowerment and the reinvigoration of civil society. Wills notes that the living wage campaign has illustrated the central importance of the development of a realizable political strategy, the organized and sustained mobilization of civil society and the proactive development of strategic alliances with partners, such as the trades unions, who share many of the same goals. It is important to recognize however that Citizens UK's reliance on the support of faith and community leaders and on the active commitment of large numbers of often hard-pressed people means that its support base is fragile and that its ongoing development rests to a large degree on the encouragement and energy created by further successes and the cultivation of an active civil society.[103]

DIVERSITY OR DIVISION? THE FUTURE OF ORGANIZING IN THE UNITED KINGDOM

Since the early attempts to develop broad-based communities in Bristol and Merseyside during the early 1990s proved ultimately fruitless, the model of community organizing promoted by Citizens UK has, to date, been largely confined to London. Over the last ten years, Citizens UK has begun to root organizing in other British cities such as Milton Keynes, Cardiff, Nottingham and Glasgow. However the story of Birmingham Citizens more effectively illuminates the possibilities and problems facing community organizing in the United Kingdom because it is the oldest community organization outside London and because in 2008 it ended its formal relationship with Citizens UK following a period of disagreement about the future direction of community organizing in the city.

The story of the growth, decline and changing face of Birmingham Citizens exemplifies the diversity of approaches to community organizing in the United Kingdom. Four key points emerge from this still unfolding story.

First, Birmingham Citizens is even more reliant on local faith groups than Citizens UK. Of its twenty-five 2005 founding members, only four were not faith-based institutions. At its 2009 annual general meeting the number of non-faith-based institutions had not grown and the board of trustees was composed exclusively of people drawn from Birmingham Citizens' faith-group members.[104] In this sense it has more in common with faith-based community organizations in the United States such as PICO and the Gamaliel Foundation than it does with the Industrial Areas Foundation to which Citizens UK is affiliated. It is not surprising, therefore, that in 2010 Birmingham Citizens began to develop a direct relationship with the former director of the Gamaliel Foundation, Greg Galluzzo. Second, Birmingham Citizens has, especially since the end of its relationship with Citizens UK in 2008, sought to adopt a more flexible partnership-based approach to the campaigns it has mounted than that employed by Citizens UK. In practical, if not theoretical, terms, Birmingham Citizens resembles an inclusive network more than the solid people's organization envisaged by Alinsky. Third, just as the early organizing of TELCO in the mid-1990s revolved around a process of one-to-one relational meetings and listening campaigns, the initial agenda for action adopted by Birmingham Citizens at its 2005 founding assembly arose directly out of a series of community dialogues across the city. Community organizing is context specific and is not likely to take root in different settings unless the particularity of towns and cities is recognized and those campaigns that are mounted arise from the concerns of local people. Such a situation begs the question, 'How far is it possible to group a variety of community organizations operating in different contexts under a single structural banner?' Fourth, since the end of its relationship with Citizens UK, Birmingham Citizens has sought to fashion a less hierarchical independent broad-based community organization that is driven by a grass-roots campaigning agenda characterized more by informal partnerships with a range of community action groups than the overriding aim of building a permanent people's organization.[105]

Such brief reflections tell only half of the story. However, it is important to note that, like other earlier British broad-based community organizations that have ended their affiliation with Citizens UK, Birmingham Citizens is characterized by fragility and provisionality. Struggles to rebuild the momentum it had built from 2004 to 2008 as an independent community organization that could no longer draw on the support systems of the more-established Citizens UK proved intensely difficult. Its capacity to mount credible broad-based campaigns became seriously limited and its tentative attempts to assert a bottom-up Birmingham-specific identity emphasize the challenges facing broad-based community organizations in the United Kingdom that seek to develop their work outside the structure of Citizens UK. The emergence of the fledging Birmingham Citizens UK in 2013 should be read against this backdrop. The post-2008 Birmingham story raises a further challenge. Changes in personnel, capacity and context led to the development of a different approach that is perhaps more easy to reconcile with community development work, wider social movement politics and networked advocacy than classical community organizing—a stimulus for change, rather than its source.

As I noted previously, Citizens UK refers to itself as the 'national home of community organizing' in Britain. This is a reasonable claim. However, it would be a mistake to infer from this that there are not other, self-consciously faith-based community-organizing networks beginning to emerge in the United Kingdom. Such tentative initiatives include the nascent broad-based organization Changemakers, which, since its establishment in 2008 has begun developing community-organizing programmes in Manchester, Bradford and Stockton-on-Tees in the north of England.[106] Changemakers is in its infancy and, although its Manchester grouping is currently developing campaigns around support for those who care full time for a family member, the destitution of asylum seekers, drug and alcohol abuse and youth employment training, it is too early to critically assess its model of organizing and the likelihood of its long-term strength. It is possible, however to note several distinctions between Changemakers and Citizens UK. First, although like Citizens UK, Changemakers describes itself as a vehicle for the rebuilding of active civil society, its mission statement points to a clearer focus on campaigning for social justice than that of Citizens UK. The Changemakers website identifies this mission in the following terms: 'Our mission is to build a powerful community-led organization whose members take action on issues of social, economic, political and environmental justice.'[107] Second, unlike the effective but pragmatic faith base of Citizens UK, Changemakers is an explicitly faith-based community organization wherein religious faith is not viewed as a key resource but as the foundation for organizing. Although its faith basis is not immediately apparent from Changemakers' literature, its programs and research are all led by Church Action on Poverty key workers. It is important to ask therefore if Changemakers should be seen as a nascent independent broad-based community organization or as a partner project of the long established Church Action Poverty.[108] Third, whereas Citizens UK is affiliated to the Industrial Areas Foundation, Changemakers is closely linked to the specifically faith-based Gamaliel Foundation and receives community-organizing training from Gamaliel Foundation organizers. The Changemakers initiative is still too young to assess whether it has the potential to become rooted in the United Kingdom in the same manner as Citizens UK. Furthermore, its close connection with the Gamaliel Foundation may raise questions about its long-term viability in light of the fact that in conversation during 2010 US-based PICO organizer Gordon Whitman suggested to me that the Gamaliel Foundation itself is under severe strain in terms of its own institutional future.[109] Consequently when assessing community organizing in the United Kingdom it is important to recognize that although Citizens UK does indeed currently represent the fulcrum of British community organizing, the model of civil society politics it exemplifies is far broader than might at first appear to be the case.

CONCLUSION

In this chapter, I have shown that, since the establishment of the Citizens Organizing Foundation in 1989, broad-based community organizers have fashioned one of the most effective grass-roots progressive political movements seen in the United Kingdom since the emergence of the trades union and labour movement in the late nineteenth century. As I conclude this chapter, I want to highlight four critical questions that have emerged from my analysis. First, is the model of civic activism that community organizing has developed in the United Kingdom since 1989 new or unique? As I will show in the next chapter, it might be the case that broad-based community organizing is, in fact, much more closely akin to wider social movement politics than has previously been suggested. Second, is UK community organizing an example of radical faith-based civic activism and the reengagement of faith with the public sphere or is its faith base borne of pragmatic multiculturalism? In chapters 5 and 6 I begin to forge a liberative theology of community organizing that is rooted in an explicit bias to the oppressed and the fluid provisionality of the third space of superdiverse societies. Such a project can feed, challenge and enrich community organizing in the United Kingdom due to its de facto faith basis. Third, what does it mean to belong to Citizens UK or Birmingham Citizens? In one sense, this is a simple question to answer. Only those faith and community groups that become dues-paying members belong and have ownership of UK community organizations. Currently individuals cannot join or become friends of London or Birmingham Citizens and, although Citizens UK has a compact of understanding with the Islamic Foundation, informal networked alliances are entered into on a largely ad hoc basis in relation to specific campaigns. In later chapters, I ask whether the fluid third space of urban society demands a more networked and informal understanding of belonging and ownership. Fourth, how open is community organizing to independent constructive critique or dialogue with alternative models of urban civic activism? I have indicated in this chapter that Citizens UK has developed important and creative partnerships with the social geographer Wills and with the political theologian Bretherton. Wills has engaged in analytical depth with the living wage campaign, and Bretherton has begun to develop a political theology that engages with Alinskyite community organizing. However, to date there has been little detailed critique of UK community organizing since the Citizens Organizing Foundation was established in 1989 and, thus far, no significant attempt to sow the seeds of a liberative theology of community organizing. It is to this task that I turn in the following chapters.

Part II
Analysis

3   Part of a 'New Politics'

INTRODUCTION

In first part of this book, I charted the development of community organizing in the United States and the United Kingdom. I now turn from 'Experience' to 'Analysis' as I bring community organizing into a critical dialogue with examples of the extra-institutional political activism that has become increasingly significant in the decades since the fall of the Berlin Wall. Over the last decade the Internet has increasingly provided a globally accessible forum for the 'new politics'. During the late 1990s the Mexican resistance movement the Zapatistas began to illustrate the potential of the Internet as a tool for social movement politics.[1] The use of texting and social media such as Twitter in the 2009 protests about the Iranian presidential elections, in demonstrations against rises in student tuition fees in the United Kingdom in 2011, as a tool in the initial months of the Arab Spring across North Africa and parts of the Middle East from 2010 to 2012 and the Occupy movement since 2011and the sharing of a YouTube video protesting against Joseph Kony, the leader of the Lord's Resistance Army in Uganda (viewed almost ninety million times in 2012) have further demonstrated the dispersed political power of the Internet. Is this a 'new politics' for a 'Facebook generation'?[2] Although in the United Kingdom and the United States active engagement in formalised political processes has declined in recent decades, the claim that politics has withered on the vine needs to be considered afresh.[3]

Where does community organizing fit on this increasingly fluid political landscape and what implications might the 'new politics' have for the articulation of a liberative theology of community organizing? In this chapter I will consider what contemporary social movements, identity politics and the politics of difference may have to teach faith-based community organizers about active citizenship in the network society described so eloquently by Manuel Castells.[4] In an arguably postideological era a dialogical model of community organizing has the capacity to exemplify a 'new' bottom-up progressive politics and the potential to resource the articulation of a postreligious and postsecular theology of liberation for a superdiverse century.

Can it, however realize this potential without clearly aligning itself with a radical liberative agenda and a conscious bias towards the oppressed? It is with this question in mind that I begin my exploration of the 'new politics'.

FAITH IN THE PUBLIC SPHERE

The role of faith groups in the public sphere in the United Kingdom and the United States has become a central theoretical question in the twenty-first century. Is religious faith a purely private personal choice which should have no bearing on the nature of civil society or on government social policy? Alternatively is faith inherently public and, therefore, political?

In the United States where, since the adoption of the American Con- stitution, there has been a constitutional separation between church and state, faith groups have historically played a central role in the fashioning of civil society as de Tocqueville noted less than a century after the American Revolution.[5] Key issues as contrasting as the campaign for the abolition of slavery, the civil rights movement, the defence of gun ownership, capital punishment and opposition to abortion and equalities legislation in relation to human sexuality cannot be adequately explained if the central role of US faith groups is ignored. Although Alinsky was at pains to stress the faith- neutral character of community organizing, the broad-based organizations that have arisen from his Industrial Areas Foundation have, for over seventy years, relied implicitly on the active involvement of faith groups. In spite of Putnam's argument that the bonds of social capital in the United States are fraying, faith groups remain powerful players in the battle over the shape and style of civil society. Michael Edwards suggests that such voluntary civic associations remain central to American public life.[6] His point is illustrated by two recent developments. From the progressive tradition of American politics Barack Obama instituted a standing White House committee focus- ing on partnering faith groups and government within months of assuming the presidency in 2009, and from the right of the Republican Party, conser- vative Christians have emerged as key players in the Tea Party since its rise to prominence in the same year.[7]

The work of the Washington, DC-based Sojourners Community and its founder Jim Wallis exemplifies the key role played by faith groups in the US public sphere. Wallis has sought for almost four decades to fashion a space in US civil society for a model of religious faith that revolves around an activist's commitment to inclusive social justice on the one hand and an evangelical rooting in the Biblical narrative on the other. Wallis served as an adviser to Barack Obama from 2009 to 2012. He writes, 'God's politics reminds us of the people our politics always neglects—the poor, the vulner- able, the left behind. God's politics challenges narrow national, ethnic, eco- nomic or cultural self-interest . . . offering a new vision for faith and politics in America.'[8] Wallis is not explicitly aligned with any formal community organizations. However the model of faith-based activism he personifies has made him a critical friend of community organizing in the United States and his focus on 'soft' power and networking rather than organization building has the capacity to critique and enrich more formalised community organizations. The space he has fashioned straddles grass-roots campaigning (as seen in his support for the Occupy movement), the evangelical Christian community and influence on the domestic policy of the Obama White House. In a society where church and state are constitutionally separated, Wallis provides an example of the ongoing influence of Christian faith on US social policy.

The story in the United Kingdom is arguably the mirror image of the American narrative. Historically faith groups have been central characters in the story of faith in the public sphere in the United Kingdom. In spite of the marked decline in attendance at worship and in the membership of faith groups, particularly since the 1960s, the historic importance of the faith-based political engagement of the Diggers, the Tolpuddle Martyrs, the Victorian Christian Socialists, the often overlooked influence of Methodism on the labor movement or the earliest incarnations of the Campaign for Nuclear Disarmament cannot justifiably be overlooked. Yet, ironically given the existence of an established church and the ongoing presence of Anglican bishops in the House of Lords, religion has been widely and assertively depicted as a private activity which has no place in the contested public sphere of a largely post religious British society. However a 2012 report by the think tank Demos suggested that people of faith are more likely to be politically active than people who do not identify themselves with a specific faith community.[9] In recent years religious faith has been described by some, such as Christopher Hitchens and Anthony Grayling, as a primary driver of intolerance, exclusivity and social division—the cause and not the cure of society's ills. Such a strong secularist perspective is clear—faith has no place in the public sphere.[10] Robert Furbey summarises their case: 'Religion has little to contribute to public life; rather it threatens mayhem. Public politics should be secular, omitting religion.'[11] Tariq Modood suggests that this implacable separation of religion and politics reflects a priori values and cultural assumptions rather than a pragmatic assessment based on balanced observation.[12]

Such strong secularism neglects the faith base of progressive social movements such as the civil rights movement in the United States from the 1950s onwards, the role of the Church in struggles against apartheid in South Africa in the 1970s and 1980s or, more recently, the central place of faith groups within campaigns against global debt, opposition to the invasion of Iraq and Tony Blair's recently established 'Faith Foundation'.[13]

Furthermore, the last decade has seen the questioning of the Weberian secularisation thesis by some former advocates like Peter Berger and the re-emergence of religion as a credible player in the public sphere in the United Kingdom.[14] Steve Bruce reasonably notes that formal church membership and regular attendance at worship has declined dramatically over recent decades in the United Kingdom.[15] To a significant degree this remains the case but the picture is far from uniform. In fact the last decade has witnessed the rapid numerical growth of African-British Christian denominations like the Redeemed Christian Church of God (especially in London) as Richard Burgess shows, and attendance at Church of England parish churches has stabilized since 2011 and, in some cases, begun to grow.[16] Furthermore, it would be a mistake to conclude that numerical decline necessarily implies a decline in faith-based community and political engagement. At grass-roots level, faith groups often remain the most significant locally rooted institutions in neighbourhoods across the United Kingdom—sometimes the only public buildings in a neighbourhood. Baker and Skinner suggest that the enduring presence of faith groups in such communities gives rise to what they call 'religious capital'—the networks, the grass-roots pastoral counselling, the neighbourhood projects and the buildings made available to local community groups.[17] Such 'capital' can resource the building of 'bonding social capital'—the strengthening of the internal ties, and relationships of groups which revolve around a single set of values or a specific 'primary' identity.[18] However faith groups in diverse neighbourhoods can, contrastingly, be the focus for 'bridging social capital' whereby faith groups use their rootedness to resource dynamic, dialogical and inclusive models of community cohesion as I showed in my study of Citizens UK in chapter 2.

Adam Dinham and Vivien Lowndes suggest that, as a result of their enduring public significance, faith groups were courted by the 1997–2010 Labour government in the United Kingdom as a key source of 'bridging social capital'.[19] Faith groups were perceived to be the networks best placed to facilitate its community cohesion and social inclusion agendas.[20] However as Furbey recognises, there has been a strong critique of New Labour's linkage of its controversial post-9/11 and 7/7 Preventing Violent Extremism strategy in relation to the perceived 'radicalization' of a minority of British-Muslim youth with the challenge of forging cohesive urban communities in the aftermath of street violence in some majority-Muslim communities in the north of England in the summer of 2001.[21] Does such an approach reduce the role of faith groups to agencies tasked with 'de-radicalising' young British-Muslims and smoothing away challenging difference? Might this co-option of faith groups as informal partners in both the United States and the United Kingdom with government sap their prophetic edge and make more radical faith-based political activism more difficult to sustain?

Such questions have taken on renewed importance since the election of the Conservative led coalition government in the United Kingdom in 2010 and Prime Minister David Cameron's adoption of the concept of a 'big society' developed by Philip Blond in his book *Red Tory*.[22] The vision of a 'big society' as defined by Blond and Cameron is of an empowered civil society where individuals and community groups take greater responsibility for the life of their neighbourhoods. Within this vision faith groups have been encouraged to take on the role of 'welfare delivery agencies' as local and national government has begun, since 2010, to withdraw financial resources from programmes and projects most widely used by the very young, the very old or the very poor. At the time of writing it is too early to tell whether the 'big society' agenda has led faith groups, to use Robert Beckford's words, to 'sell out' on a dissenting model of social engagement or attain a significant new voice at the heart of social policy.[23] The 2012 US presidential election raised comparable questions. Were faith groups nothing more than convenient foot soldiers in pragmatic political competition (delivering votes for a 'conservative' Republican or a 'progressive' Democrat) or did they provide a revealing lens through which radically contrasting theological visions of America could be viewed? Community organizing offers people of faith perhaps the most structured and focused means of responding to these questions and consciously shaping this dynamic and plural public sphere.[24] What, if anything, might it have to learn from wider social movement politics?

SOCIAL MOVEMENTS

As I noted previously community organizers in both the United States and the United Kingdom have argued that broad-based community organizations cannot reasonably be compared with social movements because they are focused on building permanent people's organisations and not ephemeral and sometimes single-issue movements. Is such perspective an accurate depiction of either community organizations or social movements? Furthermore, is it possible that community organizing might be enriched by the development of an open but critical dialogue with the world of social movements?

Charles Tilly suggests that social movements first emerged in Europe and North America in the eighteenth century as 'a distinctive form of contentious politics', citing the abolitionist movements in the United Kingdom and the United States from the 1770s onwards and the revolutionary activism of the Chartists in England during the 1830s as early examples.[25] Although this era represents the formative period of early Euro-American social movements it is important to broaden this analysis to embrace the Black social movements in the Caribbean that arose in the same period. Beckford points, for example, to the 1831 rebellion against British rule animated by the Baptist deacon Samuel Sharpe in Jamaica and to the later Morant Bay Rebellion and struggle for workers' rights of 1865 led by another Baptist preacher, Paul Bogle, as expressions of organized Black resistance to slavery, racism and economic oppression.[26] The roots of social movements, therefore, cannot reasonably be reduced to their development amongst White activists in Europe or North America.

Jeff Goodwin and James Jasper suggest that the attitude of researchers to social movements shifted during the 1960s when the socially included joined forces with the socially excluded. They argue that social movements are 'conscious, concerted and sustained efforts by ordinary people to change some aspect of their society by using extra-institutional means . . . They last longer than a single protest or riot'.[27] Social movements therefore, although not the permanent people's organizations spoken of by Alinsky, cannot be easily dismissed as ephemeral fads as even a brief examination of movements as diverse as the civil rights movement, the Stop the War Coalition, Greenpeace and the Jubilee 2000/Jubilee Debt campaign demonstrates. Anthony Giddens argues that until the 1960s social movements were largely struggles against structural inequalities such as institutionalized poverty or racism, or what he calls 'emancipatory politics'. According to Giddens, a major shift from external to internal and from need to choice occurred in the middle of the twentieth century, since which time, he argues, social movements have largely revolved around individual agency and the cultural changes needed to build a participatory and inclusive society, what he refers to as 'life politics'.[28] Giddens' work can help us to understand the 'new politics' of the socially included and of advocacy centered social movements but cannot so easily be mapped onto the struggles of socially excluded people in the global South and the fourth world of the global North whose agency is thwarted as a result of ongoing structural injustice. As we consider community organizing, it is important to ask if this is the politics of the socially included acting on behalf of the excluded or the organic politics of the socially excluded asserting their own shared agency.

WHY DO SOCIAL MOVEMENTS EMERGE?

There are four broad theoretical approaches to the emergence of social movements, each of which sheds light on the central features of community organizing that I described in chapters 1 and 2. A first approach is found in 'Relative Deprivation Theory'. Joan Gurney and Kathleen Tierney suggest that 'the concept of relative deprivation in the study of social movements is practically as old as sociology itself'.[29] It can be implicitly aligned with Karl Marx's argument that capitalism engenders 'alienation' in the proletariat and with the concept of 'anomie' first developed by Emile Durkheim and then by Robert Merton.[30] A 'Relative Deprivation' approach suggests that social movements emerge where people feel that they are economically, socially or politically deprived in relation to other groups in society.

The approach can be compared to the appeal within Alinskyite community organizing to self-interest as the central motivation for activism. Susan Stall and Randy Stoecker suggest that 'among all of the tenets of the Alinsky model, the assumption of self-interest has the strongest continuing sway'.[31] Alinsky recognized that 'to many the synonym for self-interest is selfishness'.[32] In spite of this he asserted that 'the myth of altruism' that lies at the heart of America's self-image hides from the fact that 'we are motivated by self-interest . . . but are determined to disguise it'.[33] To question the centrality of self-interest in political life is, according to Alinsky, 'to refuse to see man as he is, to see him only as we would like him to be'.[34] It is important to recognize that in Alinsky's terms self-interest is a broad relational concept rather than an individualistic grabbing. In the United States Dave Beckwith and Cristina Lopez suggest that although 'many people are uncomfortable with self-interest . . . Human nature fails the angel test every time'.[35] Citizens UK also emphasizes the importance of self-interest as a building block for community organizing but importantly aligns this with the equal significance of the 'common good', as I noted in the previous chapter.[36] Similarly David McDowell of the Chicago-based Institute for Comprehensive Community Development emphasizes the centrality of mutuality to community organizing: 'If you are in relationship with others you are much more likely to define self-interest broadly.'[37] This emphasis on self-interest is premised on the assertion that people are most likely to become involved in campaigning when they believe that it will benefit them, their neighborhood or the faith or community group to which they belong. However, the appeal to deprivation and self-interest neglects two key factors. First, why when it is in their broad self-interest do some people who are deprived not become involved in social movements or community organizing? Why, for example, is it the case that most low-paid people in either the United Kingdom or the United States have not become involved in campaigns for a living wage?[38] Second, how might an appeal to deprivation or self-interest explain the active engagement of people in campaigns which have no direct or indirect impact on them, their neighborhoods or the faith or community groups of which they are a part such as the Jubilee Debt campaign or Greenpeace?

A second approach to the growth of social movements is found in 'Resource Mobilization Theory' which from the late 1960s began to challenge a 'Relative Deprivation' approach to their emergence. Early 'Resource Mobilization' theorists such as Anthony Oberschall emphasized the capacity of organizations to effectively engage in social movements.[39] Steven Buechler suggests that by the 1980s the approach had become the dominant theoretical lens through which social movements were viewed.[40] 'Resource Mobilization' theorists emphasized organizational strength and what Buechler calls the 'rational actor model' wherein individuals who may not experience deprivation personally decide to participate in a social movement when 'the potential benefits outweigh the anticipated costs'.[41] Hence 'Resource Mobilization' approaches center around the power of institutions to effectively persuade people to invest the resource of their energy and time in a movement. Craig Jenkins suggests that we can speak of 'instrumental resources' that can be used to directly influence targeted change, 'power resources' that enable social movements to influence power elites and the 'mobilizing resources' that can be deployed by institutions in the campaigns mounted by social movements.[42] Jacquelien van Stekelenburg and Bert Klandermans remind us that it is also important to recognize the importance of the 'non-tangible' resources such as 'authority, leadership, moral commitment [and] trust' that motivate people to engage in social movements.[43] Baker and Skinner refer to this as 'spiritual capital . . . the values, ethics, belief and vision which faith communities bring to civil society'.[44] Elements of the 'Resource Mobilization' approach to social movements can be related to the stress within community organizing on the ability of key individuals within member organizations to realize the 'resource' of their congregation, student association or trades union branch in order to mobilize the maximum number of committed individuals to actively participate in a campaign. Furthermore, like the resource mobilization approach to social movements, community organizing is largely institution focused and premised on the capacity of faith groups or community projects to foster a shared sense of identity and values that translate into common action. Although the 'Resource Mobilization' approach accurately describes a number of the dynamics at play in both social movements and community organizing, it is a model that invites two major concerns. First the approach does not adequately focus on the importance of motivating values, what van Stekelenburg and Klandermans refer to as 'ideals and passion'.[45] For Buechler this neglect of the 'ideas, beliefs, values, symbols and meanings' that motivate individuals can instrumentalize struggle within a movement or a broad-based community organization and strip it of a forceful vision of a just future.[46] Second, the institutional focus of 'Resource Mobilization' and community organizing can downplay the potential of smaller and less hierarchical grass-roots faith or community groups. Buechler suggests that this emphasis on formalized organization can, 'blind investigators to the theoretical value and strategic importance of different organizational forms'.[47]

The third approach to understanding social movements focuses on wider political factors. Political process theory rose to prominence during the early 1980s and is exemplified by the work of the American sociologist Doug McAdam as seen in Figure 3.1.[48]

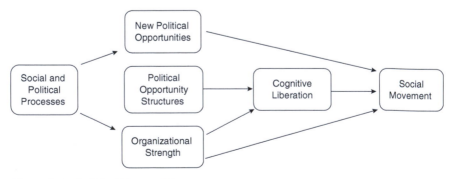

Figure 3.1   Political Process Theory

Four factors are central to the work of political process theorists as seen in Figure 3.1. First, although social movements draw upon articulated grievances and on the mobilizing of resources, these need to be read in broader historical and political terms. Hence the emergence of the civil rights movement can only be fully understood if it is set against the historic relationship between the Black Church and the struggle for racial justice stretching back into the nineteenth century. Second, McAdam suggests that the successful forging of a social movement relies on the presence of existing 'political opportunity structures' that make it possible to take advantage of emergent new 'political opportunities'.[49] McAdams describes 'political opportunity structures' as 'those collective vehicles, informal as well as formal, through which people mobilize and engage in collective action'.[50] In relation to the birth of community organizing in Chicago, 'political opportunity' was not the result of emergent new rights. Still in the grip of the Great Depression, local workers' wages were cut three times in 1939 and labour unions were unable to organize the ethnically diverse workers. Alinsky was able to fashion the first broad-based community organization (the Back of the Yards Council) by drawing on the 'political opportunity structures' represented by the local Roman Catholic parish and tenants groups. Third, the 'organizational strength' of faith or community groups is central to their ability to effectively mobilize people. Fourth, as van Stekelenburg and Klandermans note, 'mediating between political opportunities and organizational strength are people and their hopes and fears'.[51] Writing of his work alongside Brazilian peasants, Paulo Freire argues that the process of education can become part of the transformation of unjust power relations where oppressed communities become conscious of the cause of their oppression and the possibility of change.[52] Political process approaches to social movements suggest that such cognitive liberation is key, for, as Castells notes, 'whoever wins the battle for people's minds will rule, because mighty rigid apparatuses will not be a match in any reasonable timespan for minds mobilised around the power of flexible alternative networks'.[53]

'Political Process Theory' effectively captures many of the aspects of the emergence of both social movements and broad-based community organizations. However it has been increasingly criticized over the last decade by newer culture-based approaches to social movements as the work of Aldon Morris illustrates.[54] First, Morris contends that the political process approach to social movements is 'overly structural and contains rationalist biases'.[55] The Structuralist analysis of political process theory can be applied to traditional social movements which have clear organizational characteristics and draw largely on formalised faith or community groups. However, the approach cannot so easily be mapped onto inherently fluid and networked social movements, such as the Occupy movement which have no identifiable centre and draw on loose and informal 'mobilizing structures'. Second, Morris notes the emphasis within political process models on new political opportunities, 'external political opportunities must first become available before challenging groups can generate collective action'.[56] Such an emphasis can underplay the agency of grass-roots communities to fashion nascent movements for change in the face of repression or social exclusion. For example, the establishment of the first trades union in the United Kingdom by a group of agricultural labourers from Tolpuddle in Dorset in 1832, later known as the Tolpuddle Martyrs, arose against a backdrop of the lowering of agricultural wages in rural England. These labourers were stimulated by their suffering and by their Christian faith (the leader of the group, George Loveless, was a Methodist lay preacher) and not by emergent new political opportunities.[57] The example of the Tolpuddle Martyrs touches on a third question that recent culture-based approaches raise about the political process model, namely, the importance of ethical and religious motivations and the mobilizing significance of cultural identities. Writing about the civil rights movement, Morris argues that Martin Luther King 'instinctively understood that the church's transcendent belief system was the appropriate cultural material from which to frame the movement . . . This moral frame had mobilizing power because it . . . assured the participants that God was one their side, for he condoned African-American collective action that sought justice'.[58] A fourth issue raised by culture-based analyses of social movements relates to the use of collective action framing. The sociologist Erving Goffman speaks of frames as 'schemata of interpretation'.[59] Robert Benford and David Snow suggest that this process of framing is an act of internalized meaning-making for 'frames help to render events . . . meaningful and thereby function to organize experience and guide action'.[60] Hence, as Marc Steinberg notes, 'by constructing a compelling sense of injustice . . . frames provide a diagnosis and prognosis of a problem and a call to action to resolve it'.[61] Consequently a social movement is more than a response to relative deprivation, political opportunity or resource mobilization. It can reasonably be depicted as ethics, faith or ideology in action, comparable to values-led community organizing. It is for this reason that the process of critical self-reflection on the ongoing activism of a broad-based community organization is vital to its long-term health. Such reflective practice needs to be fashioned in continuing dialogue with the 'interpretive communities' (the churches, mosques, gurdwaras, synagogues, community groups, trades unions) that guide the values of people who engage in broad-based community organizing as I note in more depth in chapter 5.[62] A fifth question that the culture-based approach raises revolves around the nature of leadership within faith or community groups. Within community organizing, an emphasis is placed on the mobilizing role of the community organizer and on the training of new leaders. Where external organizers who have little knowledge of the values, history or culture of a faith or community group begin to build a broad-based community organization the important resource of existing community engagement and leadership and other local protest traditions can potentially be neglected. Robert Schreiter touches on this insider-outsider tension in the articulation of contextual theologies, suggesting that 'both the insider and the outsider are needed . . . Outsiders bring important experience but . . . can come to exercise hegemony over the community'.[63]

Castells argues that social movements have become 'critical sources of resistance to the one sided logic of capitalism, statism and informationalism'.[64] Such movements address structural issues rather than isolated examples of injustice. They depend upon an effective pattern of liberative education facilitated by a conscientized organizer and can be seen as potential new spaces for existential reflection.[65] Ron Eyerman and Andrew Jamison make the point clearly: 'social movements re-interpret established and shared frameworks of meaning which make communication and coordinated action possible.'[66] The emergence of social movements such as the Jubilee Debt Campaign, the Stop the War Coalition or the Occupy movement can be reduced to a reaction against failed institutionalized politics. Such a perspective may partially explain the growth of social movement politics, but neglects the possibility that social movements are an expression of a 'new politics' rather than a reaction to an absence.

TYPES OF SOCIAL MOVEMENTS

Whilst he wrote almost fifty years ago, the typology of social movements developed by David Aberle remains helpful.[67] Although recognizing that any typology represents ideal types, Aberle suggested that it is possible to identify four types of social movement. First, there are 'Alternative Social Movements' which engage specific groups within society and seek to bring about limited social change in relation to targeted issues, such as Bringing Hope which works alongside young adults caught up in gang culture in the city of Birmingham in the United Kingdom or the home schooling movement in the United States.[68] Second, 'Redemptive Social Movements' such as the Rock against Racism movement that arose in the United Kingdom in the late 1970s or evangelical Christian movements such as Promise Keepers target specific groups of people often united by shared values or beliefs in order to bring about radical change within individuals who can then model an alternative 'redeemed' society.[69] Third, there are 'Reformative Social Movements' like the Jubilee Debt Campaign or Greenpeace which agitate for limited reforms that will impact the whole of a society or initiatives like Movement for Change (which adopts a community-organizing methodology) launched by the former British Foreign Secretary David Milliband in 2011 as a means of reinvigorating the Labour Party in order to generate social change.[70] Fourth 'Revolutionary Social Movements' such as the Occupy movement, the Arab Spring or the civil rights movement seek to engage the widest possible cross-section of society in order to bring about radical social change. Against the backdrop of this typology and my previous comments, how might social movements enable activism in superdiverse societies?

SOCIAL MOVEMENTS, THE POLITICS OF DIFFERENCE AND THE MULTICULTURAL CITY

It is possible to view social movements not as a response to an absence but as a new politics for a society in which difference, as Leonie Sandercock argues, has become sociologically normative.[71] Andrew Davey makes the point in evocative tones: 'You only have to walk down the streets of any major city to encounter the world . . . You will see goods . . . made in the factories and sweatshops of the South . . . Magazines and newspapers . . . combine the issues of communities thousands of miles away and those in the immediate locality.'[72]

In the twenty-first century, this landscape of normative difference increasingly informs the atmosphere within which political leaders define social policy, as Loretta Winters and Herman DeBosse and also Kimberly McClain DaCosta note in a US context and Paul Gilroy reveals in relation to the United Kingdom.[73] Writing in the aftermath of the terrorist attacks on the London public transport system in July 2005, Steven Vertovec highlighted the words of Ken Livingstone, the mayor of London, following the attacks. London, said Livingstone, represents 'the world gathered in one city'—the site not just of diversity but of what Vertovec calls 'super-diversity'.[74] It is such dynamic diversity that forms the context within which social movements are forged in the twenty-first-century city.[75] Two particular responses to such superdiversity are of importance in relation to social movements and have a major influence on contemporary community organizing in both the United States and the United Kingdom—identity politics and the cultural politics of difference.

IDENTITY POLITICS

Identity politics is not new. It characterized the radicalization of political activism during the late 1960s as exemplified by the emergence of feminist and Black Power social movements. However, as Castells and Giddens observe, the growth of political activism based on ethnic, sexual or religious identity has become increasingly significant since the early 1980s.[76] In her analysis of the lesbian and gay rights movement in the United States, Mary Bernstein suggests that sexual identity becomes a source of personal and communal empowerment and effective mobilization.[77] Giddens argues that such New Social Movements reflect a shift within political activism away from the focus on externalized and structural oppression that characterized the Old Social Movement towards a self-reflexive politics of choice within which personal identity is of paramount importance.[78] For Castells, 'identity is people's source of meaning' and is constructed 'on the basis of a cultural attribute . . . that is given priority over other sources of meaning'.[79] Castells suggests that such patterns of identity politics can resource 'resistance identities' which represent 'the exclusion of the excluders by the excluded'.[80] He argues that these 'resistance identities' exemplify 'forms of collective resistance against otherwise unbearable oppression, usually on the basis of identities that are clearly defined by history, geography or biology'.[81] Castells further suggests that although these resistance identities are widely articulated, 'they rarely communicate with each other because they are built around sharply distinct principles, defining an "in" and an "out"'.[82]

Social movements premised on faith-based 'resistance identities' are neither inherently 'conservative' nor inevitably 'progressive'. Castells recognizes the mobilizing force of faith-based identities. However his selection of case studies (Christian 'fundamentalism' in the United States, Islamic 'fundamentalism', the 1995 sarin gas attack on the Tokyo transport system by members of the Aum Shinrikyo sect and Al-Qaeda) emphasises only theologically conservative or violent examples of faith-based activism. We are all selective and Castells selectivity can perhaps be explained by his a priori attitude to religious faith: 'outside us God would become homeless.'[83] Although Castells points to a clear conservative tendency within some faith-based identity politics, it is important to recognize that such activism is not inherently reactionary as cases as diverse as the civil rights movement, development charities such as Islamic Relief, the lesbian and gay Christian movement or the Sojourners Community illustrate.

Social movements that are expressions of personal-communal identity highlight two factors from which community organizing can learn. First, these bounded forms of political activism arise largely in marginalized communities or groups characterised by apparently homogeneous relationships which assert that identity is singular, enclosed or fixed. Writing of the development of 'raciological' thought, Gilroy suggests that a mindset that rests on essentialized understandings of identity fosters models of activism that are characterised by 'camp mentalities' which affirm and empower the 'insider' while excluding those who are not perceived to 'belong'.[84] For Gilroy, such thinking 'puts an end to any sense of cultural development. Culture as process is arrested. Petrified and sterile it is impoverished by the national obligation not to change but to recycle the past continually in an essentially unmodified form'.[85]

Second, however, Gayatri Spivak and Beckford argue that such primary identities-based activism can stimulate a broader united resistance to shared oppression (what they refer to as a 'strategic essentialism') which revolves around pragmatic activism rather than deeply held ethnic essentialism.[86] Such bounded identity politics has the capacity to resource existential emancipation and foster the building of powerful social movements focused around ethnicity (e.g., the Black Power movement, the National Confederation of Dalit Organisations in India, the African National Congress or the Native American Rights Fund).[87] It can underpin movements focused on gender (e.g., the women's liberation movement or the National Organization of Women) or sexuality (e.g., the gay rights movement or the lesbian and gay Christian movement).[88] However, in superdiverse societies it is important to ask how far largely introverted social movements can effect widespread social change. Castells suggests that this only becomes possible where marginalized groups forge alliances with other excluded communities and translate 'resistance' based identities into a shared 'project' identity that is premised on a vision of holistic and far-reaching change.[89]

Community organizing does not rest on an essentialized understanding of identity. However at a pragmatic level it does bear some of the hallmarks of identity politics–based social movements. It draws, for example, on the motivating force that primary identities such as ethnicity or religion have on the political choices that individuals make and on the capacity of faith or community groups to mobilize people around shared 'resistance' identities which can be fashioned into broader networked 'project' identity–based activism. Gilroy, however, suggests that within such a perspective, 'identity ceases to be an ongoing process of self-making and social interaction . . . It . . . closes down the possibility of communication across the gulf between one heavily defended island of particularity and its equally well fortified neighbours'.[90] It is important to ask therefore whether a model of activism that relies on a coalition of bounded primary identities can provide an adequate foundation for effective community organizing in a plural public sphere. Where broad-based community organizations draw upon the 're-source mobilization' and the 'political opportunity structures' that faith groups embody as a result of the 'bonding social capital' they exhibit, community organizing can become an exclusive exercise. Ring-fenced under-standings of identity and belonging, therefore, lead to a limited model of organizing incapable of engaging credibly with a superdiverse society within which injustice will not be confined within fixed categories.

The normative cultural diversity of contemporary urban life in a glo-balized world makes it increasingly untenable to claim that ethnocentric expressions of culture and depictions of the public sphere as unitary can adequately capture the increasingly fluid nature of identity and activism in the twenty-first century. Lina Jamoul makes the point clearly: 'Discourses of "impartiality" and "universality" serve to exclude; they embody a poli-tics suspicious of difference.'[91] For Jamoul the task for contemporary com-munity organizing is to unmask the hegemony of these flawed 'discourses of impartiality' and to forge a space of activism that is 'inclusive, conflic-tual and multiple'.[92] Writing of the United Kingdom, Gilroy sounds a word of caution that needs to temper such enthusiasm for third space activism: 'multicultural society seems to have been abandoned at birth.'[93] He goes on: 'hybrid urban cultures and cosmopolitan . . . history go out of the window. Instead we get transported into the frozen realm of mythic time.'[94] Following street violence in some majority British-Muslim working-class communities in northern England during 2001, an assimilationist community cohesion agenda increasingly framed the social policy of the Labour government, ex-emplified most fully by the 'Cantle Report'.[95] In the face of the renewed street-level significance of the raciological identity politics embodied by the English Defence League since 2009 and critiques of multiculturalism such as that articulated by the current British Prime Minister David Cameron in 2011, the extent to which an uncritical multiculturalism can provide a sufficiently solid basis for progressive social activism has become a central political and theoretical question.[96] Critical reflection on this question can provide new tools for community organizing on both sides of the Atlantic.

Forty years on from the murder of Martin Luther King, the first African-American was elected as president of the United States. Barack Obama is a Black man of dual heritage and his presidency has been optimistically hailed as the dawning of the era of 'post-racial' politics dreamed of by King on the steps of the Washington Monument in 1963. However Obama's election gave rise to the raciological birther movement which questioned the validity of his US citizenship and the Kenyan nationality of his father, demanded a copy of his birth certificate and questioned his Christian identity because his family name 'sounded Muslim'.[97] Barack Obama was born in the US state of Hawaii. John McCain, his white Republican opponent in 2008, was born in Panama but is a US citizen by blood because his father was born in Iowa and his mother in Oklahoma. The validity of McCain's campaign was not questioned. 'Race', it seems, still matters in America.

THE POLITICS OF DIFFERENCE

In spite of this resurgent raciological atmosphere, superdiversity has become a core component of social movements in the twenty-first century. The cultural politics of difference articulated by Tariq Modood, Iris Marion Young, Cornel West and Leonie Sandercock has provided vital new resources for contemporary social movements.[98] Young critiques the homogenizing liberal ideal of justice that 'defines liberation as the transcendence of group difference', arguing instead for a model of justice that asserts the central importance of difference in the building of holistic emancipation.[99] She suggests that whereas 'cultural imperialism involves the universalization of a dominant group's experience and culture and its establishment as the norm', a liberative politics of difference asserts the integrity and agency of those whose life experience and cultural identity differs from that of the ruling elite. Such a task rests, as Sandercock notes, on the adoption of an 'epistemology of multiplicity' which arises from an ongoing critical engagement with lived cultural and religious diversity.[100] West suggests that a defining feature of this new cultural politics of difference is to 'trash the monolithic and the homogeneous in the name of diversity, multiplicity and heterogeneity'.[101] He argues that such a paradigmatic shift in political activism is vital for people of colour for whom the ongoing attachment to 'race' is 'too costly in mind, body and soul—especially for . . . downtrodden and despised people'.[102] Such a step beyond 'race' could subvert essentialist identity politics and critiques of multiculturalism, thereby resourcing the development of new superdiverse alliances that are premised on an ethic of liberative difference.

In the search for an 'intercultural' model of activism it is the 'Hybrid Social Movement' that is best attuned to this context of superdiversity as a result of its dialogical character. This model of social movement activism parallels that of community organizing. However, as I will suggest next, it exemplifies a networked approach that has yet to fully inform the philosophical base of community organizing. Examples of superdiverse hybrid social movements abound in both the United States and the United Kingdom. In the United States such social movements have included the Students for a Democratic Society network that emerged out of the New Left movement in the early 1960s, the civil and human rights oriented Glide Memorial United Methodist Church in San Francisco, the Rainbow/PUSH Coalition established by Jesse Jackson with its strong focus on multi-issue civil rights, the Internet based Tikkun interfaith network, the Network of Spiritual Progressives and the Occupy movement that emerged from Occupy Wall Street.[103] In the United Kingdom examples of such movements include the late 1970s Rock against Racism movement, the political party Respect that was founded in the aftermath of the 2003 invasion of Iraq, the online antiracist Hope Not Hate campaign, the City of Sanctuary movement which has focused on rights for asylum seekers and refugees since its inception in 2007 and the Stop the War Coalition.[104] Furthermore as the increasing involvement of British-Muslims in political life makes plain faith-based engagement in the public sphere in the United Kingdom can no longer be reduced to Christian activism, however loosely defined. Richard Phillips and Jamil Iqbal and also Tahir Abbas write, for example, of the partnership that the Muslim Association of Britain forged with Stop the War Coalition from 2001 and Tariq Modood of the Forum Against Islamophobia and Racism (FAIR) which has worked in partnership with broader antiracist networks such as the National Assembly of Black People since its inception in 2000.[105]

GLOBALIZING SOCIAL MOVEMENTS

In the interwoven world of the twenty-first century, a pivotal site for the development of new social movements and community organizing is what Michael Peter Smith refers to as the 'translocal urbanism' that characterizes the contemporary city.[106] In her analysis of global cities Saskia Sassen suggests that 'the global city is a strategic site for disempowered actors because it enables them to gain presence, to emerge as subjects, even when they do not gain direct power'.[107] Castells argues that in the twenty-first-century urban societies are reflections of a networked globalized world.[108] He writes, 'Networks are complex structures of communication constructed around a set of goals that simultaneously ensure unity of purpose and flexibility of execution.'[109] In what he calls the 'information age', Castells argues that although this global network of power reflects the 'spatial logic of the dominant interests in our society', it can be subverted to enable 'the global connection of . . . local experience'.[110] This act of subversion can animate and connect disparate social movements, 'increasingly global movements of solidarity, environmentalists, human rights and women's groups are organized on the internet . . . on the basis of local/global connection'.[111]

Social movements such as the antiglobalization protests against the World Trade Organisation in Seattle (1999), its partner the World Social Forum, the 'culture-jamming' of Ad-Busters, the online activism of Avaaz and the dispersed Occupy movement offer contrasting examples of what might be called globalized 'third space' social movements.[112] Such 'trans-local' social movements subvert fixed ideologies, ethnicities and faith perspectives and can provide disparate marginalized communities with the 'presence' to which Sassen refers. Relying on 'political entrepreneurs', these movements draw upon the support of people from a range of settled identities and perspectives but blur the boundaries between such positions to forge movements that arise from the cracks of an interconnected networked society, a little like broad-based community organizing. The contemporary networked social movement therefore becomes more than an example of 'new' political activism; it represents an existential enterprise and a search for a new, shared identity in a post ideological age.[113] As Goodwin and Jasper observe, 'Protest is no longer . . . a compensation for some lack, but part of an effort to impose a cognitive meaning on the world, to forge a collective and personal identity.'[114]

THE RISE AND FALL OF SOCIAL MOVEMENTS

The life cycle of social movements and the ways in which their success is measured can help us to consider afresh the development of broad-based community organizations. According to Herbert Blumer and Tilly, social movements pass through five stages as Figure 3.2 shows.[115]

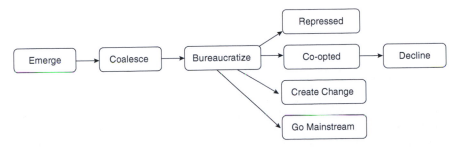

Figure 3.2 The 'Life Cycle' of Social Movements

Social movements do not simply emerge from the soil of society; they arise in specific contexts at particular historical moments, as Anthony Oberschall notes with reference to the Eastern European uprisings of 1989 and Gunther Schoenleitner discusses in relation to the emergence of the World Social Forum in 2001.[116] However, a social movement only emerges when disparate feelings are harnessed by small groups of conscientized public-political intellectuals who fashion these concerns into a focused vision and a credible agenda for action. The civil rights struggle in the United States arose from historic racism and segregation but only became a social movement when the story of Rosa Parks' refusal to leave a seat reserved for White passengers on a Montgomery bus drew Martin Luther King into the struggle. The animating role of the conscientized public political intellectual is, as the liberative educator Freire reminds us, to enable people to become conscious of the causes of injustice or oppression and to articulate a vision of an alternative future. Castells notes that urban social movements emerge when 'in their collective action and at the initiative of a conscious and organized operator, they address one or more structural issues that differentiate contradictory social interests . . . These issues, or their combination, define the movement (and) the people they mobilize'.[117]

The coalescence stage arises as this focused vision and agenda are articulated and enacted and a committed activist group begins to gather and grow. Following the emergence in September 2011 of Occupy Wall Street as a targeted protest against the influence of big corporations on US politics, the vision articulated in New York has broadened and coalesced into a global Occupy movement that is, at the time of writing, active on every continent in approximately eighty cities.[118] The rapid spread of Occupy invites us to ask how such a disparate movement will cope with the third stage in the social movement life cycle, that of bureaucratization. In this stage, Blumer and Tilly argue that previously fluid social movements begin to take on the characteristics of more stable institutions, creating bureaucracies and structures to manage the movement. It is at this point that tension can arise if activists sense that the initial impetus behind the movement has been dimmed or smothered beneath a more formalized structure.

As a social movement becomes established, it can face four possible futures. The movement can be repressed, its members driven underground and its networks damaged or destroyed (e.g., the initial protest movement in East Germany in 1989, protests against the 2009 Iranian presidential election and the Syrian uprising that began in 2011). Alternatively, a social movement can be co-opted into broader struggles or networks. Co-option can be the result of successful campaigning and can enable a movement to achieve its goals (e.g., campaigns for a living wage spearheaded in the United Kingdom by London Citizens and Church Action on Poverty). It can also, however, weaken the focus of a movement and dilute its activism as it takes its place in a bigger and broader agenda.[119] In relatively weak social movements, such co-option can also be a response to 'burn-out' amongst a small number of committed individuals who no longer have the energy to build the movement as arguably occurred in the UK community organization Birmingham Citizens following its split from Citizens UK in 2008. Co-option can sometimes therefore be an alternative to disillusion on the one hand or the slow decline that results from 'burn-out' on the other. Third, a social movement can go mainstream, adopting consensual tactics in order to influence religious, economic or political power elites (e.g., HIV/AIDS campaigns such as the Terence Higgins Trust, the Movement for the Ordination of Women in the Church of England and Earth Day).[120] Fourth, a social movement can succeed in changing the fabric of society as the antiapartheid struggle in South Africa, the nineteenth-century movement to abolish slavery, the movement agitating for Indian independence facilitated by Mahatma Gandhi or the Jubilee 2000 campaign demonstrate.

The life cycle of a social movement summarized previously is an ideal type. Real life is less clear-cut. It is, for example, difficult to measure the success of a social movement in purely pragmatic terms. The community organizing–inspired campaign for a living wage in the United Kingdom is a good example of this dilemma. At one level, the movement has succeeded in what Gramsci referred to as the 'war of position'.[121] Morally and to a degree politically the campaign led by Citizens UK has succeeded in shining a powerful light on low pay, poverty and income inequality in part through a strategic critical alliance with political leaders such as mayor of London Boris Johnson and allies in the academy like Jane Wills.[122] In pragmatic terms a significant number of key employers have committed to paying their employees a living wage.[123] Furthermore the ability of Citizens UK to gather over one thousand people in Westminster Central Hall for a Citizens Prime Ministerial Assembly ahead of the 2010 UK general election was sufficient to win promises to work towards a living wage from the then Prime Minister Gordon Brown, the leader of the Conservative Party (UK prime minister since 2010) David Cameron and the leader of the Liberal Democrats (deputy prime minister since 2010) Nick Clegg.[124] Yet figures from 2009 to 2010 and Institute for Fiscal Studies projections moving forward to 2020 suggest that poverty and inequality in the United Kingdom are now more entrenched than they were thirty years ago.[125] So is the movement for a living wage a success or not?

William Gamson alludes to this dilemma in his suggestion that 'success is an elusive idea' when applied to social movements.[126] There are actions which can be measured (e.g., numbers of people registered to vote, immunized against disease, attending school for the first time and specific victories in relation to wages, legislation or worker protection) or which clearly enhance the power base of the social movement or community organization. There are however also qualitative changes that are difficult to measure in quantitative terms such as the effect that involvement in a social movement has on an individual's self-esteem, values and broader political engagement or on the sense of well-being amongst people alongside whom or on behalf of a social movement has campaigned. Although many of the social movements to which I have alluded in this chapter have delivered important measureable results, their most significant outcome may be existential rather than material. A successful social movement changes the nature of debate in a society, shines a light on oppressive social structures and power relations and opens up the possibility of alternative futures. Is such change a priority within community organizing?

CONCLUSION—LESSONS FROM THE 'NEW' POLITICS

Community organizers have traditionally asserted that they are building permanent people's organizations and not social movements. This assertion needs to be challenged. I do not make this claim to dismiss the value of community organizing. Rather, such a debate can place community organizing alongside historic and contemporary allies in the struggle for social justice, emphasize its political importance and uncover its theological significance. As I argue in the final chapter of this book, community organizing can only fulfil its potential to model a liberative 'post-religious' (and 'post-secular') political theology in a superdiverse world when it acknowledges its place on the wider landscape of progressive social movements. In this chapter, I have explored the 'new' politics that is embodied by social movements, identity politics and the cultural politics of difference. Such political activism has the capacity to critique and enrich contemporary community organizing, thereby broadening its vision, its analysis and its campaigning. What then might community organizing have to learn from the 'new' politics? Here are twenty suggestions.

Lesson 1

Since the late 1960s, social movements have unmasked the fallacy of a singular, impartial and consensual public sphere. They have modelled a pattern of 'insurgent citizenship' that can enable community organizing to play a key role in the forging of a plural, contentious and liberative civil society.

Lesson 2

The focus within the new politics on identity and values can sharpen community organizers' reflections on the distinctions between a first-level politics of need and a second-level politics of choice. Such a focus can enable a deeper reflection on the motivation of people to engage in community organizing.

Lesson 3

The new politics illustrates the dilemma of defining 'successful' activism in purely instrumental terms and invites community organizing to consider afresh the agency that resides in 'presence' even when it does not lead to the attaining of 'power'.

Lesson 4

The ongoing significance of models of identity politics that are premised on resistance identities can offer new reflective resources to community organizing that can enable the effective use of a strategic essentialism that has the capacity to forge patterns of activism that 'exclude the excluders'.

Lesson 5

The effectiveness of identity politics can enable community organizing to reflect on the mobilizing force of primary identities and the bonding social capital to which they give rise.

Lesson 6

Contrastingly, such bounded activism can alert community organizing to the limited scope of activism that is premised on implicitly essentialized primary identities in a superdiverse society.

Lesson 7

Relative deprivation analyses of social movements remind us that where a group organizes around its deprivation in relation to other groups in society that this sense of marginalization can act as a powerful motivating factor that can inform the emphasis on mutual self-interest within community organizing.

Lesson 8

The fact that a majority of marginalized people do not engage in social movement activism and the decline of Relative deprivation analyses can stimulate a questioning of the appeal made by community organizing to self-interest as the key motivating factor behind activism.

Lesson 9

Political process analyses of political opportunities and organizational strength can inform the emphasis within community organizing on organized people, organized money and organized power. Movements that arise where there is little evidence of political opportunities or organizational strength can challenge such assumptions.

Lesson 10

Culture-based analyses of social movements which point to the central importance of individual agency, culture and values as key motivating factors behind activism can be used within community organizing to critique overly instrumental approaches to political activism.

Lesson 11

The example of fluid, networked and horizontally organized hybrid social movements invites community organizing to reflect on its more hierarchical approach and its concentrated focus on building a membership based permanent people's organizations. Fluid networks might offer a credible counterbalance to solid community organizing in the network society.

Lesson 12

Within contexts where existing faith or community groups or social movements have historically organized around issues of justice organic insights, local leadership, relationships and a track record of activism can be ignored by incoming community organizers schooled in an Alinskyite focus on organization building rather than partnership. The reflections of Schreiter on the insider-outsider relationship within contextual theologies can help to fashion more dialogical approaches.

Lesson 13

An overly instrumental measure of success can neglect more intangible qualitative progress and the possibility that existential successes that are the result of cognitive liberation may be more significant in the long-term 'war of position' than specific measurable successes.

Lesson 14

In societies where cultural and religious diversity are normative, a cultural politics of difference that is premised on an ethic of liberative difference can enable community organizing to move beyond a model of activism that can be characterized by bounded identity politics or an uncritical multiculturalism.

Lesson 15

A deep grounding in an epistemology of multiplicity that engages with diverse and dynamic theological and cultural, ethical and spiritual frameworks rather than an overreliance on a single theological or cultural perspective can foster a mutual dialogue around shared and contrasting values thereby enabling broader models of community organizing in superdiverse contexts.

Lesson 16

Models of the new politics that interweave local and global issues can resource glocal patterns of activism. Such a focus can resource a multidimensional approach to community organizing, enabling more nuanced understandings of identity, power and the interconnected character of seemingly disparate campaigns.

Lesson 17

The new politics reinforces the central importance of reflexivity in activism as a basic building block in the process of existential liberation. An open and listening reflexivity amongst community organizers can deepen an understanding of the ethical frameworks which guide the activism of those people upon whom effective community organizing relies.

Lesson 18

Effective social movements are characterized by dialogical liberative education. Such an approach to critical and open-ended reflexivity could enrich an arguably instrumental and didactic pattern of leadership training within community organizing.

Lesson 19

The use of collective action framing can foreground the foundational importance of ethical, ideological and theological values within community organizing thereby supplanting an overemphasis on appeals to mutual self-interest.

Lesson 20

A focus on reformative and revolutionary social movements could help community organizing to consider the following question afresh. Are faith-based community organizations called to a prophetic counterhegemonic model of organizing premised on an assertion of God's 'bias to the oppressed' or to a pragmatic reformative approach guided by a consensual vision of the 'common good'?

4 Enrichment and Challenge
Lessons from Social Theory

INTRODUCTION

In the first part of this book I told the story of community organizing on both sides of the Atlantic, explored its core values and methodology and the role that faith groups play within broad-based community organizations in the United States and the United Kingdom. I have suggested that community organizing can benefit from the development of a more constructive relationship with broader models of political activism and, in particular, social movement politics. I now want to build on this foundation in order to establish a dialogue between the practice of community organizing and social and political theory. Over the last decade, Citizens UK has forged strategic relationships with the social geographer Jane Wills and the political theologian Luke Bretherton. This dialogue needs to be broadened. Consequently, in this chapter I bring community organizing into a critical dialogue with a wider range of debates and ideas, thereby building a more solid foundation for the 'new politics' it is forging. This discussion will revolve around analyses of six key themes:

1. Social space and third space thinking
2. The public sphere and the political turn to civil society
3. Faith in the public square
4. The cultural politics of difference
5. Social and religious capital
6. The role of the 'intellectual' community organizer within struggles for social justice

SOCIAL SPACE AND THIRD SPACE THINKING

Community organizing represents a contextualized approach to political activism and roots the struggle for justice in particular concerns in specific places. Consequently, a deeper understanding of the social construction of shared public space can enable a more nuanced approach to community organizing. Contemporary analyses of social space are, to a significant degree, stimulated by the work of the sociologist and philosopher Henri Lefebvre and, in particular, his 1991 book *The Production of Space*.[1] Lefebvre suggested that social space is forged out of a dynamic dialogue between the 'conceptual triad' of dominant representations of space, lived spatial practice and spaces of representation.[2] It is the dialogue between 'conceptualized' space, 'perceived' space and the 'representational' spaces that gives rise to the social space within which community organizing is articulated as indicated in Figure 4.1 below.[3]

Lefebvre suggests that representational spaces are sites of existential importance within which people can either underpin or undermine dominant attitudes to civil society. He summarizes: 'Representational space is alive. It speaks.'[4] Influenced by Lefebvre's argument Edward Soja also suggests that the city embodies three 'spaces'. A 'first space' embodies material practices and institutions. A 'second space' acts as the arena of reflexive thought, what he calls 'the urban imaginary'.[5] The third space to which Soja refers is the building site of 'life stories' and the existential crucible within which the public sphere is forged, what Soja refers to as the space wherein the 'real-and-imagined' are in continuous dialogue.[6] The work of Lefebvre and Soja raises important questions about the relationship between social space, civil society and community organizing. If social space is neither inert nor neutral, it becomes a site of struggle—the crucible within which community organizing is forged. Whose interests then does social space reflect and how might community organizing use representational space to build its permanent people's organization and work for social justice?

Tim Gorringe suggests that the space we share reflects the ideological interests of those who design and govern the cities and towns within which we live because 'the ideology of space is inescapable'.[7] For Gorringe, social space 'reflects conscious decisions which in turn reflect ideologies and class positions'.[8] It is however possible to subvert the dominance of the 'conceived' space of the powerful through a creative use of varied 'representational'

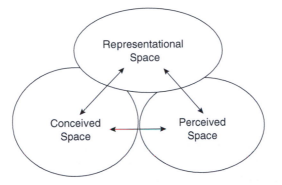

Figure 4.1   Lefebvre's Social Space Triad

spaces. Commodified and regularized space can become the site of resistance to oppression, as Kim Knott notes with reference to the way in which busy shopping streets in London became the site of what Sandercock has called 'insurgent citizenship' in the large demonstrations against the Iraq War in 2003.[9] Knott argues that faith-based narratives can transform the public sphere, but only when they are rooted in the lived realities of social space because 'without an arena of struggle . . . principles and values remain ephemeral and ungrounded'.[10] Such a subversion of regulated social space has been a defining feature of extrainstitutional politics from the civil rights movement of the 1960s to the Occupy movement of 2011–2012, as I explained in the previous chapter. The liberative potential of faith narratives to forge countercultural spaces of 'representation' has fed social movements in the past, but in a blurred superdiverse century, is it possible for disparate marginalized groups to forge a shared space of resistance in the twenty-first century?

In order to respond to this question we need to move beyond binary either-or spatial thinking. Perceptions of the public sphere that privilege the interests of the powerful while ignoring the ways in which oppressed communities perceive social space reflect such binary thinking. When the exclusivity of such an approach is recognized, it becomes possible to prioritize plural 'representational spaces' within which a range of new possible worlds are imagined, thereby subverting excluding configurations of identity, ideology and activism. Such a shift blows the myth of a universal public sphere that is the consensual space of equals and has serious implications for the ways in which we understand the 'common good'. Writing about the 'racialized geographies' of US cities Eugene McCann asserts the pivotal political importance of, 'counter-spaces where the rights to the city and to difference can be articulated'. These 'counter-spaces . . . provide hope for the production of truly open and inclusive public spaces where "marked" bodies can negotiate the future on a free and equal basis'.[11] Such 'representational spaces' are central to community organizing and provide the existential fulcrum of the liberative political activism it seeks to fashion. These are the spaces where the creative tension so central to community organizing can be forged. The dynamism of 'representational spaces' within a superdiverse society can also challenge the temptation of introversion amongst community organizers schooled in the assertion that they are not part of an open and inclusive social movement but a permanent and separate people's organization.

Taken in conjunction with the analysis of social space summarized previously, the 'third space' thinking of the postcolonial cultural critic Homi Bhabha and the emergent 'third space' public theology of Chris Baker can provide community organizers with the tools needed to fashion dynamic rather than static broad-based community organizations. Writing of the rationalist elitism that he suggests has characterized the academy, Bhabha argues that 'there is a damaging . . . assumption that theory is necessarily the elite language of the socially and culturally privileged . . . The Olympian realms of what is mistakenly labelled "pure theory" are assumed to be eternally insulated from . . . the wretched of the earth'.[12] For Bhabha, however, the disruption of this dominant narrative of intellectual disengagement is not found in its polemical dismissal but in the kind of nuanced engagement with the complexities of injustice that characterizes community organizing: 'theory becomes the negotiation of contradictory and antagonistic instances that open up hybrid sites . . . of struggle.'[13] This negotiation with complexity moves us away from an unbending rehearsal of either-or political positions that are defined at a safe distance from the messy contradiction of struggle towards a blurred both-and world within which it becomes possible to recognize the interconnected nature of seemingly disparate struggles and communities. Writing of African-American responses to racialized injustice, Anthony Pinn advocates what he calls a 'nitty-gritty' hermeneutics, which resists the temptation of predefined ethical perspectives in order to wrestle with the messy contradiction of African-American life in a manner that more completely reflects the authenticity of lived experience.[14] For Bhabha, such a nitty-gritty perspective helps us to grasp the importance of 'the hybrid moment of political change'.[15] Baker suggests that this 'third space' is 'the space produced by the collapse of the previously defining narratives of modernity based on colonialism, class and patriarchy'.[16] This space of uncertainty and difference gives rise to a contentious and fluid public sphere, what Bhabha calls the 'third space of enunciation' and is reminiscent of Lefebvre's 'representational space'.[17] It is in this in-between space that marginalized communities can subvert the 'conceived' space of the powerful, transforming the excluded edge into a new centre within which new stories can be told and new visions of a plural public sphere expressed. It is from this space that community organizing arises to challenge fixed understandings of politics, faith-based activism and universalizing analyses of the public sphere.

THE PUBLIC SPHERE AND THE POLITICAL TURN TO CIVIL SOCIETY

Established in the United Kingdom at the end of a decade dominated on both sides of the Atlantic by neoconservative social policies and monetarist economics, the Citizen Organising Foundation (now Citizens UK) declared in its founding mission statement that its aim was to enable the 're-weaving of the fabric of society'. Implicit in this pithy statement was the suggestion that the fabric of civil society had become dangerously frayed. In the United States, the campaigning of the Industrial Areas Foundation, PICO and the Gamaliel Foundation has been premised on a deeply rooted ethic of voluntarism and the historic engagement of faith groups in civil society to which de Tocqueville pointed in the nineteenth century and Putnam at the start of twenty-first. The emergence of the Citizen Organising Foundation in the

United Kingdom at the end of the 1980s provides us with a more challenging case study of the potential of the community-organizing model. In the United Kingdom, faith groups can appear marginal, religious faith a private matter and faith-based activism largely channelled through trades unions, the Labour Party or 'faith-neutral' campaigning organizations. How far is it possible for community organizing to 're-weave the fabric of society' in such a contested, fraying and atomized civil society? A deeper engagement with debates about civil society and the public sphere can help us to respond to this question.

John Ehrenberg reminds us that the discussion of civil society stretches back almost 2,500 years to Plato's exploration of the nature of political life in *The Republic* and *Politics* and Aristotle's examination of the nature of community, association and citizenship in the urban centres of the ancient Greek world.[18] In this context, the state and civil society were effectively indistinguishable. In the centuries following Augustine's *City of God*, civil society became enmeshed with Christendom. Ehrenberg describes this shift in the following way: 'The Greeks had tried to organize everything around the polis; medieval writers centered their thinking around God's organization of the cosmos.'[19] It was not until the Reformation in the sixteenth century that this framework was seriously called into question as Martin Luther began to articulate his doctrine of two distinct kingdoms. The political and the religious, the secular and the sacred began to be distinguished as separate realms, a perspective pushed further in the work of Enlightenment thinkers such as John Locke for whom civil society was a means of counteracting an unaccountable monarch or state by 'taking the executive power out of the hands of self-serving individuals and making it . . . public'.[20]

In light of this complex history, how is the term 'civil society' best understood? Edwards summarizes its opaque nature in a memorable turn of phrase, calling it 'the chicken soup of the social sciences'.[21] In spite of this lack of clarity, the term has assumed central political significance on both sides of the Atlantic in the post–Cold War world. This political shift towards civil society is of central importance when considering community organizing, although its use can reflect dramatically different visions of society. Edwards suggests that 'cited as a solution to social, economic and political dilemmas . . . civil society is claimed by every part of the ideological spectrum as its own, but what exactly is it?'[22] Edwards identifies three key strands of civil-society thinking—civil society as associational life, civil society as the good society and civil society as public sphere. Each perspective echoes aspects of community organizing and can serve to critique and enrich its development, especially in a faith-based context.

The first school of thought identifies civil society as associational life. Edwards summarizes: 'the thinkers of the Enlightenment viewed civil society as a self regulating universe of associations . . . that needed to be protected from the state in . . . resisting despotism.'[23] This depiction of civil society as a network of voluntary associations freely organizing around shared ideals and interests was a strong influence on the establishment of civic life by the first White settlers in North America. Edwards reminds us that this perspective is still 'particularly strong in the USA where it dovetails naturally with pre-existing traditions of self-governance, suspicions about the state and concerns about public disengagement from politics and civic life'.[24] The depiction of civil society as an open network of relationships safeguarding basic rights implicitly assumes equality of opportunity and an ethic of social inclusion. Where power is held in just a few hands, inequality is endemic and patterns of social exclusion are deep-seated, the free and equal exchange of citizens and the establishment of effective associational life becomes little more than an idealistic pipe dream. In spite of such questioning, at the turn of new millennium the Tocquevillian vision of civil society as freely organized associational life continues to shape academic debate and social policy on both sides of the Atlantic. Edwards summarizes: 'It is Alexis de Tocqueville's ghost that wanders through the corridors of the World Bank.'[25] And yet as Gramsci notes in his *Prison Notebooks,* although this characterization of civil society retains a hegemonic hold over marginalized communities, such a perspective can be subverted if an alternative liberative argument wins the cultural 'war of position'. In such a context, it becomes possible to forge alternative subversive civil societies and insurgent representational spaces.[26]

A second school of thought frames civil society as a synonym for a 'good' society. The years since the revolutions in Eastern Europe in 1989 have witnessed an increasingly common linkage between Western models of participatory democracy and the development of a 'good' society as seen, for example, with reference to the invasion of Iraq in 2003 and the unfolding and then stuttering of the Arab Spring in 2011–2012. However, it is worth raising a word of caution about the automatic equation between an active civil society and progressive Western social, economic and political norms. There is nothing inherent in civil-society thinking that is equated automatically with participation, plurality or social inclusion. Simone Chambers and Jeffrey Kopstein point to what they call 'bad civil society'.[27] Examples of an exclusive civil society abound from the extreme to the everyday. At one end of the spectrum, there is the Hitler Youth in Nazi Germany or the secretive Afrikaner *Broederbond* in apartheid South Africa used to inculcate xenophobia. Sat in the middle, there are networks premised on excluding raciological essentialism such as the Ku Klux Klan or the Nation of Islam and at the everyday end of the spectrum there is the neighbourhood watch group that welcomes middle-class suburbanites but implicitly excludes tenants from the so-called rough housing estate across the road. Each example could be said to exemplify civil society but none are inclusive, egalitarian or committed to the 'common good'. In light of this cautionary word it is important ask how the word 'good' is to be understood, who defines it and in whose interests. Alinsky resists the suggestion that community organizing should be self-consciously 'values-based'. However, visions of the 'good' society have shaped community-organizing networks such as the Gamaliel

Foundation and PICO in the United States since their inception. In Britain, Citizens UK identifies a commitment to 'the common good' and to the shared values of dignity, equality and social justice as the ethical basis of its declared aim to 'unlock the power of civil society'.[28] What then might it mean to view the term 'civil society' as a synonym for a 'good' society?

Edwards suggests that the roots of such an ethical framework are found in the ancient Greek idea of the engagement of citizens in the *polis*, the Enlightenment reflections of Immanuel Kant on the fashioning of an all-embracing 'ethical community' and in far older faith-based visions of human community—the Christian conception of the interdependent Body (1 Corinthians 12) and the mutuality of the *Ummah* within Islam.[29] Edwards recognizes the danger of conflating visions of the 'good' society with Western cultural norms. However, the common threads he identifies—'tolerance, non-discrimination, non-violence, trust and cooperation'—provide a reasonable foundation for what we could call an ethical civil society and bear a close resemblance to the core values of Citizens UK.[30] Moving further Edwards argues that 'too many of our existing social, economic and political systems destroy the bonds we want to have with each other . . . civil society seems to offer a way of re-constituting these relationships'.[31] On what basis then can an inclusive civil society be built within societies where social bonds have frayed or been broken? Edwards suggests that an answer to this question might be found in the thinking of Martin Luther King who characterized 'unconditional love . . . as a potentially revolutionary force for change in the public sphere, not just in out private lives'.[32] In these terms, love becomes a motivating force for movements for social justice, interlinking societal change with individual transformation. Far from being an appeal to dewy-eyed romanticism, the love to which King refers is a synonym for respect, mutuality, welcome, inclusion, egalitarian community, hospitality and social justice. A centring on love as a synonym for the 'good' society can highlight the central importance of existential liberation within struggles for social justice. Where an ethic of unconditional love underpins civil society, the systems that exclude and devalue are unmasked. Becoming aware of our own innate value and that of others can awaken us to injustice, what Paulo Freire refers to as conscientization.

Arising from this 'love ethic' we can see three expressions of civil society as the 'good' society. The first emerges from the world of faith. Often referred to as the 'golden rule', this ethic can be found across religious landscape, perhaps dating back at least to the 'Holiness Code' within Leviticus 19 (probably first written down in the sixth century BCE). At one level the 'golden rule' can be dismissed as mere pragmatism—treat other people the way you would like them to treat you. However this early expression of a 'global ethic' can also be seen as an assertion of human interconnectedness and mutuality and is summed up clearly in Jesus' 'great commandment' in Luke 10:27: 'You shall love the Lord your God with all your heart, and with all your soul, and with all your strength, and with all your mind; and your neighbor as yourself.' Seen through this lens the 'good' society is one within which the unconditional hospitality exemplified by the Sikh understanding of the *langar* (not just community kitchen but an indication of the sacramental significance of welcome and equality) enables what is referred to as *tikkun* (healing or repair) within Judaism.[33] These are ideas to which I will return in the closing chapter.

The second strand of thinking that can inform the characterization of civil society as the 'good' society is found within the emergent ideas of the 'Democratic Left' (a twenty-first-century network of democratic socialists in the United Kingdom and Germany) and the work of the think tank Compass which is focused on the renewal of the centre-left in the United Kingdom. Such thinking can be seen as the twenty-first-century inheritor of the 'third way' articulated by UK prime minister Tony Blair and Gerhard Schröder in the late 1990s which was an attempt to fashion a social ethic that combined a commitment to social inclusion with an equally clear commitment to economic dynamism and entrepreneurship.[34] The second strand of social democratic thinking upon which the 'good society' project of the Democratic Left draws is the work of the Nobel Prize–winning Canadian economist J. K. Galbraith whose ideas in *The Affluent Society* and the more recent *The Good Society* have continued to shape centre-left thinking.[35] For Galbraith, 'In the good society all citizens must have personal liberty, basic well-being, racial and ethnic equality, the opportunity for a rewarding life.'[36] Against this backdrop, Joan Rutherford and Hetan Shah suggest that in the face of endemic inequality, soaring personal debt and ingrained patterns of social exclusion in the United Kingdom, 'We are bereft of a vision of a better life'.[37] Rutherford and Shah identify the key components of the 'good' society that they seek—economic equality, the equitable distribution of power, equality of opportunity, the eradication of child poverty, an ethic of caring for the marginalized and vulnerable, equal opportunities for all children, the celebration of cultural and religious diversity and the struggle for racial justice. More recently, John Cruddas and Andrea Nahles have spoken of eight features of the good society:

1. 'rejecting the subordination of political to economic interests'
2. 'remaking the relationship between the individual and the state in a democratic partnership'
3. 'creating a democratic state that is accountable and more transparent, strengthening our institutions of democracy at all levels including the economy'
4. 'enlarging and defending individual civil liberties'
5. 'reasserting the common good . . . over the market'
6. 'redistributing the risk, wealth and power associated with class, race and gender to create a more equal society'
7. 'recognising and respecting differences of race, religion and culture'
8. 'putting the needs of people and the planet before profit'[38]

The third expression of the 'good' society that emerges from the 'love ethic' is embodied by the Roman Catholic (and to an extent Anglican) social teaching on the 'common good' that finds its origins in Pope Leo XII's 1891 encyclical *Rerum Novarum,* which sought to draw upon Christian ethics to respond to poverty and inequality in an industrializing Europe. Memorably the encyclical noted that 'it is neither just nor humane so to grind men down with excessive labor as to stupefy their minds and wear out their bodies'.[39] In a UK context, the establishment of the Christian Social Union by the Anglo-Catholic Scott Holland in Oxford in 1889 drew upon the Christian Socialism of figures such as F. D Maurice and sought to root a theologically radical 'social gospel' within the Church of England. Against this Victorian backdrop, 'common good' thinking has sought to articulate a clear faith-based vision of the 'good' society within which no person is barred from fulfilling her or his potential as a result of economic inequality, poverty, prejudice, age or place of birth as seen, for example, in the seminal 1985 Anglican report *Faith in the City* and its ecumenical 2006 successor *Faithful Cities.*[40] Just before the 2010 UK general election, the Roman Catholic Bishops Conference of England and Wales added clarity to the often rather vague concept of the 'common good', suggesting that it provided the essential yardstick for measuring the social, cultural and spiritual health of the United Kingdom. The bishops wrote that 'the common good refers to what belongs to everyone by virtue of their common humanity . . . The common good is about how to live well together . . . At the heart of the common good solidarity acknowledges that all are responsible for all'.[41] Although the bishops avoided asserting a specific political programme, they made clear links between a philosophical commitment to the 'common good' and particular policy arenas. A commitment to the 'common good', they said, implied an unswerving policy commitment to equality, to the socially excluded and to the development of an asylum and immigration agenda that arose from a core commitment to the inherent dignity of all people and a clear antiracist perspective. Much like the earlier *Faithful Cities* report, the Council of Bishops argued that 'the Christian Churches have long contributed to the promotion of the common good, as a gift and an effort that is an essential part of the Christian vision'.[42]

In the context of the twenty-first century, conceptions of civil society as the normative good society embrace centre-left political analyses such as that of Compass described previously, ancient emphases within the worlds living religions on the 'golden rule' of mutuality and Christian social teaching about the common good. Might it be that this vision can provide a yardstick against which civil-society activism, community organizing and faith-based engagement in the public sphere can be measured? Alternatively, might it be the case that the debilitating character of systemic social exclusion inhibits the translation of a consensual vision of the common good into effective action for social justice? Where part of the community is left out and left behind, whose interests does a civil society premised on a reformist vision of the common good serve and how can it be measured in an inherently superdiverse society in a globalized century?

The third strand of civil society thinking equates the concept with the 'public sphere'. Edwards summarizes: 'The concept of a 'public' that cares about the common good and has the capacity to deliberate about it democratically—is central to civil society thinking.'[43] In the context of our discussion about the capacity of community organizing to embody the foundational values of liberation theology, it is important to seek an answer to four questions. First, to whom does the word public refer? Second, are some social groups effectively excluded from active participation in the public sphere? Third, does the public sphere within the United States and the United Kingdom serve the ideological interests of the socially included or the socially excluded? Fourth, in superdiverse societies, can we speak of a single unifying public sphere or is it more credible to refer to a number of potentially conflicting public spheres? Jurgen Habermas notes that the term 'public sphere' can be understood in a variety of different ways.[44] He suggests that it is possible to trace a discursive public sphere back to the 'market place' discussion that took place amongst free male citizens within the *polis* of the ancient Greek city-states. In spite of this long back-story, Habermas argues that the public sphere as it is constituted in contemporary industrialized societies can be traced more specifically to the emergence of an eighteenth-century bourgeoisie who perceived their interests to be separate from the aristocracy on the one hand and the established church on the other.[45] Independent from the direction of the ruling class the public sphere fashioned within the coffee houses of eighteenth-century Paris and London and the town hall meetings of pre-independence New England represented a bourgeois discursive space within which *men* with the power won by their growing wealth could articulate an independent vision of society and forge a shared political agenda. Although Habermas suggests that this bourgeois public sphere became an exclusive discursive space which mirrored the interests of the new rich, he nevertheless argues that a key feature of the discourse it gave rise to is of abiding importance to those seeking an inclusive civil society: 'The bourgeois public's critical public debate took place . . . without regard to . . . pre-existing social and political rank.'[46]

Craig Calhoun summarizes the dilemma facing those seeking to theorize this exclusive public sphere: 'The early bourgeois public spheres were composed of narrow segments of the European population, mainly educated, propertied men, and they conducted a discourse not only exclusive of others but prejudicial to the interests of those excluded.'[47] Nancy Fraser raises important questions about the bourgeois public sphere as a space of free debate and consensus that are of central importance in relation to models of faith-based community organizing that arise from a conviction that God is biased towards the oppressed.[48] For Fraser the central problem is not Habermas' idealizing of the bourgeois public sphere but his failure to analyze other 'competing public spheres'.[49] She argues that the reduction of the public sphere to a bourgeois debating chamber nullifies the radical potential of public discourse, suggesting its primary purpose was to justify and rationalize a 'shift from a repressive mode of domination to a hegemonic one'.[50] In spite of the critique forwarded by Calhoun and Fraser, echoes of the idealized bourgeois public sphere, which Habermas describes, continue to ring down the years.

However, for those who seek models of community organizing and faith-based activism that reflect a preferential option for the oppressed such a depiction of the public sphere is problematic for two reasons. First, the bourgeois public sphere is premised on the assumption of an open society within which everybody has equal access to the levers of power. As Fraser reminds us within the bourgeois public sphere, 'women of all classes and ethnicities were excluded . . . while plebeian men were formally excluded by property qualifications. Moreover, in many cases, women and men of racialized ethnicities of all classes were excluded on racial grounds'.[51] Second, in a superdiverse society it is not credible to speak of a singular public sphere. Rather, as Fraser notes, it is more persuasive to speak of plural and, on occasions, conflicting, public spheres: 'Virtually from the beginning counter-publics contested the exclusionary norms of the bourgeois public, elaborating alternative styles of political behaviour and . . . public speech.'[52]

Lina Jamoul argues that community organizing provides us with the opportunity to break free from narratives that assume a singular and egalitarian public sphere in order to forge countercultural 'inclusive, conflictual and multiple' representational spaces.[53] She suggests that 'discourses of "impartiality" and "universality" serve to exclude [because] . . . they embody a politics suspicious of difference'.[54] For Jamoul, community organizing can help us to recognize that 'the starting point [for] . . . negotiating a politics of difference is not the elusive "common space" but the position of the marginalized . . . "other" '.[55] Amin Ash and Nigel Thrift make a similar point: 'Democracy requires the . . . empowering of subaltern voices', what Sandercock calls the 'voices from the borderlands', those engaged in, 'insurgent practices [which give rise to] . . . a thousand tiny empowerments'.[56] Such a perspective enables us to engage, for example, with the historic public spaces of resistance articulated by enslaved Black women and men, early trades unionists, civil rights activists, 'underground' Internet-based media collectives such as Indymedia or, more currently, the disparate Occupy movement. Edwards summarizes: 'Theories of the public sphere demand a return to the practice of politics, not as an elite occupation . . . but as an ongoing process through which "active citizens" can . . . shape both the means and the ends of the good society.'[57] It is from such empowered public spheres that a liberative model of community organizing in superdiverse societies can arise.

DIFFERENCE AND SUPERDIVERSITY

The United States and the United Kingdom are inherently diverse societies. In both contexts, it is this cultural and religious diversity that has provided community organizing with its strength. What then might community organizing have to learn from recent theoretical debates about identity and diversity in ever more dynamic and fluid societies where difference is not only normative but increasingly complex and strongly contested? Four lessons can be drawn from such current debates. Taken together they can provide community organizing with stronger theoretical base upon which to build in the future.

1—More than Diverse

Even our diversity is diverse, what the anthropologist Steven Vertovec has called 'super-diversity'.[58] Primarily focusing on patterns of migration, Vertovec notes that by the beginning of the twenty-first century people in London traced their roots to 179 different countries speaking more than three hundred languages. He suggests that, historically, 'multicultural policies have had as their overall goal the promotion of tolerance and respect for collective identities'.[59] The key word here is 'collective'. Because it rests on the mobilizing power of organized faith and community groups, community organizing, like the social policy initiatives of government, has understandably focused its energies on those organizations where such 'collective' identities are expressed and embodied. However, Vertovec invites us to step into a far more fluid and provisional world that is characterized by disorganized diversity—a world where smallness and lack of organization can render people and groups effectively invisible. The previously settled landscape of multicultural society is increasingly unsettled. We live in fluid rather than solid cities and, as a result, those engaged in community politics or contextual theology can no longer focus their attention on settled ethnic or religious background alone. This emergent superdiverse and transnational landscape demands new ways of thinking about identity and meaning that have the capacity to cope with complexity, what Sandercock calls an 'epistemology of multiplicity'.[60] Vertovec suggests that this superdiverse context is giving rise to new patterns of community, new configurations of prejudice and new expressions of segregated living alongside new forms of dialogical identity and cosmopolitanism.[61] Such dynamic superdiversity reflects the networked nature of contemporary urban life within which identity, power, community and activism arise from the continuous flow of people, ideas and culture in what Castells has called a networked 'information age'.[62] Within what Smith calls a 'trans-local urban' society, the interplay between the global and the local gives rise to increasingly complex forms of superdiversity.[63] This new landscape presents community organizing with a fresh challenge, that of finding new and creative ways of 'doing politics' that engage not only with settled and solid faith groups or community organizations but also with emergent and fluid networks that may exist 'below the radar' in back streets and on urban estates far from view.

2—Clinging to 'Race'

A second arena of debate that can inform the development of community organizing in the United Kingdom and the United States reflects the shadow side of superdiversity. In the face of normative diversity, essentialized understandings of identity and 'race' continue to provide some with a sense of existential security in an insecure world. In spite of its objective emptiness the social construction of 'race' retains cultural, political and existential significance at a subjective level because the excluding approach to identity and belonging upon which it rests continues to mould the lives of many of those alongside whom community organizers work. Gilroy makes the point sharply: ' "Race" must be retained as an analytic category . . . because it refers investigation to the power that collective identities acquire by means of their roots in tradition. These identities, in the forms of white racism and Black resistance, are the most volatile political forces in Britain today.'[64]

Essentialist race-based thinking assumes the ongoing existence of an undiluted and unchanging ethnic core. Although such a view flies in the face of sociocultural and biological realities, centuries of cultural and ethnic interweaving and the dialogical force of globalization, it is a perspective that speaks to the existential needs of some alienated communities. On the one hand, it can provide a focus for solidarity but, on the other, someone to blame for social exclusion. 'Race' based thinking can be a euphemism for racism as seen in the activism of the English Defence League, the Ku Klux Klan or one of the over one thousand White supremacist groups that the Southern Poverty Law Center identified across the United States in 2011.[65] However the feminist and postcolonial critic Gayatri Spivak suggests that in certain circumstances the adoption of a strategic essentialism can enable marginalized oppressed communities to bolster a sense of solidarity through the forging of greater bonding social capital, thereby resourcing a strong resistance identity which Castells argues serves as means of excluding the included and affirming the excluded.[66] The tension therefore between superdiversity and the appeal to ethnic or religious essentialism represents a challenge with which contemporary community organizing needs to grapple in greater critical depth if it is to develop a credible cultural politics of difference. Furthermore, such a tension poses difficult questions for those engaged in the development of a theology of community organizing that is premised on an ethic of liberative difference. This is a challenge to which I will return in the closing chapter of this book.

3—The Cultural Politics of Difference

Third, in the face of dynamic superdiversity, interwoven patterns of identity and the enduring appeal to 'race', the cultural politics of difference, which I introduced in the previous chapter, has the capacity to resource new patterns of community organizing in diverse societies that undermine the allure of essentialism. Young critiques dominant, Enlightenment models of justice that claim a universal validity while, in fact, arising from and implicitly privileging White experience and reflecting a Eurocentric worldview. Young criticizes a hegemonic color blind depiction of justice.[67] She argues that where oppressed groups are able to assert their own distinctness from the ruling class, it becomes possible to articulate a 'different ideal of liberation which might be called democratic cultural pluralism'.[68] Such a shift challenges frameworks which essentialize culture and betray 'a fear of making permeable the categorical border between oneself and the others' because 'the politics of difference . . . aims for an understanding of group difference as ambiguous, relational, shifting . . . Difference now comes to mean not otherness . . . but specificity, variation, heterogeneity'.[69] In the context of community organizing in superdiverse contexts such as the United States and the United Kingdom, the articulation of a contextualized cultural politics of difference can enable a movement beyond race-based activism. West suggests that such a shift can be 'a strengthening and nurturing endeavour that can forge more solid alliances and coalitions . . . [between] . . . people of colour and white progressives'.[70] A recognition of the importance of the work of figures like Gilroy, West and Young can enable contemporary community organizing to engage more fully with the superdiverse landscape within which it seeks to build permanent people's organizations.

In the face of normative diversity, the nature and future of multiculturalism has provided the focus for increasingly contentious debate in the opening years of the twenty-first century. In the United Kingdom this debate has largely revolved around belonging, citizenship and, in particular, British-Muslim identities in the years following the terrorist attacks on New York and Washington on 9/11 and the London bombings in 7/7, as the sociologist Tariq Modood makes plain.[71] At street level, multiculturalism is a simple descriptor of everyday urban life—diversity is ordinary rather than remarkable. However at the level of government, multiculturalism in the United Kingdom has, since the Race Relations Act of 1965 (and later 1968) and the racism exemplified by Enoch Powell's 1968 'Rivers of Blood' speech, been a policy response to the legacy of empire and to postwar migration from former colonies in the Caribbean and the Indian subcontinent. Since the late 1990s proactive multiculturalism as a political project has come under fire from both the political left and the political right. Under the Labour government of 1997–2010, narratives of Britishness took on an increasingly assimilationist tone, implying that Muslim identity and British citizenship were arguably incompatible, seemingly echoing the contentious clash of civilisations thesis of the US political scientist Samuel Huntingdon.[72] This narrative was exemplified by Labour's controversial 2007–2010 Preventing Violent Extremism policy agenda, which sought to recruit Mosques in the search for so-called radical Islamists.[73] Since the election of the Conservative-led coalition government in the United Kingdom in 2010, this attack on multiculturalism is perhaps best typified by the speech of British prime minister David Cameron in 2011 in Munich in which he suggested that multiculturalism had 'failed'.[74] Choosing his words carefully, Cameron spoke only of Islamist groups as a threat but implied that the broader British-Muslim community had failed to integrate into British society. Cameron's speech represented a selective reading of British-Muslim history, but the assertion of an ethnocentric narrative of Britishness rather than balanced historical analysis seems to have been his purpose. In this light, Gilroy's words take on a renewed importance for community organizers: 'Authoritarian modes of belonging to the national collective supply the norm . . . anyone who objects to the conduct of their government is likely to be identified as an enemy within.'[75]

In the face of such critiques of multiculturalism, the theorizing of so called hybridity has gained traction within the social sciences. Although cross-cultural relationships are far from new, the number of people of dual heritage in the United Kingdom has grown rapidly in recent decades. The 2011 National Census revealed that 1.2 million people described themselves as 'dual-heritage', almost double the number in 2001. Furthermore, 8.9% of people under the age of sixteen in the United Kingdom (just over two million) suggested that they live with parents from different ethnic backgrounds.[76] The United Kingdom in the twenty-first century is not just super-diverse but a society in which, to use Stuart Hall's words, 'new ethnicities' continue to emerge, recreating Britain in the process. Hall suggests that a hybrid society is marked by intimacy, not isolation, fusion, not so-called ethnic purity.[77] The language of hybridity enables a movement beyond binary definitions of identity and perhaps points to the future character of urbanized societies like the United States and the United Kingdom. In an interwoven superdiverse society, the emergence of dialogical identities can counter assimilationist and isolationist approaches to normative diversity. According to Gilroy, such dynamic diversity represents a threat to essentialized narratives of identity, 'hybrid urban cultures and cosmopolitan, creolized history go out of the window. Instead we get transported into the frozen realm of mythic time that has been shaped around the master analogy of immigration as a form of warfare'.[78]

However, in spite of its currency within the social sciences, the appeal to hybridity does not provide community organizing in superdiverse societies with an adequate foundation upon which to build organizing networks for two reasons. First, the language of hybridity would be better left in botany where its use originated as a means of describing the grafting of one plant species onto another to create a new hybrid plant. Although the language of fusion within botany is credible, people are not plants. The appeal to cultural hybridity implicitly gives credence to the flawed assertion that there are different human 'races' that can be fused. Instead it would be more credible to speak of dialogical identities and of people who draw upon a dual heritage. Difference remains intact, becoming the source of new models of distinctness rather than human hybrids. Second, like narratives of assimilation the deployment of hybridity as a descriptor of new dialogical identities subsumes difference within a demographic stew wherein distinctness is lost. Community organizing would do better to explore the liberative potential of a cultural fruit cocktail within which specific stories, cultures and histories are not submerged beneath a homogenizing narrative but, instead, become the basis for a creative cultural politics of difference that is capable of reflecting the dynamic realities of a superdiverse society. As Beckford notes, 'this multidimensional approach to experience means that liberation strategies will not all be the same because experience is not singular.'[79] In light of the inadequacy of the language of hybridity, another approach is required. Perhaps, as Nasar Meer and Tariq Modood argue, an intercultural approach that values commonality and distinctness can move us beyond multicultural coexistence, the aridity of excluding identity politics and assimilationist social policy.[80] Beckford makes the point clearly: 'The experience of poor whites within the inner city is similar but also dissimilar from their Indian, Bangladeshi . . . Caribbean and West African neighbours . . . Dialogue across boundaries of class, faith and gender must become an integral dimension of understanding experience if we are to be inclusive'.[81] Such a nuanced interculturalism can serve community organizers well in both the United States and the United Kingdom.

4—A Shared Humanity

On the basis of a dynamic cultural politics of difference it becomes possible to reaffirm visions of solidarity that cross the guarded borders of ethnic and religious identity and articulate new patterns of shared humanity. Over the last thirty years, the Roman Catholic theologian Hans Küng has sought to articulate a contemporary 'global ethic' that arises from the 'golden rule'. Küng's search is for an ethical framework capable of resourcing the development of a socially just and inclusive global community.[82] In 1993 Küng drafted the *Declaration toward a Global Ethic* for the Parliament of the World's Religions, which although very broad-brush, outlines a clear ethical base for a global 'good' society: 'We commit ourselves to a culture of nonviolence, respect, justice and peace. We shall not oppress, injure, torture or kill other human beings . . . We must move beyond the dominance of greed for power, prestige, money and consumption to make a just and peaceful world . . . We invite all people, whether religious or not, to do the same.'[83]

Küng's cosmopolitanism has deep roots. Such a perspective can be traced back through the work of the twentieth-century philosopher Jacques

Derrida on hospitality and the Enlightenment thinking of Immanuel Kant on the commonality of humanity to the Stoics of ancient Greece who asserted the idea that each person is not simply located in their own community but is a citizen of the world.[84] Arising from this ancient assertion of the unity and equality of all people, cosmopolitanism has assumed a renewed significance in recent decades as we have seen a shift from the bipolar certainties of the Cold War to the multipolar uncertainty of the twenty-first century. Unity and diversity here are seen to be complementary not contradictory. For David Held, cosmopolitan principles make it possible to take cultural diversity seriously, thereby enabling the development of an inclusive democratic culture characterized by 'difference and democratic dialogue'. For Held, contemporary cosmopolitanism seeks to conceptualize and sustain a shared ethic of commonality that can empower individuals and foster an inclusive pattern of social activism.[85] Cosmopolitanism echoes the commitment to unity in diversity embodied by the Christian conception of catholicity wherein people of faith from different cultural backgrounds are united by a common but contextualized faith, as I show in my exploration of the work of Robert Schreiter in the next chapter.[86]

Such a perspective resembles the core commitment within community organizing to equality, human dignity and the capacity of difference to foster shared activism. An engagement with recent cosmopolitan analyses can enrich this commitment to diversity and democratic action. However, does cosmopolitanism provide a sufficient basis for community organizing in superdiverse urban societies? Three questions are of importance. First, arising as it does from ancient Greek philosophy and the Enlightenment, is cosmopolitanism overly wedded to a Eurocentric and inherently individualistic worldview that cannot easily be translated into more communitarian cultures and communities? Second, does the cosmopolitan claim to universality and impartiality ring true, or does this mask the ideological assertion of the interests of Western models of participatory democracy? Is impartiality ever possible in an unequal society and a divided world? Third, does the commitment of cosmopolitan philosophy to common human dignity, equality and individual human agency take sufficient account of structural injustice? Does the appeal to a globalized common good provide a credible basis for community organizing in the face of systemic injustice, or is it necessary to assert instead a clear bias to the oppressed as seen within the canon of liberation theology? In spite of his commitment to a 'post-racial' politics, Gilroy asks if the laudable principles of cosmopolitanism have been co-opted by the United States and the United Kingdom in the service of the so-called War on Terror and the expansion of Westernized models of participatory democracy. Gilroy refers to this as an 'armored cosmopolitanism' that is accompanied by what he calls a 'messianic civilisationism'.[87] In spite of this critique, Gilroy suggests that the normative diversity of contemporary urban societies has given rise to an 'ordinary cosmopolitanism' that can resource the fashioning of a 'multicultural democracy' that can sustain a 'cosmopolitan solidarity from below' which is characterized by a 'planetary consciousness' and the 'cosmopolitan activism' of networked diverse oppressed communities.[88] Such a cosmopolitan politics of difference that is motivated by a prophetic commitment to a divine bias to the oppressed rather than a consensual common good can enable community organizers to build an effective alliance of the excluded on the basis of an ethic of liberative difference, as I show in the final chapter.[89]

Social and Religious Capital

Organized relational power provides the foundation stone upon which all community organizing builds. Such a focus rests upon the suggestion that associational life and networks of trust are sources of powerful and effective social action. In the early years of the twentieth century, Lyda Judson Hanifan drew upon this perspective in his work on rural school community centres in West Virginia and is possibly the first person to describe associational life and networks of trust as social capital.[90] In spite of this backstory, the language of social capital has only assumed a significant role within political and social theory in recent decades, largely in relation to social movement activism and the political turn towards an active civil society thanks largely to the work of Pierre Bourdieu and Robert Putnam.

Writing from a Marxist perspective, Bourdieu was specifically interested in the ways in which a ruling class uses its 'cultural capital' to reinforce its position of power. For Bourdieu, such symbolic power arose not only from economic capital but also from the accumulated power of relationships and networks. Hence social capital is 'the aggregate of the actual or potential resources which are linked to a durable network of institutionalized relationships of mutual acquaintance and recognition'.[91] John Field puts it more succinctly: 'relationships matter.'[92] However, for Bourdieu, in an unequal society, some people and some relationships matter more than others. Bourdieu suggests that the social capital arising from participation in these networked social relationships rested on a person's inclusion within the mainstream of society. Consequently those who are socially excluded, with little 'stake' in society, do not possess the kind of social capital that can be used to transform their situation. Bourdieu's work raises a sharp challenge for community organizers—how can a model of activism premised on the social capital of the organized power of faith and community groups engage with people and communities that are more fragile, weaker or powerless—those with little capital to 'stake'?

Over the last decade, the work of the political scientist Robert Putnam on social capital and associational life in the United States has gained a broader circulation than the earlier ideas of Bourdieu and has had a greater influence on social policy in the United States and the United Kingdom. The influence of Putnam's work has also been evident in recent expressions of urban theology in the United Kingdom, such as that exemplified by the *Faithful Cities* report. For Putnam, 'Social capital refers to connections among individuals—social networks and the norms of reciprocity and trustworthiness that arise from them. In that sense social capital is closely related to what some have called "civic virtue." '[93] Putnam describes three forms of social capital, each of which resonates with the practice of community organizing. He speaks of 'bonding' capital, which bolsters solidarity within homogeneous groups, 'bridging' capital, which can link distinct but loosely related groups, and 'linking' capital, which has the capacity to foster connections between more disparate groups. He summarizes: 'Bridging social capital can generate broader identities and reciprocity, whereas bonding social capital bolsters our narrower selves . . . Bonding social capital constitutes a kind of sociological superglue, whereas bridging social capital provides a sociological WD-40.'[94] Social capital therefore denotes the capacity of networked human relationships to bolster individual and communal agency. Relationships and the networks they foster have the power to resource effective shared values based cross-community activism within civil society.

Over the last decade, the language of social capital has begun to provide urban and political theologians with a new vocabulary of solidarity, community and discipleship. On the basis of their work with churches in the city of Manchester, Baker and Skinner speak of two levels of faith-based social capital—the practical and the existential. They note that in a number of marginalized communities, church buildings are the only public shared space in the neighbourhood. Baker and Skinner suggest that the social significance of the activities run or hosted by churches and the people power of congregations with deep roots in their community can be described as 'religious capital'.[95] Such religious capital can reflect a bonding model of social capital—building the capacity, self-confidence and health of insiders within a congregation while implicitly or explicitly excluding outsiders—those felt not to belong. Contrastingly, religious capital can reflect a bridging model of social capital—building practical bridges of understanding, dialogue and social inclusion across and between different faith, community and neighbourhood groups which, although distinct, are rooted in similar value systems. Thirdly, religious capital can move beyond facilitating dialogue between distinct but comparable groups and reflect a more outward-facing and proactive linking social capital which interconnects groups premised on quite different philosophies, theologies and ideologies but facing the same questions and challenges. In such cases, 'religious capital' can link distinct groups together in a network of common activism. The character of the specific religious capital of particular faith groups directly reflects the second form of social capital that Baker and Skinner identified—'spiritual capital'. They use this term to refer to the foundational values upon which faith communities build their common life. Spiritual capital is the energy that gives life to practical religious capital. Where the theological base of a faith group is exclusivist, the spiritual capital of such a group can tend to give rise to an excluding pattern of religious capital that bonds the group but isolates it from the wider community. However where a faith group is characterized by an inclusivist theology, its spiritual capital can resource a socially progressive pattern of religious capital that has the capacity to forge bridging and linking models of faith-based activism.

Given the key role that faith groups play within community organizing in both the United States and the United Kingdom, debates about social, religious and spiritual capital and the models of community engagement they imply can critique and enrich community organizing practice in much needed new ways. The potential benefits of such dialogue challenge community organizations to embrace a fuller and more open-ended critical engagement with theory than has been the case in the past. The emphasis within community organizing on organized people and relational networked power, for example, invites a dialogue with the key strands of social-capital thinking that I have summarized previously. Such engagement however needs to be selective, for the vocabulary of social capital is not an activist's cure-all. Two cautionary notes need to be borne in mind. First given that social capital arises from the cultivation of networks of trust, are those with no currency to contribute, people living on the edges of society, further disempowered because they do not belong to the faith, community, labour or political networks on which social capital thinking rests? Second, in light of the importance of the development of networks of trust between distinct communities, is social-capital thinking relevant in a superdiverse society where fluidity rather than solidity is increasingly the norm? The patchworks of relatively small and fragile ethnic or religious groups existing below the demographic radar can go unseen and unheard because they are not organized and have little clear social capital to contribute. Might it be the case therefore that social-capital theory and its use within theology implicitly favours the organized and settled over the disorganized and fragile? In spite of these cautionary notes, Baker and Skinner are surely right to suggest that theoretical and governmental debates about social capital have 'given the churches a new language . . . a way of re-asserting a sense of relevance for themselves within urban contexts'.[96] They argue that religious capital can 'represent a progressive spiral of influence . . . that contrasts with the apparently regressive spiral of institutional decline'.[97] How do faith groups exert such influence and what impact might this have for broad-based community organizing?

WHEN RELIGIOUS CAPITAL GETS POLITICAL

Research from the widely respected Pew Research Center suggests that ahead of the 2012 US presidential election, 54% of Americans felt that faith groups should not become involved in political matters (up from 46% in 2006).[98] However, during this period, the last two US presidents, George W Bush and Barack Obama, have both argued that faith groups have a key role to play in civil society politics and have recognized the political significance of the social capital embodied by faith communities. Indeed the Pew Research Center's Forum on Religion and Public Life noted in 2009 that 52% of Americans felt that faith groups were better placed to care for those who are homeless than non-faith-based groups (21% non-faith-based groups). What is more, 37% believed that faith groups were more effective at caring for those are socially excluded (28% non-faith-based groups), 42% that they were better qualified to mentor young people (38% non-faith-based groups) and 38% that they effectively counselled prisoners (23% non-faith-based groups).[99] The sociologist Therese O'Toole has written about the recent engagement of government with faith groups in the seemingly more secularized United Kingdom. She notes that, contrary to Tony Blair's press secretary Alistair Campbell's pithy 'we don't do God', the Labour government under Blair and his successor Gordon Brown increasingly recognized 'the role of faith leaders in fostering good community relations, and . . . faith groups, and interfaith groups especially, as possessing the ability to generate 'bridging social capital' and deliver community cohesion'.[100] Turning to the Conservative-led coalition government that won the 2010 UK general election, O'Toole highlights the launch of the Near Neighbours scheme that is coordinated by the Church of England and intended to foster greater social inclusion and community cohesion through the development of interfaith projects, particularly in socially excluded urban communities. As O'Toole recognizes, the Near Neighbours scheme, in spite of its arguably excluding linkage to the established Church (Anglican Vicars are required to countersign grant applications), reflects a renewed political recognition of the socially progressive potential of religious capital. Could this renewed confidence in 'doing God' give rise to an underexplored stream of 'linking' social capital that has the capacity to resource social inclusion and social justice in the superdiverse multifaith society of the twenty-first century? For O'Toole, 'Near Neighbours provides one test of how the Church will navigate its role as a core religious actor within a diverse, multi-faith landscape.'[101]

Citing the role of faith groups within London Citizens, a 2012 report from the think tank Demos concluded that 'people of faith are likely to be a vital base of support for any future election winning progressive coalition'.[102] The language of social capital was adopted in the ecumenical Christian report *Faithful Cities*. Alluding to the work of Sandercock, the report argues that because of their 'faithful capital' faith groups are able to empower powerless communities and give voice to the witness of voiceless groups.[103] Theoretical debates about social capital may have provided faith groups with a vocabulary that can resource a new pattern of political engagement in a postsecular context. Such reflective activism could enable faith groups to develop a more informed relationship with the broad-based community organizations that many support. Recent social capital thinking stimulates three key questions for faith groups and community organizers. First, what kind of social capital might best serve the common interests of progressive faith groups and community-organizing networks? Second, do patterns of activism that revolve around the relational power realized through the social capital of faith groups generate community cohesion without challenging structural injustice? Third, is it possible that faith-based community organizing can generate a subversive linking social capital and a new expression of the divine bias to the oppressed that is rooted in an ethic of liberative difference? Such questions place the calling of community organizers, theorists and theologians under the microscope—artisans forging fresh models of understanding that can serve the common good or agent provocateurs fermenting radically new intellectual frameworks capable of fashioning a preferential option for the oppressed that can engage credibly with the superdiverse urban societies of the twenty-first century?

WHAT'S THE POINT OF INTELLECTUALS?

The word 'intellectual' is not neutral—it is pregnant with meaning. The term evokes contrasting and emotive responses. Within the academy, the word can signify an affirmation of a person's rigorous intellect, critical mind, analytical ability and wide-ranging expertise on a specific issue. Beyond the academy, the word 'intellectual' can imply elitism, disengagement and academic snobbery. Intellectual politicians can be seen as figures of fun as both US president Barack Obama and former UK prime minister Gordon Brown have discovered—seemingly more at ease in a policy briefing than they are in street-level conversations with 'ordinary' people. Historically, as I suggested previously, community organizing has been wary of developing an in-depth critical dialogue with social and political theory because this may distract from pragmatic and results-oriented activism. In spite of this tension, I want to argue the case of the intellectual as a key ally in the development of community organizing. Indeed I would go further and suggest that without the development of a mutually respectful critical dialogue between community organizers, faith groups and intellectuals, community organizing will not fulfil its potential to model a 'post-religious' theology of liberation. Having made such a bold claim, let me explain what I mean.

The Marxist Antonio Gramsci was imprisoned by the fascist regime of Benito Mussolini in 1928. In his *Prison Notebooks,* written during his imprisonment, Gramsci wrote of the potential of culture to oppress or to liberate and of the pivotal political role played by intellectuals. Although they were smuggled out of prison in the 1930s, Gramsci's extensive reflections were not published until the 1950s and were only translated into English in the 1970s. Two of Gramsci's ideas are of direct relevance to discussions about the potential role of the intellectual within community organizing—his ideas about hegemony and education and his commentary on the role of intellectuals.

Gramsci writes of the political importance of culture as a means of social control. Unlike Leninist Marxists who underplayed the significance of culture, Gramsci suggested that it represented a key tool in the arsenal of the ruling class and was used to present the vested interests of the powerful and social inequality as part of the natural order of life. Gramsci referred to this as 'cultural hegemony'—the masking of the reality of oppression. Ideas therefore have the capacity to sustain the status quo or to subvert it. For Gramsci, this struggle of ideas was a de facto war-a *'war of position'* in which lasting social change could only be won when the idea of liberation subverted the false consciousness borne of cultural hegemony as the dominant ethic within society.[104] Half a world away in the early 1960s, Paulo Freire drew upon the Gramsci's ideas as well as the work of Frantz Fanon in Algeria in his development of liberative education programmes alongside illiterate women and men in the favellas of Brazil. Gramsci wrote of the oppression of the proletariat and Fanon of the psychological effects of racialized oppression and the force of existential emancipation from 'mental slavery'.[105] In his earliest books, *Pedagogy of the Oppressed* and *Cultural Action for Freedom*, Freire argues that through education the oppressed can become conscious of the nature and cause of their oppression.[106] In the much later *Pedagogy of Indignation*, Freire defines this process of awakening or conscientization as 'the building of a critical awareness'.[107] Education therefore can become a tool for the building of new liberative reflective networks within which the intellectual can play a vital role. Such networks could revitalise community organizing by placing a greater emphasis on open and creative reflection on the liberative potential of ideas and values than on a largely utilitarian 'means and ends' training.

Second, Gramsci writes of the role of the intellectual. Gramsci subverts elitist assumptions about the intellectual—all people have the capacity for creative critical thinking. Historically however, suggests Gramsci, intellectuals have largely been subsumed within the ruling class and their dominant role has been to serve the interests of the powerful, acting as 'the dominant group's "deputies" exercising the subaltern functions of social hegemony'.[108] However, such a role is not predetermined. Gramsci speaks of a 'new intellectualism', which subverts the perception that intellectuals inevitably serve the needs of the powerful. The 'new intellectual' is not characterized by disengagement but by an 'active participation in practical life, as . . . organiser, permanent persuader and not just as a simple orator'.[109] She or he becomes an organic intellectual reflecting and feeling the 'elemental passions of the people . . . , engaged in the task of unmasking hegemony and forging the development of conscientization amongst the excluded within the cultural "war of position" '.[110] Drawing on Gramsci (as well as the Hebrew Prophets and the teaching of Jesus), Gustavo Gutiérrez recognizes that the conscientized theologian exerts a prophetic function and becomes an organic intellectual at one with the oppressed, 'engaged where nations, social classes, people struggle to free themselves from domination and oppression'.[111] For Gutiérrez, 'the theologian is to be an "organic intellectual," a thinker with organic links to the popular liberation undertaking, and with the Christian communities that live their faith by taking this historical task upon them-selves as their own.'[112]

Within the struggle for justice, the organic intellectual is therefore in solidarity with oppressed communities, playing a key conscientizing role. Cornel West and Edward Said sharpen this role in their discussion of the public-political intellectual. For West, 'To be an intellectual means to speak a truth that allows suffering to speak [to] . . . create a vision of the world that puts into the limelight the social misery that is usually hidden or concealed by the dominant viewpoints of a society.'[113] The intellectual is a key figure who, in the words of Said, is tasked with 'speaking truth to power' within the cultural war of position because, says Said, 'the purpose of the intel-lectual's activity is to advance human freedom and knowledge'.[114] Said has translated his writing into active support for Palestinian self-determination. West has been an active supporter of civil rights struggles since the 1970s and a cochair of the Tikkun interfaith peace movement. He has been an active campaigner for African-American Democrat politicians and a strong supporter of the Occupy movement since 2011. More recently he worked with the broadcaster Tavis Smiley and organized a Poverty Tour of schools, churches and community centres across the 'battleground states' ahead of the 2012 US presidential election. This Poverty Tour led to the publication of *The Rich and the Rest of Us* in 2012.[115]

In spite of such activism, it is possible to argue that the political-public intellectual can become more of a commentator on injustice rather than an advocate speaking organically out of her or his own experience of op-pression as they have entered into solidarity with the oppressed. Does this mean that only intellectuals who are born as part of the oppressed com-munity can be seen as organic intellectuals? Alternatively, is it possible as Gutiérrez suggests, that the liberation theologian can become an adopted organic intellectual when she or he makes a conscious preferential option for the oppressed, what the urban theologian John Vincent calls 'a journey downwards'?[116] Schreiter grapples with this insider-outsider tension in his exploration of what he calls 'local theologies'. He clearly argues that the 'author' of a local theology is the community. This has to be the case if the resulting contextual theology is to represent an authentic reflection of the experience and struggles of the people. However Schreiter also suggests that the outsider, the conscientized theologian, has a key role to play in the forg-ing of a contextual theology because she or he brings a specific set of skills which, when offered to the community in authentic solidarity, can help to give rise to a liberative theology. Hence, for Schreiter, the theologian acts as a facilitator—challenging a community with new questions, offering new resources, stimulating action-reflection but never exercising hegemony over the community.[117]

In the context of community organizing, the community organizer has historically acted as a trainer, a facilitator, a fundraiser, a networker and a lead worker managing and coordinating campaigns. Organizers have often been conscientized 'outsiders'—women and men with an ability to explore localized concerns alongside neighbourhood organizations and faith groups, explain the model of activism embodied by community organizing, empathise with local people and harness mutual self-interest in order to forge a coherent community organization capable of mounting effective actions. An engagement with the debates I have summarised about the role of the intellectual in struggles for social justice can critique and enrich broad-based community organizing, thereby helping the movement to become more capable of engaging effectively in the cultural war of position. Community organizers can legitimately be viewed as political intellectuals in the terms described by West and Said. They 'speak truth to power' and bring the suffering of marginalized and often unheard groups into the light within the cultural war of position in order to generate the tension that can move debates about issues like the living wage from the sidelines to the centre of political debate. However, it is not clear that community organizers can be seen as the organic intellectuals described by Gramsci and Gutiérrez. On occasions, organizers are conscientized 'outsiders' rather than people who organically belong to the communities they seek to organize. Bearing in mind Schreiter's comment about the valuable skills that the conscientized outsider brings to a community, this need not be problematic. It does however raise the possibility that those community organizers who are outsider political intellectuals may not feel, as Gramsci puts it, 'the elemental passions of the people', the questions that go unspoken or the perception of impotence by smaller, more fragile faith and community groups. Such organizers may instead be more comfortable with pragmatic strategic goals, 'successful' campaigns and building the strength of the local broad-based community organization. This tension invites further reflection within community organizing on the extent to which community organizers are exposed to the kind of ideas I have considered previously. Is the training of a community organizer an apprenticeship in the received principles of community organizing—how to do a one-to-one, chair an assembly and mount campaigns that are likely to succeed—or the immersion of a conscientized woman or man in the broader and more challenging questions I have raised in this and the previous chapter? Engagement with this wider debate can enable community organizing to move beyond its current status as an effective model of bottom-up civic politics to that of a people's movement capable not only of winning a living wage but of shifting the pendulum in favour of the oppressed in the cultural war of position.

CONCLUSION

Since its inception more than seventy years ago in Chicago, community organizing has largely resisted a critical dialogue with social and political theory, seeing this as a diversion from the urgent task of building a permanent people's' organizations. In the early years of the twenty-first century, this perspective remains the dominant position. It must be noted that through its online educational work, the US-based Comm-Org has, since the mid-1990s, sought to develop such a critical dialogue.[118] However, the norm in both the United States and the United Kingdom is that of a utilitarian dialogue whereby relationships with theorists or theologians are seen in terms of the strategic support they can provide for existing campaigns rather than as empathetic but critical dialogue partners.

In this chapter I have argued that community organizing would benefit from the adoption of such a critical, creative and mutual dialogue with social and political theory, as well as with political and liberation theologies. I have shown that such a dialogue can critique and enrich community organizing, thereby enabling it to fulfil its potential to move beyond the pragmatic goal of building permanent people's organizations and mounting effective campaigns to embody a new cultural politics of difference and a 'post-religious' liberation theology capable of shifting the balance in the cultural 'war of position'. Specifically, I have demonstrated that current theoretical discussions about social space and the liberative potential of representational space can enrich community-organizing practice. I have illustrated the ways in which debates about civil society, the nature of the 'good society', the cultural politics of difference, superdiversity, social and religious capital and the role of political-organic intellectuals in struggles for social justice can provide community organizing with the theoretical tools to realize its undoubted potential. In the closing chapters, I draw history, narrative, the 'new politics' and social and political theory into a dialogue with political and liberation theology in order to begin to forge the outline of an interdisciplinary liberative theology of community organizing. It is to this dialogue that I now turn.

Part III
Reflection

5 Finding the Faith to Organize

INTRODUCTION

This book is an example of contextual political theology. It has arisen from my own involvement in community organizing since the mid-1990s. I have brought this experience into a critical dialogue with the story of community organizing on both sides of the Atlantic, with what I have called the 'new politics' and with recent theoretical debates within social and political theory. In an attempt to be faithful to the contours of the pastoral cycle, I now turn to theological reflection in the final two chapters. Within this chapter, I will identify a range of theological themes that arise from the practice of community organizing and the theoretical debates of the last two chapters. These are the themes that will form the key ingredients in the liberative theology of community organizing which I offer in the final chapter. I will engage in a dialogue with four of the theologians whose work can resource such a theology—Robert Schreiter, Chris Baker, Robert Beckford and Luke Bretherton—and will root this discussion in a reframing of the foundational touchstones of liberation theology.

A theology of community organizing will be rooted in the streets. Drawing on the work of Lefebvre, Knott, Soja and Gorringe, it will be a political theology that is in dialogue with constructed social space. Rooted in contextual theological methodology, a theology of community organizing will model the pastoral cycle. Theological reflection and community organizing practice will be molded by the interdisciplinary social analysis of the experience of those engaged in specific actions and the foundational values from which their activism arises. Because, as Lefebvre notes, social space is constructed rather than given, oppressed communities and activists alike are able to forge spaces of representation within which theological visions, political narratives and actions can be articulated that subvert the purposes for which the powerful have designed public space. Social space therefore is not simply the arena within which community organizing is practiced but the existential crucible from which liberative new theologies can emerge. Without such rooting in the concrete and steel of the city, as Knott reminds us in relation to the protests against the Iraq War in 2003, the potential of the spiritual capital that motivates faith-based community organizers will remain unrealized because it is only in the context of actual struggle in specific situations that liberative values can be translated into credible and subversive activism.

Such a theology will resemble the praxis model to which Stephen Bevans points because it is a theology intended to facilitate liberative social change.[1] It will be an inductive theology, resembling Bevans anthropological model, within which theological insights about faith-based community organizing emerge from what Pinn calls a 'nitty-gritty' dialogue with the liberative resources found within contemporary culture rather than the translation of existing universal dogmatic truths into local contexts.[2] The task of the organizer therefore within faith-based community organizing is to work alongside a diverse range of faith and community groups to forge multiple spaces of representation and subversive reflection. Such plurality will be aligned with the cultural politics of difference and based, as I will show, on a hermeneutics of liberative difference. This kind of community organizing demands a radical openness to 'the other' and a commitment to a 'nitty-gritty' search for liberative insights rather than a concern for doctrinal or faith-specific orthodoxy. Such an approach will rest upon a shared liberative spirituality, forged in the context of struggle and energizing faith-based organizers. Only such radical openness can facilitate the development of a faith-based community organizing that is committed to the fashioning of liberative patterns of activism which accurately reflect the translocal and dynamic nature of superdiverse societies in the twenty-first century. What is sought therefore is a model of discipleship that envisions faith groups as values-led social movements animated by common patterns of social ethics rather than enclosed religious institutions that cooperate with each other while remaining essentially unchanged. A theology of community organizing in a superdiverse context needs fluid rather than solid communities of faith. In this vein it is important to recognize that spaces of representation are not limited to official or organized social space but are to be found on the street, in the gym, the school, college, doctor's surgery and office just as often as they are within places of worship, interfaith gatherings and community organizing assemblies.

Within this chapter, I draw upon the dub hermeneutics of Robert Beckford in order to explore the extent to which Robert Schreiter's exploration of a 'new' catholicity, Chris Baker's emergent third-space thinking and Luke Bretherton's Christian cosmopolitanism can resource such a theology of community organizing. However, in order to provide a sounding board for this analysis, I turn first to a reimagining of the core themes of liberation theology which, I suggest, can provide the theological foundations for a liberative theology of community organizing and empowering resources for faith-based community organizers.

REIMAGINING LIBERATION THEOLOGY

Although the theological thrust of liberation theology cannot be confined to one region, for the purposes of my work, I draw upon its earliest incarnation in Latin America because the themes hammered out there during the 1960s and 1970s continue to provide the golden thread that runs through theologies of liberation in Africa, Asia, Oceania, the Caribbean, the Americas and Europe. In particular, I want to highlight two key themes which have a direct bearing on the development of a liberative theology of community organizing.

The birth of Latin American liberation theology is often dated either to the emergence of base ecclesial communities in the early 1960s or to the Conference of Roman Catholic Bishops at Medellin in Colombia in 1968. However in many respects liberation theology bears witness to a far older conviction. The pioneer of liberation theology, Gustavo Gutiérrez, summarizes: 'All through history there has been a repressed but resurgent theology, born of the struggles of the poor. To follow in footsteps of the poor in this history is the urgent task of liberation theology.'[3] It is, Gutiérrez goes on, 'a theology done primarily by history's nameless ones'.[4] In this light, he suggests that although those who are poor are considered blessed by Jesus and the Hebrew prophets, 'poverty is an expression of sin, that is, of a negation of love. It is therefore incompatible with the coming of the Kingdom of God'.[5] Because, as Gutiérrez asserts, the 'radical gift of liberation is the gift which Christ offers us' is for all people God necessarily has to be biased towards the poor in an unjust and unequal society.[6] As a result of God's self-identification with those who are oppressed, Leonardo and Clodovis Boff suggest that 'the Holy Spirit becomes a participant in the struggles and resistance of the poor'.[7] In other words, those who struggle for justice do not struggle alone.

The earliest expressions of liberation theology in Latin America arose from a decade of revolution and a continent wracked by the crisis of endemic poverty and economic inequality. Given that all theology is contextual, it is completely understandable that Gustavo Gutiérrez, Jon Sobrino, Leonardo Boff and their compatriots focused their work on developing a liberative theological response to poverty. Their focus was on uncovering a God who heard the cry of and was in solidarity with those who had no bread to eat, no wage, no home and no future—the women and men whom Gutiérrez suggested were effectively 'non-people'.[8] Increasingly however the inheritors of the mantle of liberation theology have recognized that oppression cannot be reduced to poverty alone. Marcella Althaus-Reid and Ivan Petrella, for example, argue that an exclusive early focus on economic poverty led to a neglect of patterns of oppression that arose from racism, sexism or homophobia.[9] Ironically, therefore it is possible, like Daniel Bell, to argue that the theological reductionism of the earliest expressions of liberation theology inadvertently erected a stumbling block on the road to holistic liberation as revolutionary praxis was replaced by a political turn towards civil society.[10]

It is very easy from the vantage point of the twenty-first century to criticize the way in which, as a result of their laser-like focus on poverty, early liberation theologians neglected forms of oppression based on ethnicity, gender and sexuality. Like others before me I have argued that such reductionism forgets that oppression is multifaceted and that only a holistic model of liberation can resource the building of a just society.[11] Therefore rather than referring to a God who is biased to the poor, we need to speak of a divine bias to the oppressed—to the marginalized, the left out and the left behind. Only such a reimagined divine bias to the poor can adequately resource credible theologies of liberation in the twenty-first century and provide a solid foundation for faith-based community organizing.

In spite of this critique, it is vital to remember the paradigm shifting significance of the witness of the first theologians of liberation—God is not neutral but is biased to the poor. It is a conviction that has revolutionized contextual theologies across the globe in the forty years since Gutiérrez published his seminal *A Theology of Liberation*. It remains an uncomfortable and prophetic word which unsettles the Church and the political left in a post religious and post ideological century. In a context where left-of-centre politicians and theologians theorize and theologize the idea of the 'good society', the acerbic assertion of a divine bias to the oppressed which critiques even-handed negotiations about the 'common good' raises uncomfortable but pivotal questions for community organizing on both sides of the Atlantic.

Liberation theology provides the perfect theological partner for community organizing because it is a theology intended to bring about radical social change. It is a political theology intended to transform the public sphere. Gutiérrez writes, 'This is a theology which does not stop with reflecting on the world, but rather tries to be part of the process through which the world is transformed.'[12] Writing of the task of the theologian, Gutiérrez amplifies this point and throws down a challenge to all who would isolate academic theology from those social movements engaged in the struggle for justice. He writes, 'They are poor theologians who, wrapped in their manuscripts and scholastic disputations, are not open to these amazing events.'[13] As a result of its commitment to social transformation, liberation theology asserts the primacy of action. Boff and Boff argue that liberation theology necessarily demands that people of faith engage in political struggle within the public sphere because 'it starts from action and leads to action . . . It is a theology that leads to practical results'.[14] However, because it arises from a faith response to the liberating nature of God, Gospel and Kingdom, liberation theology is more than an activist's 'how-to' handbook. Gutiérrez makes the point with clarity: 'Only authentic solidarity with the poor and a real protest against the poverty of our time can provide the concrete, vital context necessary for a theological discussion of poverty.'[15]

As I write this chapter early in 2013, the fallout from the deepest recession since the Great Depression of the 1930s, which resulted from the 'credit crunch' of 2009–2010, continues to scar the communities of the dispossessed and deepen already-ingrained inequality in both the United States and the United Kingdom. In this context, these core themes within the canon of liberation theology provide faith-based community organizing with an incomparable theological foundation upon which to build. The divine bias to the oppressed, the challenge to take on a preferential option for the oppressed, reflecting and acting out of the experience of and in solidarity with the oppressed in order to build a liberated, just and inclusive society that reflects the intention of God challenge community organizing to question its ongoing emphasis on self-interest as the key motivating factor behind activism for social justice.

IT'S ABOUT MORE THAN SELF-INTEREST

In his *Rules for Radicals,* Alinsky recognized that 'to many the synonym for self-interest is selfishness'.[16] As I noted in chapter three, Alinsky argued that, although it may disturb America's image of itself, self-interest and not altruism is the primary building block of civil society politics. To suggest otherwise, he goes on, is wish fulfillment.[17] Seventy years after Saul Alinsky's Back of the Yards campaign in Chicago, community-organizing networks in the United States and the United Kingdom retain his focus on self-interest as the most powerful motivating force behind activism, echoing the 'Relative Deprivation' approach to the emergence of social movements. It is important to recognize that in Alinsky's terms, self-interest is a broad relational concept rather than an individualistic grabbing. Although it is aligned with the Alinskyite Industrial Areas Foundation, Citizens UK tempers its emphasis on the importance of self-interest by emphasizing the significance of a commitment to the 'common good'.[18] Dennis Jacobsen is the director of the National Clergy Caucus within the Gamaliel Foundation in the United States. In his *Doing Justice: Congregations and Community Organizing,* Jacobsen seeks to defend an appeal to self-interest and to distinguish it from selfishness on the basis of his Christian faith. He writes, 'Organizers organize people around self-interest. They claim that the concept of self-interest is necessary to understand and embrace if one is to think clearly and to act directly in the public arena.'[19] Jacobsen critiques a Christian focus on selflessness in assertive terms as 'the art of destructive self-denial'.[20] He argues that those who would point to Jesus' call to his friends to self-denial 'live theologically on the surface' and misunderstand that Jesus' call is to turn away from the 'false self that is afraid of life' in order to find our true self in relationship with others. It is, he says, 'the highest form of self-interest'.[21] Jacobsen suggests that 'organizers view self-interest as the only true way of relating to another person because self-interest respects the two sides of the relationship. Selfishness denies the "other" in the relationship. Selflessness denies the "self" in the relationship. Self-interest honors both the "self" and the "other" in the relationship'.[22] For Jacobsen therefore it is self-interest and not selflessness that characterizes Christian discipleship.

Notwithstanding Jacobsen's arguments, the appeal to self-interest as the central motivating force behind faith-based organizing is flawed for two reasons. First, it caricatures selflessness and represents a selective reading of the ministry of Jesus within the Gospels which ignores or rereads key passages that contradict the dominant depiction of self-interest within community organizing. It is not clear, for example, how Jesus' beatitudes in Matthew 5, his call to his first disciples to a wandering life of homelessness and insecurity or his washing of the disciples feet in John 12 can be reframed as an appeal to enlightened self-interest. Second, the foregrounding of self-interest ignores examples of what might be called selfless organizing. Jacobsen claims that 'the civil rights victories of the 1960s were the result, not of impassioned moral suasion, but of a convergence of self-interests' without offering clear evidence for his bold claim.[23] Such an assertion rules out the possibility that progressive White northern students and clergy committed themselves to a struggle from which they would not directly or even indirectly benefit on the basis of ethical or theological convictions. Equally, it is difficult to interpret the active and energetic support for organizations such as Amnesty International amongst millions of people whose human rights are not in any way threatened or the engagement in social movements such as the Jubilee 2000 and Jubilee Debt campaigns, environmental movements such as Greenpeace or the Free Burma movement within a self-interest frame of reference.

In spite of its enduring hold on community organizers on both sides of the Atlantic, I suggest therefore that even a carefully rephrased commitment to self-interest cannot provide an adequate foundation upon which to build a liberative theology of community organizing. It instrumentalizes struggles for social justice and brackets out the possibility that activism may arise from deeply held ethical or religious values, as I demonstrated in chapter three in relation to 'Frames of Reference' approaches to social movements. Where then might a more solid foundation for such a theology and for faith-based organizing be found?

It would not be socially credible or ethically acceptable to tie an interfaith community organization in a superdiverse society to a particular doctrinal template or a specific faith tradition. However, drawing on 'frames of reference' models of social movement theory I do want to suggest that it is possible to provide a theology of community organizing and faith-based community organizers with a unifying and socially progressive ethical foundation upon which to build an inclusive people's organization. Such a motivating principle is found in the situational ethics of Joseph Fletcher.

In *Situation Ethics: The New Morality*, Fletcher stirred up impassioned debate as a result of his suggestion that attempts to apply absolute moral codes on the basis of Biblical texts, historic creeds or religious tradition fail to take account of the context or situation within which people live. For Fletcher, belief, activism, ethical practice and doctrinal systems are all relative, judged on the basis of the single absolute principle of love. He writes, 'Love is a universal norm . . . Christian situation ethics reduces law from a statutory system of rules to the love canon alone.'[24] It is important to recognize that an ethical framework that depicts love as the only absolute can be inconsistent, localized and individualized. Furthermore, it is an approach within which those with power can define love to serve their own interests. Consequently it becomes important to ask, how is love to be defined, by whom and in whose interests? In spite of these critical questions, I want to argue that love rather than self-interest can provide a theology of community organizing with its guiding hermeneutical principle. Those who assert the self-interest principle may argue that a theology of community organizing which is founded on a love ethic is insubstantial, overly subjective and politically naive. In anticipation of such a potential critique, I would suggest the following.

First, a theology of community of organizing that revolves around a hermeneutical principle of love is strong and relational rather than insubstantial and overly subjective. It is not an appeal to individualized or romantic love but to the broader notion of agape—an inherently outward-looking commitment to stranger and enemy as well as to friend, family or neighbour. Love as agape is an approach to human community that arises from the Biblical conviction that that all people are created equally in the divine image and is characterized by an unconditional commitment to human wholeness, or *shalom*. Such an ethic is not ephemeral but can be clearly depicted as we see in the Apostle Paul's first letter to the Christian community in Corinth. 'Love [he says] is patient, love is kind. It does not envy, it does not boast, it is not proud. It does not dishonour others, it is not self-seeking, it is not easily angered; it keeps no record of wrongs. Love does not delight in evil but rejoices with the truth. It always protects, always trusts, always hopes, always perseveres' (1 Corinthians 13: 4–7). How though does such a generalized hymn to love translate into specific ethical guidelines or particular forms of activism? Remaining within the Christian scriptures, the short first letter of John offers part of an answer to this question: 'God is love. Whoever lives in love lives in God, and God in them . . . Whoever claims to love God yet hates a brother or sister is a liar. For whoever does not love their brother and sister, whom they have seen, cannot love God, whom they have not seen' (1 John 4: 16 and 20). Love demands clear action that is intended to affirm, include and honour all people for all are sisters and brothers. It is the ethical basis of the 'golden rule' to which I referred in the previous chapter and necessarily critiques models of community organizing which implicitly adopt a utilitarian attitude to 'means and ends'. A theology of community organizing premised on the hermeneutics of agape love measures 'ends and means' in relation to the extent to which they reflect the subversion of oppressive social relations embodied in Jesus beatitudes in Matthew 5 and Luke 6. Such a foundation leads us to reflect on Jesus' challenge in Matthew

25:31–46 and to ask the organizer if an action has meant that the stranger has been welcomed, the hungry fed, the naked clothed, the homeless person given shelter. When premised not on self-interest but on love, a theology of community organizing can begin to embody the 'global ethic' to which Hans Küng points, the planetary humanism described by Paul Gilroy and the political radicalism of the unconditional love and the beloved community espoused by Martin Luther King. Such faith-based community organizing becomes an expression of the Jewish ethic of *tikkun*, or healing.

Second, a theology of community organizing that revolves around the hermeneutical principle of love need not be politically naive when it is rooted in a process of conscientization and a commitment to the divine bias to the oppressed. Such a theology therefore is not reducible to vague good intentions, nor is it any more open to ideological abuse than a model of community organizing that revolves around self-interest. A theology of community organizing that rests on a love ethic will be held to account and measured against its capacity to embody a model of organizing that places the cry of the most marginalized before the louder voices of the bigger and stronger faith and community groups which send more 'organized' people to community organizing assemblies. A theology of community organizing that is premised on love will necessarily interrogate its own activism, asking whose interests' actions serve. When aligned with a commitment to liberative education and the divine bias to the oppressed, such faith-based organizing will not be satisfied with a 're-weaving of the fabric of society' but will be judged on the basis of its capacity to forge a credible and effective preferential option for the oppressed in its organizing structures, representative committees and actions. Furthermore, within a model of faith-based organizing that revolves around the hermeneutical principle of love and an alignment with the divine bias to the oppressed, the community organizer is not simply a conscientized activist who agitates around self-interest. Instead, the organizer becomes the organic intellectual who feels the passions and pains of the people alongside whom they work (Antonio Gramsci) and a political intellectual who shines a light on suffering and gives voice to the voiceless (Cornel West) as a result of their love for the community.

WHEN THE EDGE BECOMES THE CENTRE

Thus far I have argued that a place-based theology of community organizing should be premised on a hermeneutics of love rather than the principle of self-interest if it is to provide a solid foundation for faith-based organizing and fulfil its potential to resource the building of a 'post-religious' liberation theology. Is such a challenge best served by an alignment with recent theological and theoretical reflection on the 'common good' and the 'good society' or a reimagined divine bias to the oppressed? It is to this question that I now turn.

Christian theological reflection on the common good arises most clearly from two sources—the social thought tradition of Anglicanism and the social teaching of the Roman Catholic Church that stems from Pope Leo XII's 1891 encyclical *Rerum Novarum* which drew upon Christian ethics to respond to the growing problem of poverty and inequality in an industrializing Europe. Memorably, the encyclical offered a critique of unfettered capitalism: 'It is neither just nor humane so to grind men down with excessive labor as to stupefy their minds and wear out their bodies.'[25] The establishment of the Christian Social Union by the Anglo-Catholic Scott Holland in Oxford in 1889 drew upon the Christian Socialism of figures such as F. D. Maurice in an attempt to root a theologically radical Social Gospel within the Church of England. This English tradition which influenced writing of the *Faith in the City* report in the middle of the crisis-laden 1980s echoed the slightly earlier articulation of the 'social gospel' in the United States during the 1870s. As Chris Baker summarizes, 'The social gospel rejected the prevailing theological belief that all present social structures were ordained by the will of God . . . It challenged both *laissez faire* capitalism and Protestant individualism with a reformulation of Christian faith that stressed the doctrine of God's immanence . . . in the suffering of the world.'[26] On the basis of a strong focus on the ethics of the Kingdom of God, the life, death and resurrection of Jesus were reframed to emphasize God's engagement with humanity and the 'political and social dimensions of [Jesus'] proclamation of the Kingdom of God with regard to the commitment to practice justice . . . to the poor and marginalized'.[27]

The utopian optimism of the Social Gospel withered during the twentieth century in the face of the horrors of the trenches of World War I, the gas chambers of the Nazi Holocaust, the purges of Stalin's Soviet Union and the institutionalized racism of the Jim Crow laws in the United States and apartheid in South Africa. However, its commitment to a social reading of the Christian Gospel and a negotiated and gradualist approach to social justice shaped the Christian Realism of William Temple during the 1930s and 1940s, the work of Ronald Preston in the 1970s and 1980s and John Atherton in the early years of the twenty-first century. In particular, the values of the Social Gospel informed renewed conceptions of the common good and models of discipleship characterized by active citizenship as theological imperatives in the face of deepening levels of inequality during the neoliberal 1980s and early 1990s.

Against this backdrop, recent 'common good' thinking has sought to articulate a clear faith-based vision of the good society within which no person is barred from fulfilling her or his potential as a result of economic inequality, poverty, prejudice, age or place of birth as seen, for example, in the seminal 1985 Anglican report *Faith in the City* and its ecumenical 2006 successor *Faithful Cities*. On the basis of more than a century of the social teaching that emerged out of Pope Leo XII's encyclical *Rerum Novarum,* the 1996 Catholic Bishops' Conference of England and Wales reasserted a theology of the 'common good': 'We believe each person possesses a basic dignity that comes from God, not from any human quality or accomplishment, not from race or gender, age or economic status. The test therefore of every institution or policy is whether it enhances or threatens human dignity and indeed human life itself.'[28] The bishops went onto argue that because human beings are made in the image of God, people are created to live in community making the protection of democracy and active citizenship central aspects of Christian discipleship. As a result, they asserted that 'Catholic Social Teaching sees an intimate relationship between social and political liberation on the one hand, and on the other, the salvation to which the Church calls us in the name of Jesus Christ . . . That must include liberating humanity from all forces and structures which oppress it, though political liberation cannot be an end in itself'.[29] Just before the 2010 UK general election, the Roman Catholic bishops added further clarity to the rather vague concept of the 'common good', suggesting that it provided the essential yardstick for measuring the social, cultural and spiritual health of the United Kingdom. The bishops wrote that 'the common good refers to what belongs to everyone by virtue of their common humanity . . . The common good is about how to live well together . . . At the heart of the common good solidarity acknowledges that all are responsible for all'.[30] Although the bishops avoided asserting a specific political programme, they made clear links between a philosophical commitment to the common good and particular policy arenas. A commitment to the 'common good', they said, implied an unswerving policy commitment to equality, to the socially excluded and to development of an asylum and immigration agenda that arose from a core commitment to the inherent dignity of all people and a clear antiracist perspective. Much like the earlier *Faithful Cities* report, the Council of Bishops argued that 'the Christian Churches have long contributed to the promotion of the common good, as a gift and an effort that is an essential part of the Christian vision'.[31]

A theology of community organizing that is premised on the hermeneutics of love will necessarily be rooted in this theological vision of the common good and in the recent thinking about the good society amongst centre-left politicians to which I pointed in the previous chapter. However, although such reflections clearly imply a preferential option for the oppressed, does a theological vision of the common good provide a sufficiently substantial foundation for a liberative theology of community organizing? Such a perspective implicitly relies upon the existence of a shared and inclusive public sphere from which no one is excluded—the space where we can find common ground and forge a good society together. As I showed in previous chapters, the superdiverse societies of the United States and the United Kingdom are characterized by multifaceted social exclusion, endemic inequality and the existence of plural and, on occasions, antagonistic public spheres. In such a context, a theology of community organizing that is premised on a hermeneutics of love and a vision of the 'common good' needs to be rooted in an explicit and culturally credible articulation of the divine bias to the oppressed which takes account of the multifaceted nature of oppression and social exclusion. The prophetic outweighs the pragmatic. Only such a theology can provide faith-based community organizations with the foundation they need if they are to fulfil their liberative potential and forge actions which build a bottom-up common good that ensures that the fabric of a superdiverse society is rewoven.

DIVERSITY AND LIBERATION

In the United States and the United Kingdom, a theology of community organizing will foreground a cultural politics of difference. Such a perspective will be rooted in grass-roots realities and forged out of a dialogue between enduring race-based thinking, essentialist identity politics, introverted religious resistance identities, everyday multiculturalism, increasingly superdiverse communities and the practice of interfaith broad-based community organizations. If it is to resource effective faith-based organizing in such contexts, a theology of community organizing will necessarily wrestle not only with the need to root actions in an ethic of liberative love but also in a proactive cultural politics of difference and a clearly defined hermeneutics of liberative difference.[32] Such a perspective, as Cornel West notes with reference to the ongoing struggle for civil rights and social justice in the United States, would have the capacity to translate bonding and bridging models of social capital activism into a more subversive and risky linking social capital approach to faith-based organizing which moves beyond the relative safety of settled religious communities animated by comparable ethical frameworks towards an engagement with more fragile, fluid and superdiverse spiritualities. In a post-9/11 era shaped by a strident othering of people and communities increasingly defined as 'them' rather than 'us', a hermeneutics of liberative difference clashes with populist variations on Samuel Huntingdon's 'clash of civilizations' thesis.

For more than a decade, broad-based community organizations in the United States have been at the centre of debates about the rights and citizenship of up to an estimated eleven million undocumented immigrants who have lived and worked in the United States for many years but have no legal rights. A clear example of such an ongoing action is the PICO Campaign for Citizenship.[33] In the United Kingdom, the Citizens Organising Foundation and its successor Citizens UK have mounted similar high profile campaigns: Strangers into Citizens and Citizens for Sanctuary.[34] Such actions have typically revolved around specific measurable goals. In 2009, Citizens for Sanctuary launched its Sanctuary Pledge, working with faith-group partners to persuade parliamentary candidates to sign the pledge ahead of the 2010 UK general election.[35] A second example of targeted Citizens UK activism around sanctuary and diversity was its 2010 campaign to persuade the

UK government to end the practice of imprisoning the children of asylum seekers in detention camps. At a Citizens UK general election assembly in May 2010, the party leaders Gordon Brown (Labour), Nick Clegg (Liberal Democrats) and David Cameron (Conservatives) were all challenged to pledge to end child detention and to sign the Sanctuary Pledge.[36] In June 2010, the Conservative–Liberal Democrat coalition government committed itself to end child detention, although by 2013 this pledge had still not been fulfilled.[37]

DUBBING DIFFERENCE—BECKFORD, SCHREITER, BAKER AND BRETHERTON

In a superdiverse society still in thrall to excluding race-based thinking a theology of community organizing that is premised on an ethic love and a reimagined preferential option for the oppressed will necessarily subvert the demonizing of difference. Rather than remaining a threat to community cohesion or something that is subsumed within new hybrid cultural identities, difference becomes the dynamic that energizes a liberative theology of community organizing.

Dub practice has been widely used in reggae and dancehall music for almost half a century. A producer, record engineer or DJ strips away keyboards, guitar and vocals leaving only the track's foundational melody and beat upon which a new lyric is laid. Dub practice revolves around a process of deconstruction and reconstruction. Beckford writes, 'Dub is more than sound: it is the product of a sophisticated signification and the raw material for a dynamic interplay between word, sound and power.'[38] Beckford argues that 'dub is more than a musical technique: it is . . . a quest for meaning'.[39] Dub practice is not inherently socially progressive. However, when it is informed by a liberation ethic it can provide political theology in a superdiverse century with a creative new hermeneutical tool in the long 'cultural war of position'.[40] Consequently, for Beckford, 'rebuilding is guided by an emancipation ethic which seeks out redemptive themes in history, culture and society that can be the focus for transforming the original thesis . . . to "dub" is to engage with the social world through prophetic action'.[41] Within a liberative theology of community organizing, the dub practice explored by Beckford can provide an emancipatory hermeneutical technique capable of resourcing an ethic of liberative difference through a critical rereading of Schreiter's new catholicity, Baker's third space theology and Bretherton's Christian cosmopolitanism.

In his book *The New Catholicity: Theology between the Global and the Local*, Robert Schreiter dubs the ancient Christian emphasis on catholicity in his search for a liberative new contextual theology that can engage credibly with a globalized world where superdiversity has become normative. Schreiter roots his search in the unfolding story of contextual theologies which began to emerge in the 1950s and 1960s in the global South in resistance to dominant universalizing theologies which 'extended the results of their reflections beyond their own contexts to other settings usually without an awareness of the rootedness of their theologies within their own contexts'.[42] In what he calls a multipolar world, Schreiter suggests that although contextual theologies must speak beyond a localized context, it is vital that they avoid 'a suppression of difference and a claim to be the sole voice'.[43] The liberative 'new catholicity' that Schreiter explores rests on four key themes, each of which have relevance for the articulation of a liberative theology of community organizing in a superdiverse century.

First, Schreiter argues that globalization is as much about how we think and make meaning as it is a political, economic and cultural process. In a globalized world where time and space have been compressed but inequalities deepened, Schreiter suggests that 'theology . . . finds itself between the global and local'.[44] Schreiter goes on to argue that this 'hyper-differentiated' glocal landscape where identities and cultures are increasingly hybrid provides theology with a fluid new context within which theological reflection becomes an increasingly provisional exercise. At the heart of such contextual theological reflection is the negotiation of difference. Schreiter writes, 'Boundaries today are increasingly not boundaries of territory but boundaries of difference . . . [which] . . . intersect and crisscross in often bewildering fashion.'[45]

Second, Schreiter suggests that this new hybrid and superdiverse context is inherently dynamic. In this context theologians of culture need to recognize the molding significance of such fluidity because 'flows . . . like a river, define a route, change the landscape and leave behind sediment and silt that enrich the local ecology'.[46] The theological task is always unfinished and the theologian becomes a restless traveller for, as Schreiter makes clear, 'a theology of culture will have to focus especially on moments of change rather than moments of stasis. For it is in the experience of moving from one place to another . . . of negotiating multiple identities and logics that insight into where God is at work in a globalized culture will be found'.[47]

Third, for Schreiter, and for those engaged in forging a theology of community organizing in a superdiverse context, a progressive new model of theological reflection necessarily rests on egalitarian intercultural meaning-making. Can such a theology have any grass-roots credibility in contexts where difference is perceived to be a threat to so-called cultural purity? In order to forge a culturally credible theology in situations where the stranger is depicted as an outsider who does not belong, it is necessary to move beyond eloquent but empty liberal affirmations of inclusivity. Schreiter, like the urban planning theorist Sandercock, recognizes that although 'syncretic borrowing' characterizes everyday life in many communities, tension surrounding difference continues to mark many urban contexts.[48] Nevertheless, Schreiter reasserts the central importance of an inclusive conversational intercultural hermeneutics in situations 'where a common world is not shared by the speaker and hearer'.[49] Such intercultural hermeneutics revolves around responses to difference. Although committed to the liberative tenor of diversity, a credible intercultural hermeneutics (like a credible theology of community organizing) cannot smooth away the significance of cultural difference beneath a blanket of affirming but superficial sound bites. Schreiter makes the point: 'Denial of difference can lead to the colonization of a culture and its imagination. Denial of similarities promotes an anomic situation where no dialogue appears possible.'[50] On the basis of such a 'nitty-gritty' approach, Schreiter reminds us of the resource that glocal cultures can provide for those seeking a liberative theology in a superdiverse urban world: 'Diversity is prized but difference is valued even more highly. Culture, especially from the perspective of minority groups . . . disrupts the homogeneous narratives of the powerful.'[51]

Fourth, Schreiter suggests that a theological emphasis on reconciliation can provide a clear basis for a 'new catholicity'. Schreiter makes it plain that reconciliation should not be reduced to a comfortable coexistence. Instead he speaks of a reconciliation which sees 'God taking the world to a new place, transformed out of its suffering but not forgetting the wounds of the past', suggesting that 'reconciliation portends to be a capacious enough theme both to recognize and struggle with the dividedness of the world . . . It becomes a key aspect in understanding the new catholicity'.[52] Such a focus on liberative reconciliation would, argues Schreiter, need to be built upon the 'recognition of diversity [for] . . . without recognition there is invisibility which demeans and dismisses those who are different'.[53] Second, liberative reconciliation in a superdiverse context needs to be built upon a 'respect for difference . . . [which] goes beyond acknowledgement of the otherness of diversity . . . [and] explores the nature of difference and the consequences for living together'. When premised on an ethic of liberative difference, such a commitment, according to Schreiter, 'involves a struggle against those forces in society that, using the signifier of race or other means of demarcation, make difference a warrant for discrimination and oppression'.[54] Third such a theological focus on reconciliation demands an activist's commitment to the forging of a 'forum of cooperation and communication' and a recognition that 'those who have been in the struggle for justice together can see better what one group may contribute to the other and to the common good'.[55] Such a commitment to an egalitarian and inclusive model of intercultural hermeneutics and the liberative potential of diversity echoes the expression of reconciliation expressed in the New Testament letter to the Ephesians, for we are 'strangers and aliens no longer' but sisters and brothers engaged in a shared struggle (Ephesians 2:19).

On the basis of these four markers, Schreiter argues the need to dub received understandings of catholicity that have historically focused on formally defined Christian communities in order to articulate a new inclusive and dynamic understanding of wholeness, or *shalom,* that has the capacity to engage with superdiverse urbanism in the twenty-first century. For

Schreiter, 'A new catholicity is marked by a wholeness of inclusion and fullness of faith in a pattern of intercultural exchange and communication.'[56] Schreiter writes of the task of doing contextual theology in multiple contexts in a globalized world. A theology of community organizing arises from a more specific context given that this model of faith-based action for social justice is still primarily associated with the United States and the United Kingdom. However Schreiter's dubbing of the ancient Christian emphasis on catholicity offer theologians and community organizers new resources. His recognition of the multiple and dynamic nature of particular contexts in an era of globalization, his exploration of the theological centrality of difference, his articulation of an inclusive intercultural hermeneutics and the liberative potential of reconciliation offer important insights for all who seek a theology of community organizing that has cultural credibility in superdiverse societies and the capacity to resource effective interfaith community organizing.

In his book *The Hybrid Church in the City: Third Space Thinking*, Chris Baker dubs binary understandings of identity and social space as he articulates a third-space theology that has the capacity to resource new and dynamic Christian theological reflection in a culturally 'hybrid' superdiverse urban world. Whereas Schreiter writes of contextual theological reflection on a global scale, Baker's primary focus is on the transformed nature of urban space, identity, the search for meaning and the struggle to forge the common good in the cities of the global North. Baker invites us to step into the dynamic, unstable and provisional third space that has emerged within the city as previously dominant narratives of meaning relating to class, religion and race have fragmented and increasingly lost their power to define identity, political struggle and spirituality for more than a declining minority of citizens. Baker writes, 'Hybridity is here to stay and there is no going back. My passionate argument in this book is that it is a category of human thought and experience that profoundly influences how we 'do' our politics, live in our cities and consume culture and spirituality.'[57] Although in the previous two chapters I argued against the use of the currently ubiquitous term hybridity as a retreat from the challenge of difference, Baker's journey into the dynamic both-and world of the contemporary city offers those seeking a culturally credible theology of community organizing in the twenty-first century creative and liberative new tools for the task. Baker's work presents three challenges to those seeking a liberative theology of community organizing in the United States and the United Kingdom.

The first challenge posed by Baker's work relates to the way we define ourselves and other people. Baker argues that 'we are moving further and further away from the binary either/or definitions that the Enlightenment and Marxism bequeathed to the nineteenth and twentieth centuries'.[58] Within such thinking we were one thing or another but not a number of different and shifting things at the same time. We were either Black or we

were White. We were either gay or we were straight. We were either working class or bourgeoisie.

Baker notes that figures from the 2001 UK National Census showed that
677,177 people self-defined as 'mixed' race, making people of dual heritage
the fastest growing ethnic identity in the United Kingdom between 1991 and
2001. As I noted previously, four years after *The Hybrid Church*, the 2011
National Census revealed that by that point 1.2 million people self defined
as 'mixed' race, making this the fastest growing ethnic community in the
UK. It is, therefore, with justification that Baker writes, 'Today binary systems and hierarchies have lost considerable power to influence and dictate
behaviour.'[59]

Dynamic fluidity increasingly characterizes ethnicity in the United Kingdom. During the 1990s when I was a Methodist minister in the East End
of London, I got to know a group of young men whose parents had mi-
grated from Bangladesh to the United Kingdom in the 1970s and 1980s.
On the street these young men walked with the stereotypical bowling gate
of a 'gangsta', dressed like New York rappers, listened to both Bhangra and
Public Enemy and spoke Cockney English laced with elements of Jamaican
patois, conscious Black Power tones and occasional Bangladeshi phrases. At
home or in the mosque, they were respectful Muslim sons who dressed and
spoke conservatively, studied Arabic carefully and read the Qur'an dressed
in the traditional clothing of the Bangladeshi diaspora. These young men
were not reducible to one thing or the other. They were not pretending on
the street, at home or at the mosque but were both respectful young Muslims who wanted to learn about Islam and young men whose self-identity
was shaped on the superdiverse and globalized streets of inner London.
Baker, like Paul Gilroy and Cornel West within sociology and Iris Marion
Young within political philosophy, notes the disruptive challenge that 'both/
and' identities pose to the political, popular, ideological and theological narratives of cultural separateness and essentialized difference that emerged out
of nineteenth century anthropological notions of othering.

Within the binary world of ethnic essentialism culture was given, blood-
bound and static allowing the non-White 'Other' to be defined, objectified
and distanced as Jonathan Hearns notes in his exploration of primordial
nationalism.[60] In spite of Edward Said's searing 1978 critique of such Orientalism this process of othering continues unabated. Such binary separat-
ism homogenizes dynamic cultures, making a liberative cultural politics of
difference an even more subversive act. Whether it is the evocative title of
Gilroy's first book *There Ain't No Black in the Union Jack* and his assertion
that as a Black British man he continues to be 'Other', or Samuel Huntingdon's contentious clash of civilizations thesis (which strongly suggested
that so-called Western civilization and so-called Islamic civilization were
incompatible), the theoretical significance of othering has retained its grip.
Whether it is the rise of the introverted resistance identities to which Manuel
Castells points such as the Nation of Islam, far-right groups such as the

English Defence League and the Ku Klux Klan or certain Islamist groupings like Hizb ut Tahrir, the binary insider-outsider world of othering continues to play out on the streets of superdiverse societies in the twenty-first century. In the context of such enduring othering and over a decade of social policy in both the United Kingdom and the United States that specifically homogenizes Muslim communities, depicting them as the potential enemy within, mixing and hybridity represent a transgression of closely guarded ethnic boundaries. Yet superdiverse both-and culture continues to rise. It may be seen as 'transgression' by some, but as Baker makes plain, a movement beyond the insider-outsider world of binary politics, religion and culture is a tide that cultural King Canutes will not be able to hold back. I suggest it offers us perhaps the most creative resource in the building of a liberative theology of community organizing and the sustenance of interfaith community organizations.

The second resource that Baker's work provides for those forging a theology of community organizing in the twenty-first century relates to ideas about a cultural third space. Drawing on postcolonial critic Homi Bhabha's *The Location of Culture* (1994), Baker describes the third space as 'the space produced by the collapse of the previously defining narratives of modernity based on colonialism, class and patriarchy'.[61] It subverts the damaging domain of essentialist othering and enduring race-based thinking. This in-between third space is the context within which community organizing is forged, and its plurality provides faith-based community organizations with their strength. However, the third space is more than just another name for a superdiverse public sphere. The third space is a place of existential challenge and the arena within which we understand and interpret both ourselves and those alongside whom we live, worship and struggle for justice. The fluid third space is pregnant with power. It embodies the force of the representational space to which Lefebvre refers. It is a place of dialogue between attempts to objectify and define cultural, ethnic, social, ideological and theological identities (the 'Said') and the dynamic fluidity of interpretation and self-representation (the 'Saying').[62] In the context of faith-based community organizing in the twenty-first century, the third space is the fulcrum of reflective activism and the crucible within which the liberative theological and educational process to which I have referred previously is forged. The egalitarianism of the third space enables a shared activism to arise that subverts the occasionally hierarchical approach of existing broad-based community organizing. As I noted previously, Sandercock cites this 'terrain of difference' as a defining feature of contemporary urban life and the oxygen which feeds insurgent patterns of citizenship. The dynamic open-endedness of the third space can provide 'voices from the borderlands' with the presence and agency to forge third-space insurgencies that challenge those committed to social inclusion, community cohesion and the common good to adopt an organic ethic of liberative difference. The third space is a site of self-expression, translation and negotiation amongst equals and, as a result, a representational space which has the capacity to give rise to what Bhabha calls a 'counter hegemonic process' that enables a movement towards 'the hybrid moment of political change'.[63] Such a potentially liberative process however cannot be systematized as a result of the dynamism of a super-diverse third space. Baker summarizes: 'The Third Space is, in its essence, epistemologically unstable and politically enigmatic . . . Attempts to build coherent political and community development programmes on the basis of hybridity and multi-discourse politics are notoriously difficult.'[64] Activism, therefore, in the third space represents more than a pragmatic alliance of diverse communities which face the same struggles and share similar ethical or spiritual values. Third space community organizing can change who we are in relation to one another, enabling a new relationship and a new understanding of faith to arise from the crucible of our shared actions. It has the capacity to revolutionize attitudes to activism and what could be called 'solid' political theologies and will form a central plank of a liberative theology of community organizing in the superdiverse twenty-first century.

The third challenge that Baker's work poses to faith groups that are committed to engagement in the struggle for social justice and to a theology of community organizing relates to the theological significance of fluidity. Baker's emergent third-space theology has implications for Christian ideas about the nature of the Church, the person of Jesus, mission and interfaith relationships. First, in comments echoing the work of Pete Ward on ecclesiology, Baker suggests that third-space living demands a dubbing of received conceptions of catholicity and a shift from the solid church of modernity towards a more relational and liquid networked model of discipleship better suited to an increasingly fluid postmodern landscape.[65] Such a 'liquid' Church, says Baker, can only fashion a credible third-space missiology if it adopts what he calls 'an open-ended and fluid Christology' and an ethic of 'risky' hospitality which moves beyond an often implicit host-guest power dynamic towards an 'unconditional hospitality' that revolves around the inclusive Kingdom feast imagery which characterizes the ministry of Jesus within the Gospels.[66] Such a step represents a challenge to personal identity, for 'to open oneself unconditionally to the Other is potentially to allow one's own identity to be deconstructed . . . allowing the normal barriers that separate . . . yourself from the demands and cultures of others to be blurred'.[67] As Baker notes such a movement demands the commitment to a 'risky theology which will often lead to messy or blurred encounters . . . subvert the status quo . . . [and] point towards the *telos* of justice, inclusivity and reconciliation'.[68] A theology of community organizing in the superdiverse worlds of the United States and the United Kingdom must be prepared to engage in such a risky journey if it is forge a holistic and liberative foundation for faith-based community organizing in the twenty-first century.

In *Christianity and Contemporary Politics*, Luke Bretherton dubs dominant depictions of the 'stranger' as he seeks to develop a Christian cosmopolitanism that is characterized by an ethic of radical hospitality.

Bretherton's incisive exploration of the role of the Christian community in civil society politics uses reflections on neighbourliness and hospitality on a local, national and global scale to navigate an arguably postsecular cultural landscape characterized by a resurgent role for faith communities in the public sphere. Bretherton's work can be seen as a critical expression of the 'theological politics' that he suggests characterizes the work of figures like John Milbank, Stanley Hauerwas, William Cavanagh and Oliver O'Donovan.[69] For Bretherton, such a task is necessarily outward-facing and dialogical, emphasizing the 'political dimensions' of Christian discipleship.[70] His focus is less on the internal identity of the Church and more on the manner in which it translates this into pragmatic but prophetic action for the common good in liberal democratic societies. Although Bretherton's analysis is wide-ranging, here I focus just on the challenges that his exploration of neighbourliness and hospitality have for those of us who are engaged in the forging of a liberative theology of community organizing. In particular, three themes are of importance: loving, hallowing and listening.

The first theme of importance for those seeking to build a theology of community organizing in a plural public sphere is that of loving and welcoming. Bretherton makes his own view clear: 'What we need is a politics that can live with deep plurality over questions of ultimate meaning and can encompass the fact that many communities and traditions contribute to the common good.'[71] For Bretherton, the challenges posed by such dialogical politics can only ever be understood in the context of specific struggles and particular relationships. Although he recognizes 'that it is not the case that community organizing constitutes the only way of faithfully pursuing a just and generous political order', Bretherton suggests that it is 'a means by which we encounter strangers—sometimes as their guest and at other times as their host. It is thus a form of tent making where a place is formed in which hospitality is given and received between multiple traditions'.[72] Community organizing facilitates the development of representational space. It is in this context that neighbourly love is shared and the stranger transformed into a compatriot in the struggle to 're-weave the fabric of society'. Such an ethic of neighbourly love and hospitality characterizes the Christian cosmopolitanism advocated by Bretherton. He describes this vision of hospitable politics: 'To welcome the other is to recognize one who is the same as me . . . to welcome the other is to be at home and thus in relationship . . . to truly welcome another is to welcome one who is like nobody else.'[73] Rooting his reflections on neighbourly love and hospitality in a context of working alongside asylum seekers and refugees, Bretherton bemoans a tendency to 'maintain refugees as bare life excluded from the political community and exposed to death at every turn'.[74] Bretherton suggests that two factors must shape a Christian cosmopolitanism as it relates to refugees. First, echoing words from Matthew 25:31–46 and Hebrews 13:2, he asserts the central spiritual importance of welcoming the stranger saying, 'Hospitality towards strangers constitutes part of the church's witness to the Christ-event.'[75]

Hospitality towards the stranger is not therefore reducible to humanitarian concern alone; it is a necessary faith response to the Incarnation. As Bretherton notes, 'For Christians, welcoming the vulnerable stranger inherently involves a process of decentring and re-orientation to God and neighbor . . . Welcoming the stranger re-orientates us to ourselves, our neighbor and to God by raising a question mark about the "way we do things round here."'[76]

Second, drawing on Jesus' parable of the Good Samaritan, Bretherton notes that although this paradigmatic story makes it plain that neighbourly love must not be restricted by ethnicity, gender or religion, it can only be expressed or experienced in specific contexts: 'the extension of solidarity is particular . . . the Good Samaritan responds to one he finds nearby, not some generalized 'Other' who exists nowhere and everywhere.'[77] Hence in a superdiverse society the universality implied within the Christian emphasis on catholicity is only ever made real in particular moments, places and acts of solidarity. Consequently a theology of community organizing that is animated by a hermeneutics of liberative difference can only energize those struggling for liberation if it is deeply rooted in the specifics of place, people and time. Bretherton reminds us that solidarity therefore is always particular, citing the Sanctuary movement in the United States and the Citizens UK Citizens for Sanctuary campaign in the United Kingdom as examples of such neighbourly love.[78]

Bretherton suggests that this ethic of neighbourly love and hospitality towards the stranger emerges from the doctrine of Creation and the resulting Christian anthropology because 'concentric circles of sociality are central to what constitutes . . . personhood in the image of God'.[79] To assert that all people are created in the divine image is to indicate the innate dignity and worth of all people, the centrality of communal life to human experience and a mutual responsibility for one another. We are indeed, it seems, our sister and brother's keeper. In the context of a structurally unequal society still in thrall to race-based thinking, the welcoming of the stranger that is so central to a liberative theology of community organizing in a superdiverse context represents a subversion of the sociocultural status quo. Bretherton makes the points clearly: 'Politics within this Christian cosmopolitan vision involves the formation of a common world of meaning and action within particular places. The formation of such a world entails . . . the breaking down of those structures and patterns of relationship that exclude vulnerable strangers.'[80]

The second theme that arises from Bretherton's work that it is of potential importance in a theology of community organizing emerges from the Lord's Prayer which Jesus taught his disciples in Matthew 6:9–15. This most ancient of Christian prayers begins, 'Our Father in Heaven hallowed be your name'. Bretherton reminds us that 'to hallow something means recognizing the irreducible worth of what is before one'.[81] We can go a step further than this however because when we hallow somebody we do not just recognize their worth but acknowledge them to be a child of the God who made them in Her or His own image. People, we might say, are not just valuable, they are holy. Consequently, as Bretherton recognizes, hallowing becomes a fundamental expression of Christian discipleship and a subversive political act because 'to hallow the name of God involves us in standing against that which desecrates God's holy name. The rendering of creatures as bare life constitutes just such a desecration'.[82] As a result, when we 'welcome the stranger' and show them neighbourly love, those whom society excludes and objectifies are acknowledged as subjects of their own destiny and people with agency. To hallow socially excluded asylum seekers and refugees is more than hospitality. Such an action embodies the divine bias to the oppressed and the preferential option for the oppressed that needs to undergird a theology of community organizing which is founded on an ethic of liberative love.

The third theme within Bretherton's work that is of importance within faith-based community organizing in an arguably 'post-religious' society is that of listening. For Bretherton it is vital that Christians engaged in political activism listen in prayer, listen to the witness of the Bible and listen to those they seek to serve because 'listening is a way for churches to practice humility in their negotiation of political life, ensuring that they glorify God rather than glorifying themselves'.[83] Such an orientation implies a need for openness and a warning against exclusivity for two reasons. First, as Bretherton notes, listening opens us up to the person before us, ensuring that their experience and not a predetermined ideological, theological or community-organizing goal is the sole determinant for action. Bretherton writes, 'In listening one must take seriously who is before one and attend to the situation rather than predetermine what to do in accord with some prior agenda, ideology or strategy of control.'[84] For Bretherton, listening is a key feature of authentic hospitality and neighbourly love because 'listening trusts and gives space and time to those who are excluded from the determination of space and time by the existing hegemony'.[85] Second, the act of listening to the witness of the Bible places Christian political activism on a wider plane and enables people to bring their activism and the narrative of Scripture into a critical dialogue 'through listening to Scripture and others so as to discern who is the neighbor to be loved a sense of obedience to the Word is nurtured'.[86] A listening-shaped activism that is shaped by an ethic of hospitality and neighbourly love can ensure that a theology of community organizing embodies the divine bias to the oppressed rather than limiting itself to the strengthening of specific broad-based community organizations. Bretherton's openness invites us to consider community organizing more as networked movement than permanent people's organization. He writes, 'In both hospitable politics and a politics of the common good there is a wide scope for an exploratory partnership with those committed to democratic politics.'[87] Such a networked approach must form a vital element of a theology of community organizing if it is to exemplify a radical new catholicity in the third space, a hermeneutics of liberative difference and a preferential option for the stranger.

Robert Schreiter's exploration of the diverse unity of the worldwide Church gives rise to a new catholicity which, although still rooted in Christian tradition, foregrounds open-ended dialogue with other faith communities, an egalitarian mutuality and human wholeness as the key hallmarks of a new contextual theology for a globalized century. The liberative potential of such a new catholicity can be realized when aligned with the third-space theology of Chris Baker. In his exploration of identity, faith and the common good in the fluid and dynamic third space that exemplifies the public sphere of superdiverse societies like the United States and the United Kingdom, Baker challenges people of faith to embark on a risky journey. A commitment to the uncertainty of third-space theology dares us to cast aside either-or, in-out, insider-outsider thinking, theology, mission, discipleship and activism. However, a new third space catholicity implies more than a revolution in thinking. Such a step demands a reimagined model of discipleship that emphasizes equality, inclusivity and a vision of the common good that is premised on a divine bias to liberative difference. Such a risky step lies at the heart of Luke Bretherton's carefully argued examination of the relationship between Christianity and contemporary politics. Third-space catholicity revolves around a reframing of ideas about neighbourliness and hospitality which moves beyond binary 'us' and 'them' thinking. Bretherton's exploration of the theological foundations upon which socially progressive Christian political activism for the common good can be built has rightly become a yardstick in contemporary political theology. His work arises from a thoughtful dialogue with a wide range of traditions, themes and theologies and marks his place as one of the foremost political theologians of the early twenty-first century. However, the Christian cosmopolitanism which he expounds so clearly needs to be brought more fully into dialogue with the emergent third space articulated by Chris Baker if it is to resource faith-based organizing in the twenty-first century. A culturally credible theology of community organizing that is premised on a hermeneutics of sisterly and brotherly love needs to move beyond an ethic of 'hospitable politics' into the much messier, provisional and risky world described by third-space thinking. Such a move when combined with an even broader new catholicity than that envisaged by Robert Schreiter has the capacity to resource the unconditional listening, hallowing of life, prophetic hospitality and unconfined neighbourly love advocated by Bretherton. When supplemented by my examination of the cultural politics of difference in previous chapters, insights drawn from the work of Schreiter, Baker and Bretherton can provide us with the tools needed to begin to build the hermeneutics of liberative difference that needs to characterize a theology of community organizing in a superdiverse urban world. It is to this task that I turn in the final chapter.

AWAKENING AND ORGANIZING

Historically, broad-based community organizations such as the IAF, the Gamaliel Foundation and PICO in the United States and Citizens UK in Britain have placed a strong emphasis on the training they provide for faith and community groups.[88] Training programmes largely focus on preparing people to engage in community organizing, providing a series of pragmatic sessions on key organizing skills such as the development of one-to-one meetings, negotiation, power analyses and leadership. Although such a utilitarian 'how-to-organize' approach to community organizing training is arguably the norm, it is important to recognize another strand of education for organizing, which adopts a more critical and reflective approach. Both PICO and the Gamaliel Foundation National Clergy Caucus offer a range of reflective resources for those engaged in faith-based community organizing that moves beyond the more widely practiced pragmatic approach. From a non-faith-based organizing perspective, Comm-Org represents an Internet-based educational resource bank and forum that interconnects academics and organizing practitioners.[89]

A theology of community organizing needs to adopt this broader approach if it is to facilitate the development of genuinely radical faith-based organizing that recognises the liberative potential of critical and dialogical reflection. In his iconic track 'Redemption Song', Bob Marley sings, 'Emancipate yourselves from mental slavery. None but ourselves can free our minds.'[90] Marley's appeal echoes of Jesus' challenge to his disciples to ask, seek and knock and his promise in John 8:32 that 'the truth will set you free'. As I noted in previous chapters, Gramsci argues that existential emancipation has a key role to play in the 'cultural war of position' and the unmasking of hegemony and Castells, like Freire, suggests that mobilized minds have the capacity not only to resource resistance to oppression but to defeat it in the long term. Such an approach reframes training as liberative education—a process similar to that of conscientization within the work of Freire. Such an approach to a theology of community organizing views the community organizer not as trainer but as conscious companion, akin to the role of theologian as facilitator in the work of Schreiter. Such a perspective represents a challenge to existing community organizing and views reflection on specific actions, values and broader organizing as an evolving dialogue within which new insights can be drawn from other social movements, faith traditions and academic disciplines. Such an approach is shaped by the open-ended 'nitty-gritty' hermeneutics of Pinn to which I referred previously rather than a more introverted banking model of training.

It is possible to envisage the development of reflective groups within which faith-based community organizers bring their ongoing engagement in organizing into dialogue with the ethical and theological values upon which their activism is built. Such groups, when premised on the ethic of love, the divine bias to the oppressed, a preferential option for the oppressed, the cultural politics of difference and a hermeneutics of liberative difference could provide a reflective engine room for faith-based community organizing. An ethic of liberative difference would enable participants to draw upon the liberative strands of their own faith tradition and bring these into a creative dialogue with the theological and spiritual resources of practitioners whose commitment to forging the common good arises from a different faith tradition. These reflective groups would not act as the guardians of orthodoxy nor would they subvert the necessarily pragmatic strategic planning or execution of actions and campaigns within a broad-based community organization. They would however provide a more substantial reflective foundation upon which faith-based organizing in superdiverse contexts could build through their capacity to draw upon the subversive spiritual capital present within their scriptures, tradition or religious teaching. Such groups could enable deeper reflection on the nature of discipleship and of broad-based community organizations. Their theological dialogue could help to reposition faith-based community organizations as dynamic and inclusive networked social movements rather than solid and implicitly exclusive permanent people's organizations.

CONCLUSION

In this chapter, I have drawn upon the story of the development of community organizing on both sides of the Atlantic and my critical dialogue with what I have called the 'new politics' and social and political theory to begin to identify the key ingredients in a liberative theology of community organizing. I have argued that faith-based community organizing has the potential to model a reimagined theology of liberation and to offer people of faith a powerful and effective means of taking on a preferential option for the oppressed in the superdiverse twenty-first century. However, I have also suggested that this potential can only be fulfilled if attention is paid to the development of a theology of community organizing that moves beyond brief theological reflection. Such a theology must be inherently interdisciplinary, cross-cultural and intrafaith if it is to reflect, analyse and speak with credibility to the fluid world of third-space community organizing. In the final chapter, I begin to articulate this liberative theology of community organizing.

6   A Theology of Community Organizing
Becoming Yeast in the City

INTRODUCTION

Having told the story of community organizing, explored the new politics, engaged with social and political theory and identified the key ingredients of a liberative theology of community organizing, it is now time to pull these threads together. What might a theology of community organizing look like in practice? It is this question that I hope to answer in this final chapter. I do not aim to delineate a carefully calibrated systematic theology of community organizing because this would contradict what I have said thus far about the blurred fluidity of third-space urban life, the dynamic nature of culture, the provisional character of contextual theology and the necessary open-endedness of a community organizing approach to the struggle for social justice in a superdiverse society. Instead, these final pages represent a call to action for others to respond to and make their own. This chapter will point to the ways in which faith-based community organizing has the potential to model a twenty-first century liberation theology.

In the weeks of Lent during the Middle Ages, cloths were placed over church altars depicting the suffering of Jesus. In recent decades Christians from the global South, as well as development agencies such as Misereor (the German Roman Catholic Church's development agency), have drawn on this heritage to create what are often called 'hunger cloths'. The hunger cloth interweaves global suffering with a liberative reading of the passion of Jesus. A graphic example of the contemporary hunger cloth is the 'Tree of Life', which was created by the Haitian artist Jacques Chéry in 1982.[1] The cloth arises organically from the Haitian experience of oppression, dictatorship and poverty but it has become a transnational symbol of solidarity and struggle in recent decades. Although the Haitian roots of Chéry's hunger cloth are of intrinsic importance, in a globalized and superdiverse century, the sense of interconnectedness, solidarity, empowerment and holistic liberation that he has woven perfectly summarizes the thrust of a liberative theology of community organizing. The roots and branches of the 'tree of life' on which Jesus hangs reach into every shadowy and celebratory corner of human life. Chéry's Jesus is Black—incarnate in Haitian life and the wider

Black struggle for emancipation. He is present in every small design on the hunger cloth—in the classroom and at the feast as well as under the boot of a soldier with a baton and with the refugees in their small leaky boat. Chéry's hunger cloth reflects a Christology of a 'thousand tiny empowerments' and a theology where those whom society treats as 'insignificant' are prioritized. The Black Jesus is a brother in their struggles. The 'tree of life' however does more than reflect a spirituality of solidarity because it spans the divide between oppression and liberation. Consequently, as the fruit-laden branches reach into the light a series of liberative reversals take place. This image of holistic solidarity weaves its way through the theology of community organizing that I outline in this final chapter.

CORE PRINCIPLES—A BIAS TO THE OPPRESSED IN A SUPERDIVERSE SOCIETY

The liberative capacity of a theology of community organizing rests on the adoption of three fundamental theological principles: prioritizing insignificance, liberative reversals and a hermeneutics of liberative difference. When combined these three principles embody a reframing of the divine bias to the oppressed that is culturally credible in the fluid third space of superdiverse societies such as the United States and the United Kingdom. Since these fundamental principles give life to a theology of community organizing it is necessary to explore them in a little more detail.

PRIORITIZING INSIGNIFICANCE AND LIBERATIVE REVERSALS

Elsa Tamez argues that the God of the Jewish and Christian scriptures 'identified himself with the poor to such an extent that their rights become the rights of God himself'.[2] In Mark 10:32–34, Jesus blesses a child whom his disciples have pushed aside, telling them that children will have pride of place in the Kingdom of God. In Luke 7:37, 'a woman in the city who was a sinner' bathes Jesus feet with her tears and dries them with her hair. When challenged by a local religious teacher, Jesus suggests that she and not his devout host is a symbol of faithfulness. In John 4:1–42, Jesus meets a Samaritan woman who has come alone to collect water from the well in the heat of the day. John tells us that she lives with a man even though they are not married. As a Samaritan, this stranger is the demonized 'other'. As a woman, she should not speak to Jesus in public. Jesus astounds his disciples by asking her for a drink and debating faith with her. A gentile woman becomes a key early evangelist.

A theology of community organizing will necessarily prioritize those who are marginalized and considered insignificant. Such a theological perspective draws on the practice of Jesus as it is described in the Gospels in order to reframe the preferential option for the poor as the prioritizing of insignificance. It models an approach to community organizing that utilizes the subversive social capital of faith groups to forge a series of liberative reversals as seen in Figure 6.1.[3]

The theological commitment to prioritizing insignificance and a model of discipleship characterized by the practice of liberative reversals dubs dominant narratives about worth and value. As a result, it critiques models of faith-based community organizing and political theology that are premised on a consensual understanding of the common good as it is defined by those on the inside and the upside of society. In her analysis of the nature of the global city, Saskia Sassen points to the way in which the 'the city has emerged as a site for new claims: by global capital . . . but also by disadvantaged sectors of the urban population . . . The formation of new claims raise the question—whose city is it?'[4] In a low-wage capitalist service economy within which perceived worth is largely tied to wealth, possessions and power, socially excluded post-industrial communities are often regarded as worthless. Such a perspective ran through the media coverage of and political commentary on the urban riots in England during the summer of 2011. The unemployed were depicted by Prime Minister David Cameron as symbols of a 'broken Britain' in 'moral decline'.[5] Although equally strongly condemning the violence, Ed Milliband, the leader of the Labour Party, aligned himself more closely with a London School of Economics report into the 2011 riots, suggesting that they should be seen as part of a bigger and deeper social problem related to the social exclusion of those with no stake and little interest in David Cameron's 'big society'.[6] Sassen suggests that it might be possible to break the cycle that leaves the marginalized powerless: 'The global city is a strategic site for disempowered actors because it enables them to gain presence, to emerge as subjects, even when they do

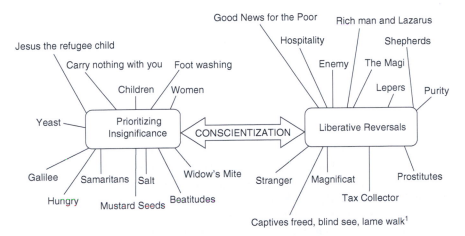

Figure 6.1 Prioritizing Insignificance and Liberative Reversals

not gain direct power.'[7] It is in this contested and plural public sphere that community organizing is forged—but whose voices are listened to most attentively amidst the static of the city?

Within the Christian tradition, Jesus' Beatitudes mark the beginning of his public ministry in Matthew's Gospel. The language of the Beatitudes continues to carry cultural currency, even in arguably post religious societies like the United Kingdom. However, the revolutionary character of Jesus announcement of a Kingdom of liberative reversals is softened in Matthew's recording of His words where it is the 'poor *in spirit*' (Matthew 5:3) and those who 'hunger and thirst *for righteousness*' (Matthew 5:6) who are blessed. In the less widely quoted 'blessings and woes' in Luke 6:20–26, we find a theology of liberative reversals that is less tentatively worded— 'Blessed are you who are poor, for yours is the kingdom of God. Blessed are you who are hungry now, for you will be filled' (Luke 6:20–21). Those often considered worthless—the asylum seeker, the unemployed young man on a housing estate, the redundant car worker, the Muslim woman wearing the *niqab*—become the blessed ones, those whom God favours. The writer of Proverbs 14 amplifies the point: 'Those who oppress the poor insult their Maker, but those who are kind to the needy honour him' (Proverbs 14:31). Tamez suggests that the Jewish and Christian Scriptures reveal a God who prioritizes insignificance: 'God takes sides and comes on the scene as one who favours the poor, those who make up the masses of the people.'[8] As Figure 6.1 indicates those whom society considers insignificant or worthless are placed centre stage by Jesus (the widow, the child, the woman, the Samaritan, the worker, the prostitute). Such an approach is vital within progressive faith-based community organizing if it is to model a theology of liberation for the twenty-first century.

Furthermore, images of apparent powerlessness and smallness become metaphors of faithfulness and liberative reversal (the widow's mite, foot washing, salt and yeast) within a theology of community organizing. Power, it appears, is not to be equated with strength, size or muscle—after all, you do not need much yeast to bring life and energy to a lump of lifeless dough or more than a pinch or two of salt to preserve and give flavour to meat. Hidden from view, yeast and salt transform, even though their presence may not be recognized. In her Magnificat, Mary embodies the divine prioritizing of insignificance as she sings, 'My soul magnifies the Lord . . . for he has looked with favour on the lowliness of his servant' (Luke 1:47–48). It is an unmarried pregnant teenager who first declares a gospel of liberative reversals. God has 'brought down the powerful from their thrones and lifted up the lowly . . . filled the hungry with good things and sent the rich away empty' (Luke 1:52–53). Here is the liberative sound of the 'voices from the borderland' to which Sandercock refers—the source of what she calls 'insurgent citizenship.' A liberative theology of community organizing that is premised on a commitment to prioritizing insignificance and liberative reversals will emerge from the socially excluded margins rather than from the socially included centre. It will draw upon that which is considered small and weak and arise from the subversive social capital of fragile faith and community groups to fashion what Sandercock calls a 'thousand tiny empowerments'.[9]

Such an ethic of liberative smallness and the interweaving of loose communities of the excluded challenges the appeal within much community organizing to organized people, organized money and organized power and the goal of building a powerful permanent people's organization. It critiques the temptation to listen most attentively to the big and the strong faith and community groups that are members of a broad-based community organization when actions are being discussed and campaigns enacted. A theology of community organizing that prioritizes insignificance will dare faith-based community organizers to engage in a process of liberative reversals whereby the smallest and the most fragile take centre stage and forge the path that a broad-based community organization takes. In the context of such a theological commitment within a superdiverse society the hermeneutics of liberative difference becomes essential.

TOWARDS A HERMENEUTICS OF LIBERATIVE DIFFERENCE

A theology of community organizing that is premised on an ethic of liberative love and a reimagining of the divine bias to the oppressed in a superdiverse society will be aligned not with current narratives of hybridity but with the cultural politics of difference. This hermeneutics of liberative difference borrows from the dub practice pioneered by Beckford in order to deconstruct and then reconstruct attitudes to difference in a superdiverse context in order to subvert the resurgent Orientalism that has surfaced since Samuel Huntingdon published his *Clash of Civilisations* in 1996.[10] Such a hermeneutical principle can resource interfaith community organizing in the plural and contested public sphere to which Jamoul and Fraser refer in a manner that does not sideline or subsume difference but foregrounds it as a central strength in the struggle for justice.

A hermeneutics of liberative difference has six key features. First, because it is animated by a 'nitty-gritty' approach comparable to that found in grounded theory a hermeneutics of liberative difference will not theorize away diversity under the convenient cloak of hybridity or freeze cultures on the basis of ideological, ethnic or theological essentialism. A hermeneutics of liberative difference has the capacity to resource a theology of community organizing within a superdiverse society because it resists attempts to homogenize the heterogeneous cultures that characterize the fluid third space of the twenty-first century.

Second, a hermeneutics of liberative difference can help to critique all forms of reductionism, thereby enabling faith-based community organizing to engage with the both-and world that characterizes the third space of a superdiverse world. Such a perspective can also enable an honest wrestling with the multifaceted nature of oppression and the need for a model of mutual liberation that honours diversity rather than subsuming it under the banner of community cohesion or pragmatic organizing actions.

Third, because it is characterized by a prioritizing of insignificance, a hermeneutics of liberative difference cannot be equated with an uncritical multiculturalism or a theological pluralism within which no judgments can be made about truth or justice. Although it is inherently dialogical, a hermeneutics of liberative difference is dialogue with an edge. The liberative potential of difference will be judged on the basis of clear criteria and a hermeneutics of suspicion. Key questions to be asked by those engaged in interfaith community organizing therefore include:

1. Are we all open to discovering new truths from those whose faith is different from my own?
2. Are we all motivated by a radical hospitality and a clear preferential option for the 'stranger'?
3. Are we all committed to shared liberative struggle, or is partnership motivated solely by pragmatic concerns?
4. Are we all committed to a multidimensional equality that is not bound by age, ethnicity, gender or sexuality?
5. Are we all committed to giving priority to people perceived to be 'strangers' and to marginalized faith and community groups rather than 'insiders' and those people and groups with strength and power?

Fourth, because it is rooted in the cultural politics of difference and the guiding values of liberation theology, a hermeneutics of liberative difference will enact and extend the model of radical and unconditional hospitality introduced by Bretherton in order to reflect a divine bias to the stranger and the outsider. In this sense, liberative difference reflects a hermeneutics which does not only prioritize perceived insignificance but also proactively privileges the demonized.

Fifth, because it reflects an organic and nitty-gritty engagement with the blurred world of the third space and the glocal nature of urban communities, a hermeneutics of liberative difference can enable a new relationship with social space. As a result of its engagement with the theorizing of social space and its ideological use, a hermeneutics of liberative difference can enable faith-based community organizing to understand the contested nature of social space more fully. Such a hermeneutical perspective can subvert the dominance of conceived social space by the powerful or its ideological ghettoization into Muslim space, Christian space, Jewish space, Sikh space, Hindu space, Buddhist space, Black space or White space through the conscious creation of the kinds of shared representational spaces of which Lefebvre speaks and the radically inclusive reflective groups to which I referred previously. Such spaces of neighbourly love and egalitarian hospitality need to be free and unregulated spaces that are not controlled by community organizers or religious leaders if they are to resource an organic model of shared liberative praxis. Such shared liberative representational spaces have the potential to model new third space interpretive communities that subvert all forms of race-based essentialism or theological exclusivism. Such third-space representational spaces can become the sites within which blurred base communities can be forged as the engine rooms of twenty-first-century faith-based community organizing. Open, inclusive, networked and motivated by an ethic a liberative difference, such interpretive communities would resemble movements rather than permanent people's organizations, thereby reflecting the dynamic nature of third-space superdiversity, an expanded new catholicity and hospitable listening.

Sixth, because it is animated by a commitment to the importance of the conscientization to which Freire refers, a hermeneutics of liberative difference will emphasize the central importance of critical reflection and debate. I am not here referring to the practice of brief evaluations after people's assemblies that are common within community organizing. Rather I am suggesting that a hermeneutics of liberative difference can help those involved in faith-based community organizing to cultivate the intercultural hermeneutics described by Schreiter and the practice of listening to which Bretherton refers—not in separate faith or cultural groups but as one diverse body. Liberative difference, therefore, reminds us of the importance of inclusive and open-ended reflection and liberative education. It dares us to recognize that this process cannot be confined to specific community organizations or single faith groups, imprisoned within a theological or ethnic camp mentality or a pragmatic community organizing agenda. It belongs to, challenges and enriches all.

Drawing on a critical correlation methodology such as that pioneered by Paul Tillich and revised by Don Browning and Gordon Lynch, a hermeneutics of liberative difference will utilize Beckford's dub practice to deconstruct prevailing responses to difference before reconstructing them on the basis of the guiding ethic of a prioritizing of the demonized stranger.[11] A hermeneutics of liberative difference adopts a conversational approach to theological reflection reminiscent of that envisaged in revised correlation methodologies. However, although a hermeneutics of liberative difference seeks to engage in an honest nitty-gritty manner with diversity, it is not directionless. Rather, it is shaped by an *a priori* commitment to liberative action. Like the liberation theology from which it draws its inspiration, a hermeneutics of liberative difference will be judged by it capacity to facilitate social change. The hermeneutics of liberative difference provides a theology of community organizing with a radically inclusive interpretive framework that has the capacity to resource reflective interfaith community organizing in a manner that subverts an appeal to hybridity on the one hand and ethnic essentialism or theological camp mentality on the other. Such an interpretive tool critically privileges difference on the basis of the liberative plumb line introduced previously and the cultural politics of difference explored in previous chapters. It can provide people of faith engaged in community organizing with the tools with which to forge the liberative third-space theology envisaged by Baker, the expansive wholeness that characterizes Schreiter's new catholicity and the prophetic hospitality and unconditional neighbourly love advocated by Bretherton. Only such an approach can awaken those who seek to organize to the power of mobilized minds in the 'cultural war of position'.

BUILDING BLOCKS—EMANCIPATING DOGMA

A theology of community organizing will build upon the foundation provided by these core principles in an attempt to emancipate liberative theological themes from the grip of dogmatic camp mentality. Three emphases will be placed centre stage in such a theology: creation in God's image, incarnation and *shalom*.

CREATED IN GOD'S IMAGE TO LIVE IN COMMUNITY

Regardless of whether we read the first chapter of the Bible as history or creation myth, the following verses from Genesis 1 provide people of faith with a pivotal resource for egalitarian community organizing: 'Then God said, "Let us make humankind in our image, according to our likeness . . . So God created humankind in his image . . . male and female he created them"' (Genesis 1:26–27). In *sura* 49:13 the Qur'an asserts a similar perspective: 'People, we created you all from a single man and a single woman and made you into tribes and races so that you should get to know one another.'[12] The central commitment within community organizing to human dignity and equal worth finds a theological foundation in Biblical and Qur'anic anthropology. Humanity is created in the image of God to live together within egalitarian communities. Consequently, all people are of equal worth as members of a single human family, neighbours scattered across the earth.

It is on the basis of this ethic of fundamental human worth and intimate interconnectedness that a theology of community organizing necessarily asserts a hermeneutics of liberative difference in the face of historic and contemporary othering, persistent race-based thinking and ethnic essentialism. When agape love, rather than self-interest, provides the ethical foundation for a theology of community organizing the neighbourly love and radical hospitality to which Bretherton refers become a necessary means of asserting a priority of insignificance and the open-ended 'new catholicity' considered by Schreiter in the both-and third space explored by Baker. In a superdiverse society within which those perceived to be strangers are cast as suspicious outsiders, a reclaiming of the narrative of creation subverts theoretical, theological and political critiques of multiculturalism and provides a solid foundation upon which faith-based community organizing can build inclusive and egalitarian broad-based community organizations.

Within Sikhism, the innate worth of all people forms the spiritual foundation of the community kitchen, or *langar*. From its birth in the Punjab, Sikhism emphasized the sacramental nature of hospitality. The principle of welcoming and equality is rooted in the life of the founder of Sikhism Guru Nanak, although it was the third Guru, Amar Das, who instituted the *langar* as a key feature in all Sikh gurdwaras. Within the *langar* all people, regardless of gender, class, caste or ethnicity sit together on the floor as one body. All are welcome and all are served the same food, implicitly echoing the advice of the writer of the letter to the Hebrews in the Christian scriptures: 'Do not neglect to show hospitality to strangers, for by doing that some have entertained angels without knowing it' (Hebrews 13:2). Within the gurdwara and within Hebrews 13, hospitality is elevated from welfare to sacrament—a physical action exemplifying the welcoming presence of God and the equality of all people. Such a commitment challenges all exclusivist theologies, immigration policies and assimilationist models of community cohesion wherein difference is to be feared or subsumed. Against this backdrop, actions such as Strangers into Citizens and Citizens for Sanctuary in the United Kingdom and the PICO Campaign for Citizenship in the United States become more than examples of socially progressive activism intended to foster an inclusive diverse society.[13] Such campaigns become enacted parables of our common humanity and judgments upon racist immigration and citizenship mechanisms on both sides of the Atlantic, perhaps reminding people of faith of the words of Jesus in Matthew 25:43: 'I was a stranger and you did not welcome me.'

INCARNATION—UNITY AND SOLIDARITY

Elsa Tamez suggests that 'the poor in the Bible are the helpless, the indigent, the hungry, the oppressed, the needy, the humiliated . . . it is not nature that has put them in this situation; they have been unjustly impoverished and despoiled by the powerful'.[14] If the theological narrative of creation articulates an egalitarian anthropology and a vision of the divine image that is imprinted on all people then an emphasis on incarnation builds this into an assertion of God's solidarity with the oppressed. Within the Christian community this focus is exemplified by a single verse at the beginning of John's Gospel—'And the Word became flesh and lived among us' (John 1:14). Historically Christians have pinpointed the birth of Jesus as the key tipping point in human history—the particular moment when God became a person in a specific time and place thereby identifying completely with humanity. This confluence of human and divine in the person of Jesus has become a key distinguishing marker of the Creeds of the Church within which Christians declare their faith 'in one Lord, Jesus Christ, the only begotten Son of the Father . . . being of one substance with the Father, by whom all things were made . . . For us and for our salvation he came down from heaven, was incarnate from the Holy Spirit and the Virgin Mary and was made man' (the Nicene Creed, 325CE).

The British theologian Kenneth Leech argues that the Incarnation represents a revolutionary moment in human history: 'God took to himself human flesh . . . raised [humanity] into God. To believe this is dangerous and controversial' rather than an individualized dogmatic marker.[15] The Methodist urban theologian John Vincent emphasizes the implications of the Incarnation (more than its divine origins) and the solidarity of the human Jesus with oppressed communities in the city as a result of he calls Jesus' 'journey downwards'.[16] Jesus becomes the archetypal organic intellectual whose 'good news to the poor' is embodied by his conscious alignment with the marginalized of first century Palestine. Writing out of the dramatically different context of the civil rights movement and the Black Power struggle in the United States, James Cone adds substance to the reflections of Leech and Vincent in *God of the Oppressed*. Cone argues that the liberative force of the Incarnation rests on a contemporary translation of Jesus' life within an oppressed and colonized first-century Jewish community into culturally resonant contemporary terms. In light of African-American history, Cone offers such a translation. He suggests that in a society where Blackness has historically been a symbol of oppression, powerlessness and worthlessness Jesus must be Black 'because he was a Jew' in occupied Palestine.[17] For Cone, 'the validity of any Christological title in any period of history is not decided by its universality but by . . . whether in the particularity of its time it points to God's universal will to liberate particular oppressed people from inhumanity'.[18] In light of such reflections, how might an engagement with the Incarnation and Christology inform a theology of community organizing that is premised on a hermeneutics of liberative difference? Three things can be said.

First, although it would not be intellectually credible or ethically appropriate to uncouple Incarnational thinking from the particularities of Jesus life, death and resurrection and their central importance for Christians, it is possible to place a greater emphasis on the implications of the Incarnation for liberative activism rather than its dogmatic significance. Cone and Vincent imply that the power of Christology is found in its capacity to resource liberative praxis in particular contexts rather than in its universal doctrinal significance. Consequently, in a superdiverse society it becomes possible, as I have argued elsewhere, to follow Cone's example and fashion new culturally resonant Christological titles that can signpost solidarity, interconnectedness, the prioritizing of insignificance and liberative reversals. Jesus therefore becomes 'the insurgent', 'the stranger', 'the unheard', 'the story-teller', 'the organic intellectual' and a model of faith-based activism and the solidarity of God with the oppressed rather than one on whom an individual's personal salvation rests.[19]

Second, an emphasis on incarnation within a theology of community organizing can resource subversive discipleship in atomized and unequal societies for two reasons. First, Incarnational activism critiques the individualization of oppression wherein the marginalized are judged to be oppressed as a result of their own lack of effort or skill and attempts to stand alongside such people viewed as individualized attempts to 'love our neighbor' or 'help the disadvantaged'. An emphasis on Incarnation reminds us of our commonality and of the systemic nature of injustice and when allied with a hermeneutics of liberative difference has the capacity to resource creative action-reflection within the interfaith reflection groups that could play such an important role within faith-based community organizing in the future. Second, an emphasis on incarnation within a theology of community organizing can offer a critical counterpoint to the effects of multifaceted social exclusion and the geographical, political, cultural and existential isolation of marginalized groups and communities. The excluded are not just included but prioritized as a result of the ethic of solidarity and commonality that runs through Incarnational thinking.

Third, Incarnational thinking reminds us of the interwoven nature of injustice. In words that find an echo in the Islamic conception of the diverse unity of the worldwide Muslim *ummah*, the apostle Paul makes the point clearly in his first letter to the church in Corinth: 'we are one body and whenever one person is hurt the entire body is damaged' (1 Corinthians 12). The African-American vocal group Sweet Honey in the Rock graphically expresses the significance of such Incarnational thinking in the context of global injustice: 'Chile your waters run red through Soweto. The hand that choked the spirit of Allende pulls the trigger of a gun on the children of Soweto . . . The hand that cut short the song of Victor Jara put young Steven Biko in a dusty hill grave.'[20] As Martin Luther King noted from his prison cell in Birmingham, Alabama, in 1963, 'Injustice anywhere is a threat to justice everywhere.'[21] Such an emphasis can help to align community organizing campaigns such as the living wage actions in the United States and the United Kingdom with wider social movements and struggles for justice and set these in a holistic analysis of interconnected systems of oppression.

SHALOM AND THE STRUGGLE FOR WHOLENESS

The writers of the Talmud (the central teaching resource of Rabbinic Judaism) suggest that 'the name of God is "Peace"', a phrase echoed in the first letter of John within the Christian scriptures—'God is love and whoever lives in love lives in God' (1 John 4:17). Within the Hebrew Scriptures, this focus revolves around the term '*shalom*', a rich word implying holistic well-being as a counterpoint to brokenness, injustice, exclusion and despair. Such *shalom* expresses an emphasis on human interconnectedness and is related to the well-being of other people within an extended family (e.g., Genesis 43:27 or Exodus 4:18), to the 'stranger' (e.g., Deuteronomy 10:19 or Psalm 146:9) or to the well-being of communities, cities and nations (e.g., Jeremiah 29:7). Within Jewish tradition, such *shalom* finds fulfilment in the development of a just and inclusive community that places people before systems and emphasizes existential as well as material well-being.

In theological terms, *shalom* can be compared with the Christian social teaching about the common good to which I referred in the previous chapter. A focus on the theme of *shalom* within a theology of community organizing will enable the development of integrated models of organizing that recognize the central importance of spiritual and ethical values as the drivers of holistic activism. The work of Leech and Beckford can resource such reflection within faith-based community organizing. Like Young within political philosophy and Sandercock within urban studies, Leech notes that both oppression and liberation are multifaceted, embracing existential as well as sociopolitical factors. Social exclusion can, he suggests, sap psychological or spiritual well-being, leading to the internalization of cultural hegemony. If we are treated as if we have no worth for long enough, we may begin to believe that we have no value to such a degree, says Leech, that we become eaten away by 'emptiness, void and loss of meaning'.[22] Furthermore Beckford points to the need to forge holistic models of liberation which are characterized by emancipation from corrosive race-based thinking and enacted liberative love which transforms not only social structures but also the relationship between oppressed and oppressor.

A theology of community organizing that is characterized by such an emphasis on *shalom* will recognize the need for a holistic approach to campaigning, which heals the internal as well as the external wounds of oppressed communities, thereby enabling the 'reweaving of the fabric of society'. An example of such an approach is seen the work of the US-based interfaith Tikkun community which arises from the work of the Californian rabbi Michael Lerner.[23] The Hebrew word '*tikkun*' means 'to heal' or 'to repair'. This integrated approach to interfaith action for social justice arises from an engagement with the deep human need for a psycho-spiritual well-being that stimulates the critical awareness and conscientization needed to underpin effective ongoing activism. A further example of *shalom*-based activism is found in the work of Glide Memorial United Methodist Church in San Francisco.[24] A central focus at Glide is on unconditional welcome and the suggestion that all people—be they oppressor or oppressed—are damaged. Holistic liberation in this context can only emerge when it is recognized that we are all 'in recovery'.[25] Such a *shalom* emphasis characterizes aspects of the community organizing of the Gamaliel Foundation in relation to health care, education and housing campaigns, all of which recognize the need for a holistic internal-external approach to organizing.[26]

When built upon the core principles which will underpin a theology of community organizing (prioritizing insignificance, liberative reversals and a hermeneutics of liberative difference) the key themes of *shalom* or wholeness, incarnation and solidarity and creation in the image of God and unity can begin to shape a liberative future for faith-based community organizing and resource subversive patterns of discipleship.

SUBVERSIVE DISCIPLESHIP

In all four of the Christian Gospels, we read about the calling of the first disciples. What we encounter in the Gospels is not the establishment of the institutional Church but the emergence of a dynamic social movement, which subverts excluding social and theological attitudes towards ethnicity, gender and class. We witness a movement that lives in a Palestinian third space and is characterized by radical hospitality, a preferential option for the oppressed and open-ended unconditional activism. This is a both-and not an either-or community—more network than permanent people's organization. Those who become part of the movement are the marginalized and the dispossessed. They bring their vulnerability and openness to change rather than the power of organized people or organized money. On the edge of Jewish society, the fragile communities of interpretation and resistance that we read about in Acts 2 and 4 are more like yeast which energises the dough of society while remaining unseen than mustard seeds sown in the ground which grow into a bush that is strong enough for the birds to nest in.

The development of an action-oriented theology of community organizing that revolves around such an open-ended conception of community and activism has significant implications for faith groups. This is a theological model that demands an ethic of openness to change on the part of faith communities. Embracing this liberative openness transforms faith groups from solid communities with clear borders into fluid movements with blurred boundaries. Animated by a vision of an unfolding Kingdom spirituality, such faith groups will become interlinked in a network of other communities shaped by the same commitment to prioritizing insignificance and liberative reversals. Pete Ward argues that as modernity shifts into postmodernity the solid church forged in the centuries following the Reformation that was characterized by fixed boundaries needs to be supplanted by a liquid and open-ended model of Christian fellowship.[27] Ward speaks out of a post-evangelical search for a culturally credible church that rests on a dispersed and relational rather than a gathered and organizational model of community. However his focus on inclusive fluid community when allied with the egalitarian ethic of the base ecclesial communities (BECs) that found their origins in Latin America can provide a template for people of faith who are engaged in community organizing in a superdiverse society.

In *The Church from the Roots*, José Marins, Teolide Trevisan and Carolee Chanona explore the rise, character and significance of BECs. They emphasize the fact that although the BEC represents a rediscovery of the Christian calling to be yeast and salt in society, it is not 'a protest group', 'a discussion group' or a naturally occurring social grouping but a 'sacramental event' which embodies the mission of the Church to become 'the dynamic reality of an evangelical, liberating and prophetic community opting preferentially for the poor . . . and a seed for the growth of a new model of society'.[28] In a Latin American context the BEC represented a grass-roots expression of the Church, built from the underside of society on the basis of a liberative model of theological reflection and education. Although shaped quite clearly by Christian spirituality, the BECs that emerged in Latin America were, according to Marins, Trevisan and Chanona, 'open-ended, thus avoiding the temptation to lapse into a ghetto mentality or to form elitist groups'.[29]

BECs arose in a very different context from that facing faith-based community organizing in a superdiverse century and so the temptation to simply lift them from their Latin American soil and then transplant them uncritically in the very different earth of the United States and the United Kingdom must be avoided. Furthermore, the open-endedness of base communities can perhaps be overstated. The BEC was not a completely independent faith group but a contextualized Christian fellowship that grew out of the specific experience of a particular oppressed community and a clear preferential option for the oppressed. The BEC was intended to be an expression of the wider Church and was interconnected with other similar communities in a network of solidarity. Bearing these two words of caution in mind, it is nevertheless possible to draw upon the example of the BEC and that of the broader small Christian communities movement it stimulated as we seek to develop an ecclesiology capable of resourcing a liberative theology of community organizing in the twenty-first century for four interlinked reasons.

First, the BEC reminds us of the critical importance of deep listening within and to a context. Faith groups that are animated by a liberative theology of community organizing will necessarily root their activism in ongoing deep listening to the context within which they are set, using this as the basis for activism rather than attempting to squeeze their communities into a predefined dogmatic template. The pastor or community organizer in such a context becomes an organic intellectual shot through with what Gramsci calls the 'elemental passions of the people'.

Second, the BEC reminds us of the foundational importance of holistic liberative education within a faith group that is committed to prioritizing insignificance. Such holistic existential emancipation must be seen as a vital aspect of faith-based community organizing if broad-based community organizations are to change cultural norms as well as political institutions. Holistic social change rests therefore on a model of liberative education which draws theological reflection together into a dialogue with a critical analysis of the nature, cause and impact of oppression. Without emancipated minds and spirits, those engaged in faith-based community organizing will only ever be able to change surface-level structures whilst leaving underlying systems untouched.

Third, the BEC reminds us of the importance of a model of faith-based activism that prioritizes insignificance. A community organizing ecclesiology that is premised on the divine bias to the oppressed is one that takes sides. It will necessarily listen more attentively to those who are left out and left behind than to the powerful in order to foster the common good in an unjust society. Such an orientation is vital and subversive in equal measure because it overturns models of community organizing that implicitly measure success in terms of size and strength—the numbers of people attending assemblies or companies paying a living wage. It reflects an understanding of liberative struggle that focuses on systemic injustice as well as the pain that social exclusion causes individual children, women and men. Rooted in a BEC style yeast based model of discipleship, rather than a mustard seed ecclesiology, faith groups that embrace a liberative theology of community organizing will, therefore, emphasise the power of smallness and perceived insignificance.

Fourth, the BEC reminds us of the dangers of isolationism. Conscientized faith groups that are involved in community organizing in superdiverse societies need to be characterized by the open and unconditional ethic of hospitality introduced by Bretherton, the new catholicity explored by Schreiter and the third space dynamism described by Baker. When animated by a hermeneutics of liberative difference such groups will be dynamic and open-ended, shaped more by Kingdom values than doctrinal fidelity. Such a perspective challenges bounded conceptions of 'Church', the institutionalism of much community organizing and the common goal of building solid, powerful and permanent people's organizations amongst community organizers. A focus on values rather than dogma will present faith communities with a theological challenge—as we meet together in the struggle for justice, how is our own framework of faith challenged? Faith-based community organizing does not just have the potential to facilitate a new theology of liberation for a post religious society, it might also subvert wider patterns of theological camp mentality and exclusivism. Such an approach can resource those struggling to unmask all forms of oppressive hegemony, be they political, ideological, cultural or theological, in the 'cultural war of position' thereby not only 'reweaving the fabric' of society but pointing towards a new liberated world.

On the basis of my discussion in previous chapters, I have argued that a model of faith-based community organizing that is founded on a theological commitment to prioritizing insignificance, a process of liberative reversals, a hermeneutics of liberative difference and an ethic of agape love needs to revolve around what could be called subversive linking capital. In order to ensure that such a commitment has the capacity to generate liberative change subversive linking capital within faith-based community organizing must be earthed in specific moments, places and struggles. Consequently, the development of grass-roots representational spaces within which subversive linking capital can be articulated, explored and critiqued is of vital importance.

In this vein, the interfaith reflective groups to which I referred previously become a key resource within a theology of community organizing. As I have noted, such groups would revolve around a bottom-up dialogue between the diverse spiritual resources of specific faith traditions, a theological commitment to prioritizing insignificance, a process of liberative reversals, an ethic of agape love and a hermeneutics of liberative difference as they relate to and arise from particular community organizing campaigns. Such reflective groups would need to be facilitated by those who attend rather than clergy from specific faith groups or professional community organizers if they are to fulfil their potential to become the independent educational and theological engine rooms of faith-based community organizing rather than semi official focus groups which do not offer critical guidance to broad-based community organizations.

STRENGTH FOR THE JOURNEY—A SPIRITUALITY OF COMMUNITY ORGANIZING

Burnout is a constant danger within all forms of civic activism and community organizing is not immune from this problem. In his *Dreams from My Father,* Barack Obama recognizes this danger as he reflects on his own work as a Gamaliel Foundation community organizer during the 1980s.[30] The enthusiastic faith-based community organizer will run dry unless she or he can draw on a well of nourishment. Dennis Jacobsen puts his finger on the problem: 'action can . . . be frenetic, mindless and damaging to the human spirit . . . a whirlwind that swoops down upon the soul of a person and sends her or his life into a crazy spin.'[31] In light of this danger, I will use these final pages to sketch out the broad contours of a spirituality that can energize community organizers, thereby providing strength for the journey. Inevitably, the reflections that follow are tentative suggestions that need to be tested out in the heat of grass-roots activism because a spirituality of community organizing is necessarily contextual. They arise, however, from the core principles of the theology of community organizing that I outlined previously—prioritizing insignificance, liberative reversals and a hermeneutics of liberative difference. It is a spirituality which will emphasise a liberative re-imagining of Scriptures and deep contemplative listening.

Within this book, I have outlined the shape of a theology of community organizing in superdiverse societies. It has not been my intention to comment upon debates about conflicting truth claims within the theology of religions. What can be said, however, is that the hermeneutics of liberative difference which helps to underpin a theology of community organizing necessarily implies a person-centred spirituality that honours difference (rather than demonizing or subsuming it) while still providing the resources to energize faith-based community organizers from diverse religious traditions. Recent debates within the sociology of religion can help to inform the search for such a liberative person-centred spirituality of community organizing. Paul Heelas and Linda Woodhead suggest that the dawning of the twenty-first century marked an existential watershed in Western societies characterized by a turning away from objective and dogmatic belief systems and the embrace of subjective spiritualities within which 'the goal is not to defer to a higher authority but to have the courage to become one's own authority'.[32] Gordon Lynch suggests that such new spiritualities can be aligned to a degree with progressive left-of-centre political activism.[33] For Gutiérrez such a liberative spirituality will centre on 'a conversion to the neighbor, the oppressed person, the exploited class'.[34] It is such a subject centred, anti dogmatic and liberative spirituality that is required if a theology of community organizing is to energize exhausted community organizers. Furthermore, as Christine Dodds reminds us, it is important to resist the remnants of binary attitudes towards spirituality which divorce it from grass-roots political struggle. Dodds argues that a liberative spirituality will bind together understandings of immanence and transcendence rather than depict them as polar opposites, so that it becomes possible to discover 'the transcendent in our midst'.[35] Such a perspective, Dodds suggests, can never be forged in isolation. It is not an individualized spirituality fashioned apart from others but a person-centred spirituality which is forged in relationship. As a result, it is a spirituality that leads us deeper into the lives of others and an affirmation of our common life. Dodds argues that it is on this foundation that we can then build a listening incarnational spirituality because, 'contemplation gives us the "squint" with which we glimpse those Kingdom moments and events where God is already acting and begin to co-operate with God in that action'.[36] Such spirituality rests on the cultivation of deep listening and the subversive reimagining of Scripture.

DEEP LISTENING

The practice of holistic listening can foster patterns of faith-based community organizing that are characterized by a contemplative resistance, which is capable of deepening activism and energizing activists. Such contemplative resistance embeds frenetic organizing and the attention to important but short-term campaigning goals in the life-giving soil of rich and often ancient spiritual traditions.

The one-to-one conversation forms a core part of community organizing methodology. However, these strategic conversations can tend to be focused on the pragmatic goal of encouraging the person with whom we speak to become involved in a specific broad-based community organization or on persuading a person with power to support an organizing campaign. Deep listening can resource but also critique these commonly used one-to-one conversations. When we listen, we need to stop and wait, to pay concentrated attention to our conversation partner rather than remaining focused on our own predetermined agenda. We need to be critically open to the possibility of learning new truths or finding our own perspective challenged. Within a spirituality of community organizing, we are challenged to listen to a range of 'voices'. In particular, there are three forms of holistic listening that can resource a spirituality of community organizing—listening in prayer and meditation, listening to the communities within which we organize and listening together. On the basis of the core principles of prioritizing insignificance and liberative reversals, it is important for faith-based organizers to consider who is speaking and in whose interests when they listen and to prioritize the 'voices' of the unheard and unseen as they seek to forge a spirituality rooted in the divine bias to the oppressed.

Holistic listening within a spirituality of community organizing begins with the act of listening in prayer and meditation. In the twenty-first century, we are surrounded by noise. Community organizers are often ruled by the deadlines and overwhelmed by targets. Such frenetic activity can also characterize the faith groups to which many within a broad-based community organization belong. A spirituality of community organizing requires us to step back from the fray, to look within and be renewed. Such a step demands a quietening of the soul and a stillness that opens us up to new, often unimagined, insights and marginalized voices. Within the Christian Gospels, Jesus often withdraws to 'lonely places' to listen for the 'still small voice of God' (1 Kings 19:12) and to be renewed (e.g., Matthew 14:13, Mark 1:35, Luke 4:42 or John 6:15). This contemplative listening forms a central feature of Quaker worship (a waiting in stillness for the voice of the Spirit). It characterizes the Buddhist practice of meditation which is intended to help people to cultivate a calm spirit and an awareness (or mindfulness) of others and our relationships with them.

A spirituality of community organizing that is premised on a hermeneutics of liberative difference cannot revolve around excluding listening. Consequently, a focus on such contemplative listening within can also provide an energizing resource for those whose community organizing does not arise from a religious faith but from a deep humanitarian commitment to social justice. Leonie Sandercock makes the point well in her study of the superdiverse global city: 'It is time to reintroduce into our thinking about cities . . . the importance of the sacred, of spirit . . . How can cities nurture our unrequited thirst for the spirit, for the sacred? In the Middle Ages it was in the building of cities around cathedrals. But that was long ago.'[37] In answer to her own question, Sandercock envisions a city where 'there are places of stimulus and meditation; where there is music in public squares'.[38] If Sandercock is right and the meeting of our 'thirst for the spirit' is part of what it means to be human, then it is upon this that a holistic listening within community organizing must focus.

A second expression of the holistic listening that can feed a spirituality of community organizing is that of listening with critical openness to the neighbourhoods within which we organize and to those most affected by the issues upon which campaigns focus. Such attentive listening is vital if a spirituality of community organizing is to arise organically from and speak to the context within which actions are developed. Such contextualized listening will root spirituality in specific communities, thereby recognizing the impact that the built landscape, public space, social policies, global economic factors and localized cultural characteristics have on the lives of those communities alongside whom faith-based organizers will be campaigning. Such contextualized listening will enable faith-based organizers to engage with the stories which shape specific communities thereby ensuring that a spirituality of community organizing arises from the bottom-up rather than reflecting a decontextualized top-down spiritual tradition. Such listening to context takes place in dialogue with prayerful/meditative listening. As a result, prayerful and meditative listening is informed by context and contextualized listening is deepened through a listening in prayer and meditation, thereby enabling a more organic and empathetic approach to community organizing.

The third key aspect of holistic listening within a spirituality of community organizing revolves around listening together. Because community organizing rests on the power of relationships and the commonality that lies at the heart of the religious traditions that shape the activism of faith-based community organizers, it is vital that our holistic listening and the spirituality it feeds is not isolationist. We listen within specific mosques, synagogues, churches, temples and gurdwaras. We listen in relationship and the faith groups which provide the building blocks of community organizations represent the crucible within which our spirituality is forged, shared, affirmed and challenged. Such interpretive communities can provide a framework within which we site our prayerful and meditative listening and our listening to context on a broader and bigger spiritual landscape. However, it is important to ensure that our common listening remains true to the core principles of a theology of community organizing. Consequently, on the basis of a commitment to prioritizing insignificance and the practice of liberative reversals, listening in community will pay particular attention to those within the interpretive communities that shape us whose lives are most clearly damaged by social exclusion rather than deferring to those with power or a position of authority. Furthermore, a focus on the hermeneutics of liberative difference will challenge us to listen in dialogue—unafraid of contrasting perspectives and open to being changed as we listen to others whose organizing arises from a different spiritual tradition.

REIMAGINING SCRIPTURE

Scripture is of foundational importance to faith-based community organizers from different religious traditions although the way it is approached differs widely. It is not my intention here to offer a detailed comparison of,

for example, Qur'anic and Biblical studies because the purpose of a liberative theology of community organizing that arises from a hermeneutics of
liberative difference is not to pit religious traditions against one another or
to attempt to subsume them within a pluralistic framework that fails to honour difference and disagreement. Rather such a theology seeks to identify
and draw upon the liberative potential of diversity in order to resource the
struggle for justice amongst faith-based community organizers from different faith traditions. Having said this, an attempt needs to be made to enable the subversive reimagining of Scriptural traditions in order to supplant
the uncritical translation of what might be called 'surface' readings and the
political neutering of Scripture inherent in what we can call 'spiritual' readings. The tools of critical awareness and liberative education can be used
to resource a subversive reimagining, which has the capacity to energize
faith-based community organizers and provide them with strength for the
journey ahead. Such subversive reimagining will draw upon reader-response
approaches to the engagement with Scripture, the liberative power of imagination and the intersubjective force of narrative and story.

Reader-response approaches to Scripture are most clearly formalized
within Christian Biblical hermeneutics, but they are implicitly present
within other faith traditions even if they are not as widely named. The postcolonial Biblical critic Fernando Segovia suggests that the power of reader-
response approaches lies in the fact that they recognize that meaning rests
not within the text or the interpretive community but in the relationship
between reader and Scripture. Meaning is made and remade as a result of
this dynamic dialogue.[39] As a result, as Robert Fowler, notes, 'no longer can
meaning be understood to be a stable determinate content that lies buried
within the text . . . meaning becomes a dynamic event in which we ourselves
participate'.[40] Consequently, a reimagining of Scripture can give rise to a
range of alternative readings rather than a unifying orthodoxy. Such fluidity reflects the dynamic third-space character of faith-based community
organizing in a superdiverse society but need not dissolve into a relativism that makes critical judgements impossible because a reader-response
reimagining of Scripture within a spirituality of community organizing will
be premised on a commitment to prioritizing insignificance and liberative
reversals. These core principles will sharpen and contextualize the reimagining of Scripture and the commitment to a hermeneutics of liberative difference will guard against the implicit imposition of homogenized re-readings
within which diversity is smothered.

A further tool in the faith-based organizers' Scriptural reimagining kit
bag is that of conscientization. As I noted previously, the liberative education methodology based on the work of Freire and Gramsci's focus on
the central importance of existential liberation emphasizes the liberative
power that is released when the oppressed become critically aware of the
causes of their oppression. Such an approach to the reimagining of Scripture, when allied with Cornel West's conviction that the intellectual must

be one who perceives their calling to be that of shining a light on suffering and empowering those whose voice is rarely heard, can enable emancipated readers in their liberative rereadings, thereby further resourcing faith-based community organizing. An example of this approach to Scripture is seen in Ernesto Cardenal's *The Gospel in Solentiname* which emerged out of his work establishing a BEC and a community of artists on the Solentiname Islands in Nicaragua during the 1960s and 1970s.[41] Within these imaginative reflections on the Christian Gospels, paintings and re-imaginings of Biblical passages were allied with a grass-roots commitment to liberative education and liberation theology. Such a creative reimagining of Scripture can resource the development of imaginative new patterns of faith-based community organizing.

Imagination is a neglected resource within the engagement with the Scriptures of different religious traditions, particularly those characterized by a mode of Enlightenment reasoning that revolves almost exclusively around rationalism. Such an approach to Scripture can marginalize hermeneutical perspectives that validate experience, creativity, culture or non-Eurocentric epistemologies as R. S Sugirtharajah, Mukti Barton, Michael Jagessar, Elsa Tamez and Robert Beckford demonstrate.[42] One way of subverting such an excluding approach to Biblical hermeneutics and enabling the liberative reimagining of Scripture is found in the Ignatian spirituality that is based on the model of prayer set down by Ignatius Loyola in his *Spiritual Exercises* in the sixteenth century. Ignatian spirituality revolves around the conviction that God is personal, evidenced in the life of Jesus and actively present today. The model of imaginative prayer that arises from this Incarnational spirituality focuses on a creative engagement with the Biblical text. Imagining we were there, we ask what it is that we see, hear, feel, think and do.[43] Beckford suggests that Jesus engaged in such creative reimagining: 'Jesus challenges and dismantles the prevailing order . . . He disrupts and overturns the status quo . . . Jesus disruption includes re-ordering the centre and locus of divine activity.'[44] When we ally an Ignatian reimagining of Scripture with the dub practice advocated by Beckford it becomes possible to reengage with familiar stories in a new, conscientized and liberative manner which can help to resource a liberative spirituality of community organizing.

Two examples from the Gospels illustrate the practice of the reimagining of Scripture within a spirituality of community organizing. Although these examples are drawn from the Christian Scriptures, it is an approach that could be used in an amended form in relation to the Scriptures of other faith traditions. It is a model that can be used by individuals and in the setting of the faith-based community organizing reflection groups to which I referred previously. Premised on the core values of a theology of community organizing (prioritizing insignificance, liberative reversals and a hermeneutics of liberative difference), the same simple approach to reimagining is followed in each case. It is for people of faith to fashion their own liberative reimaginings in relation to their own community-organizing context. Here I simply offer brief reflections and outline the approach that a group might take:

1. The passage is read to the group, who are asked to imagine themselves within the story—What is happening? Who is there? Who speaks and who listens? How do you feel within the situation? What might happen as a result of the encounter and how might it impact on the wider community?
2. Each person within the group shares their responses to the passage and to the previous questions.
3. A nominated facilitator encourages the group to draw on their re\imagined engagement with the passage to reflect on the following questions:

    a) What might the passage teach us about the practice of prioritizing insignificance within our community organizing?
    b) What might the passage teach us about the practice of liberative reversals within our community organizing?
    c) What might the passage teach us about a commitment to liberative difference within our community organizing?
    d) How does this passage reenergize us as faith-based community organizers?
    e) What implications does this passage have for the practice of community organizing and for one specific action or campaign in particular?

EXAMPLE 1—NEIGHBOURS AND ENEMIES: THE PARABLE OF THE GOOD SAMARITAN (LUKE 10:25–37)

The parable of the Good Samaritan is one of the best-known passages in the Bible. This familiarity can rob it of its subversive force. Nevertheless, the parable provides faith-based community organizers in superdiverse societies with a rich reflective resource that has the capacity to both enrich and critique organizing practice. The story is familiar. A lawyer asks Jesus what he has to do 'to inherit eternal life' (10:25). He is aware of the command to love God, his neighbour and himself but asks Jesus what this means in practice. Jesus tells him a story of a man who was mugged while travelling from Jerusalem to Jericho. A priest came by and a Levite but neither helped the man (10:31–32). And then a Samaritan on the road stopped and 'bandaged his wounds' before taking the man to a local inn to care for him further (10:33–34). Jesus asks the lawyer, 'Which of these three, do you think, was a neighbour to the man who fell into the hands of the robbers?' (10:36).

Drawing on Ignatian spirituality, we can imagine ourselves into the passage on the basis of our own experience of power or powerlessness. As we inhabit the role of the mugged man, the priest, the Levite or the Samaritan, the tools provided by reader-response approaches to the Bible can enable a critical dialogue between our own experience of exclusion or inclusion, our engagement in community organizing campaigns and the actions of the priest, the Levite and the Samaritan. We attribute meaning to the passage as a result of this internal dialogue and through the discussions of the community organizing reflective group to which we belong. As we 'dub' Luke 10:25–37, we strip away the layers of meaning and domestication that have accrued over the centuries. Such a 'Good Samaritan dub', when guided by a commitment to prioritizing insignificance, liberative reversals and a hermeneutics of liberative difference, identifies three insights that can resource ongoing community organizing. First, the passage raises ethical questions about the nature of neighbourly love and the ethnic or religious limits we place on it— 'Who is my neighbor?' (10:29) Within the context of community organizing in superdiverse societies that are racked by enduring xenophobia, this question is crucial. The Samaritan does not obviously act out his own self-interest but on the basis of agape love, raising questions about the motivation of community organizers. Second, the passage invites community organizers to consider their own use of tension as they reflect on its creative use as a means of liberative education within the ministry of Jesus (10:25–29). The lawyer wants to test Jesus who uses a culturally subversive narrative to challenge the dominant theology of his day. Jesus does not appear to be focused on engineering a measurable change in ethnic power relations but on a potent question demanding an internal response from the lawyer—How do you decide who is your neighbour? Third, the passage invites faith-based community organizers to reflect on the inversion of power dynamics within the parable. It is the so-called insignificant person whom Jesus prioritizes (the Samaritan), inviting the question, who do community organizations prioritize? The passage illustrates the practice of liberative reversals as the marginalized and demonized Samaritan (the stereotypical 'other') becomes the source of radical hospitality and inclusive neighbour love. The Samaritan becomes the template for faith-based community organizers.

EXAMPLE 2—A WOMAN SUFFERING WITH BLEEDING (LUKE 8:40–55)

Drawing on the same approach used in relation to example 1, the faith-based community organizer imagines herself or himself into the passage. Are they part of the crowd, making their own demands on Jesus? Are they Jairus or the woman suffering with continuous haemorrhages? Again, arising from their own social location and experience of community organizing, the faith-based organizer will ask different questions of the passage, of their fellow organizers and of the broad-based community organization to which they belong. Luke 8:40–55 offers a subversive meditation on the nature and use of power that is of direct relevance to the activism of faith-based community organizers. Power is classically perceived in relational terms within community organizing. Its goal has historically been to forge a powerful permanent people's organization that uses the power of organized people to bring about meaningful social change.

This Biblical passage invites community organizers to ask three questions of the broad-based organizations to which they belong—How do we understand power? Who is powerful? Who should be listened to most closely? Luke 8:40–55, like Luke 10:25–37, utilizes narrative tension as an organizing and teaching tool. Power here is understood in hierarchical terms. The passage opens as a powerful man approaches Jesus asking him to heal his dying daughter. He is given a name (Jairus, 8:41) and a status (a synagogue leader, 8:41). As Jairus speaks to Jesus, a powerless woman touches him (8:43–44). She is not given a name but, in spite of her debilitating illness and poverty (8:43), she recognizes and uses her power to reach out, touch and be healed. Luke tells us that Jesus stops and talks with the woman before she is healed. As they talk, Jairus daughter dies, although as the passage concludes she, too, is healed (8:49–51). Priority is given to the powerless and nameless woman and social relations are inverted as Jesus engages in the practice of liberative reversals. He listens first to the woman who has been suffering from bleeding for twelve years and only then to the powerful Jairus.

What might such an encounter have to say to faith-based community organizers? The passage offers an affirmation of the excluded and marginalized within broad-based community organizations but also raises an important question about whose voice is listened to most carefully by community organizers. Is it to the large churches, mosques, synagogues or gurdwaras that send most people to assemblies that community organizations listen to most sympathetically? Alternatively, is the voice of the small and fragile groups that send fewer people and contribute less in terms of membership dues given priority? Luke 8:40–55 invites faith-based organizers to draw upon the practice of liberative reversals to invert power relations within broad-based community organization so that priority is given to those often perceived as insignificant.

Both of these examples draw on well-known passages from the Christian Gospels. However, when the dub practice introduced by Beckford is allied with a reader-response approach, an Ignatian reimagining and the previous questions, such passages can assume new meanings and become energizing resources within a spirituality for community organizing.

CONCLUSION

Within this final chapter I have drawn upon my engagement with the story of the development of community organizing in the United States and in the United Kingdom, my examination of the new politics, my critical dialogue with social theory and my exploration of key theological themes and discussions in order to begin to articulate a liberative theology of community organizing. Such a theology is characterized by three core principles—prioritizing insignificance, liberative reversals and a hermeneutics of liberative difference. When allied with a focus on three key themes—created in the divine image, incarnation and *shalom*—these core principles have the capacity to resource the development of a liberative theology of community organizing in the superdiverse contexts of the United States and the United Kingdom. The emancipatory potential of such a theology rests on the adoption of a liberative model of education and reflexive practice that can foster a critical awareness of the multifaceted nature of oppression and the need for a holistic approach to liberation. Aware of the tendency to burn out amongst activists, I have begun to sketch out the shape of an energizing spirituality of community organizing characterized by deep listening and a reimagining of Scripture. Such a spirituality is an integral aspect of the theology of community organizing and is intended to foster a critical approach amongst faith-based community organizers and to provide strength for the long journey ahead.

As I draw to a close, I will outline a challenging 'Theology of Community Organizing Charter' intended to resource faith-based community organizers in their struggle for justice and to stimulate fresh questions and approaches as we seek a liberative theology of community organizing for the twenty-first century. It is to that concluding task that I now turn.

Part IV
Action

Conclusion

In this book I have begun to fashion an interdisciplinary theology of community organizing, which reframes the core values of liberation theology in order to engage in a credible and holistic manner with the dynamic complexities of life within superdiverse societies in the twenty-first century. In the preceding chapters I have shown that the broad-based community organizing that Saul Alinsky first established in Chicago seventy years ago represents a powerful and widely practiced expression of grass-roots civil society politics and suggested that it provides people of faith with the most effective means of translating their ethical or theological values into ongoing action for social justice in superdiverse societies where faith groups retain significant social capital in socially excluded communities.

To date, analyses of broad-based community organizations have been largely uncritical, and very few studies have offered a multidimensional picture of community organizing. Some articles and books have offered largely uncritical theological reflections aimed at Christian congregations, and others have focused on specific sociological case studies without engaging in broader social analyses or an examination of the nature and motivation of faith-based community organizing. As I noted in the introduction, I am not a neutral observer of community organizing but a long-term critical friend. Consequently, my development of a wide-ranging and interdisciplinary analysis of community organizing has been stimulated by my conviction that it is perhaps the most significant expression of faith-based political activism to have emerged in either the United States or the United Kingdom in the last fifty years and by my desire to see it fulfil its potential to model a cross-cultural and interfaith post secular theology of liberation for the twenty-first century.

Throughout I have argued that community organizing will only fulfil its enormous potential if it embraces its status as a social movement and engages in a more inclusive manner with the broader sweep of social-movement politics, from which it has much to learn. I have also suggested that a far deeper and creative dialogue with social and political theory, urban studies, the cultural politics of difference and cultural studies can enable community organizing to fashion more wide-ranging and multifaceted actions, a deeper understanding of identity in a fluid twenty-first century and grasp the multidimensional nature of networked power, social exclusion and oppression and social justice and liberation.

This book has been framed by my own deep engagement with contextual theology and, as a result, has been implicitly shaped around the contours of the pastoral cycle as shown in Figure 7.1.

In part I ('Experience', chapters 1 and 2), I explored the emergence, development, values, methodology and activism of broad-based community organizing in the United States and the United Kingdom, placing a particular focus on faith-based organizing. In part II ('Analysis', chapters 3 and 4), I brought community organizing into a critical dialogue with what I called the 'new politics' exemplified by social movements and some forms of identity politics and with key insights drawn from social and political theory, urban studies, the cultural politics of difference and cultural studies. On the basis of this dialogue, part 3 ('Reflection') drew upon key foundational values within liberation theology, contextual theology and political theology in order to argue that faith-based community organizing has the capacity to model a post secular theology of liberation for the twenty-first century. In the last chapter, I drew these threads together to outline the key features of a liberative theology of community organizing, which was premised on a hermeneutics of agape love and the reimagining of the classical foundations of liberation theology—a prioritizing of insignificance, the practice of liberative reversals and a hermeneutics of liberative difference. On the basis of the liberative theology of community organizing that I forged in the last chapter, the pastoral cycle moves towards the final stage—'Action'. I close therefore with a call to action and 'A Theology of Community Organizing Charter' which is intended to stimulate further reflection amongst community organizers and faith groups. The twenty statements within the charter are intended to be an invitation to further reflection. It is my hope that

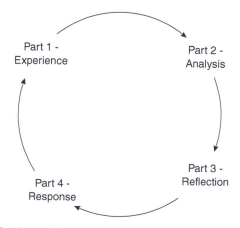

Figure 7.1   The Theology of Community Organizing Cycle

people will embrace it, critique it, develop it further or take it in new directions, thereby forging a liberative theology of community organizing that arises organically from the contexts within which people of faith organize.

A THEOLOGY OF COMMUNITY ORGANIZING CHARTER

1. A theology of community organizing is a contextual political theology.
2. A theology of community organizing is rooted in holistic interdisciplinary social analysis.
3. A theology of community organizing is a theology intended to facilitate social change.
4. A theology of community organizing is founded on a guiding ethic of agape love, not self-interest.
5. A theology of community organizing prioritizes insignificance.
6. A theology of community organizing prioritizes the narratives of marginalized communities.
7. A theology of community organizing enacts the practice of liberative reversals.
8. A theology of community organizing is intercultural and rooted in the both-and third space.
9. A theology of community organizing is shaped by a hermeneutics of liberative difference.
10. A theology of community organizing focuses on dialogical difference rather than hybridity.
11. A theology of community organizing is characterized by a new catholicity and networked activism.
12. A theology of community organizing is committed to radical hospitality.
13. A theology of community organizing emphasizes the importance of holistic liberative education.
14. A theology of community organizing roots liberative education in interfaith reflective groups.
15. A theology of community organizing recognizes the importance of energizing spiritualities.
16. A theology of community organizing emphasizes shared listening: in prayer, in context, to scripture.
17. A theology of community organizing frames communities of faith as liberative social movements.
18. A theology of community organizing is fashioned within subversive spaces of representation.
19. A theology of community organizing resources the common good.
20. A theology of community organizing enables the reweaving of the fabric of society.

Speaking in Fort Wayne, Indiana, on the fortieth anniversary of the murder of Martin Luther King, Jr., the former Chicago community organizer and first African-American President of the United States, Barack Obama told the crowd, 'Dr. King once said that the arc of the moral universe is long but it bends towards justice. It bends towards justice, but here is the thing: it does not bend on its own. It bends because each of us in our own ways put our hand on that arc and we bend it in the direction of justice'.[1]

Community organizing has travelled a long way since it first emerged in the 'Back of the Yards' in Chicago. It has grown into a powerful movement in both the United States and the United Kingdom that is capable not only of building a just and inclusive society but also of harnessing the grass-roots social capital of faith groups even in an age of apparent religious decline. Can community organizers on both sides of the Atlantic embrace the world of broader social movement politics more fully, enter into a deeper and more creative dialogue with social theory and recognize that liberative love, rather than self-interest, provides the strongest foundation for the new politics? If they can then community organizing has the potential to model a post secular theology of liberation capable of transforming our superdiverse twenty-first century and bending the arc of the universe more fully towards justice. Can this book play some small part in this critically important task? That is my hope, but it is a question only others can answer.

Notes

NOTES TO THE INTRODUCTION

1. Peter Berger, 'The Desecularization of the World: A Global Overview', in *The Desecularization of the World: Resurgent Religion and World Politics,* ed. Peter Berger, (Grand Rapids, MI: Eerdmans, 1999), 2.
2. Luke Bretherton, 'A Postsecular Politics? Inter-Faith Relations as a Civic Practice', *Journal of the American Academy of Religion* 79, no. 2 (2011): 353.
3. Bretherton, 'A Postsecular Politics?', 355–356.
4. Robert Beckford, *God and the Gangs: An Urban Toolkit for Those Who Won't Be Sold Out, Bought Out or Scared Out* (London: Darton Longman and Todd, 2004), 8–10.
5. Michel Foucault, *The Archaeology of Knowledge* (Abingdon: Routledge Classics, 2002), 211.
6. Stephen Pattison, *Pastoral Care and Liberation Theology* (London: S.P.C.K, 1997), 34.
7. Gustavo Gutierrez, *A Theology of Liberation* (London: SCM Press, 1974), 11.
8. Chris Shannahan, *Voices from the Borderland: Re-Imagining Cross-Cultural Urban Theology in the Twenty-First Century* (London: Equinox, 2010).
9. Kenneth Leech, *The Sky Is Red: Discerning the Signs of the Times* (London: Darton Longman and Todd, 1997), 50.

NOTES TO CHAPTER 1

1. Andrew Bradstock and Christopher Rowland, eds. *Radical Christian Writings: A Reader* (Oxford: Blackwell Publishing, 2002), 109–125; Alexis de Tocqueville, *Democracy in America,* Volume I, trans. Henry Reeve (London: Oxford University Press, 1946); and Joyce Marlow, *The Tolpuddle Martyrs* (London: Deutsch, 1971).
2. Manuel Castells, *The Network Society; The Power of Identity: The Information Age ... Economy, Society and Culture.* Oxford: Blackwell Publishers Ltd, 2010, 9ff; and Paul Gilroy, *After Empire: Melancholia or Convivial Culture?* (Abingdon: Routledge, 2004), 27 and 39.
3. See, for example, bell hooks, *Feminist Theory: From Margin to Center* (Boston: South End Press, 1984); Robert Corber and Stephen Valocchi, eds. *Queer Studies: An Interdisciplinary Reader* (Oxford: Blackwell, 2002); and Gordon Lynch, *The New Spirituality: An Introduction to Progressive Belief in the Twenty-First Century* (London: I .B. Tauris, 2007).

4. Michael Edwards, *Civil Society* (Cambridge: Polity Press, 2009).
5. Website, http://www.mkgandhi.org/nonviolence, accessed 22 February 2010.
6. Martin Luther King, Jr., 'Letter from Birmingham City Jail' (1963), in *A Testament of Hope: The Essential Writings of Martin Luther King Jr.,* ed. James M. Washington (New York: Harper & Row, 1986), 290ff.
7. Martin Luther King, Jr., 'Love, Law and Civil Disobedience' (1961), in Washington, *A Testament of Hope,* 46.
8. See the work of Stokely Carmichael, formerly a key supporter of King and the Southern Christian Leadership Conference. The phrase formed the title of a key speech by Malcolm X in 1965, the last year of his life.
9. For a description the work of Glide in San Francisco, see the Glide website, accessed 1 February 2010, http://www.glide.org, and Cecil Williams, *No Hiding Place: Empowerment and Recovery for Our Troubled Communities* (San Francisco: Harper & Row, 1993). For further details about Jesse Jackson's involvement in the Rainbow/PUSH coalition, see the Rainbow/PUSH website, http://www.rainbowpush.org, accessed 2 February 2010 For details about Civic Frame, see the Civic Frame website, accessed 2 February 2010, http://www.civicframe.org.
10. For a summary of the work of the Stop the War coalition, see the coalition's website, accessed 1 February 2010, http://www.stopwar.org.uk.
11. Website, http://www.jubilee2000uk.org, accessed 2 March 2010, and http://www.makepovertyhistory.org, accessed 2 March 2010.
12. Jubilee Debt Coalition website, http://www.jubileedebtcampaign.org.uk, accessed 4 May 2013, and Enough Food IF website, http://enoughfoodif.org, accessed 4 May 2013.
13. Paul Henderson and Harry Salmon, *Community Organizing: The UK Context* (London: Community Development Foundation Publications, 1995), 4.
14. Sanford D. Horwitt, *Let Them Call Me Rebel: Saul Alinsky, His Life and Legacy* (New York: Vintage Press, 1992), 525ff; and Jennifer Frost, *An Interracial Movement of the Poor: Community Organizing and the New Left in the 1960s* (New York: New York University Press, 2001), 72.
15. Saul D. Alinsky, *Reveille for Radicals* (New York: Vintage Press, 1946), ix.
16. Saul D. Alinsky, *Rules for Radicals: A Pragmatic Primer for Realistic Radicals* (New York: Vintage Press, 1972), 29 and 34ff.
17. Alinsky, *Rules for Radicals,* 127 and 130.
18. Edward T. Chambers and Michael A. Cowan, *Roots for Radicals: Organizing for Power, Action and Justice* (New York: Continuum, 2003).
19. Website, http://www.industrialareasfoundation.org, accessed 5 May 2013.
20. Website, http://www.industrialareasfoundation.org/content/mission, accessed 5 May 2013.
21. Jay Macleod, *Community Organizing: A Practical and Theological Appraisal* (London: Christian Action, 1993), 4.
22. Macleod, *Community Organizing,* 4.
23. Website, http://www.gamalielfoundation.org, accessed 25 January 2010. The vision statement was approved by the Gamaliel Foundation's National Council of Presidents on 30 November 2005.
24. Website, http://www.gamaliel.org/AboutUs/History.aspx, accessed 5 May 2013.
25. Website, http://www.gamaliel.org/NewsRoom/NewsGamaliel/Today, accessed 26 January 2010.
26. Barack Obama, *Dreams from my Father* (Edinburgh: Cannongate Books, 2007), 133–206.
27. Website, http://www.barakobama.com/learn/about_ofa.php, accessed 27 January 2010.
28. Website, http://www.gamaliel.org/Platform.htm, accessed 26 January 2010.

29. Website, http://www.gamaliel.org/NewsRoom/NewsGamalielToday.htm, page 1 of 2, accessed 26 January 2010.

30. Website, http://www.piconetwork.org/about, accessed 27 January 2010.

31. Website, http://www.piconetwork.org/about, accessed 27 January 2010.

32. Website, http://www.piconetwork.org/issues, accessed 21 February 2010.

33. Website, http://www.piconetwork.org/lifelines, accessed 5 May 2013.

34. Website, http://www.piconetwork.org/bringhealthreformhome, accessed 5 May 2013.

35. Website, http://www.piconetwork.org/about, accessed 27 January 2010.

36. With reference to Paul Seer, see website, http://peabody.vanderbilt.edu/docs/pdf/faculty/vita/2013/Speer_Paul_CV_0113.pdf, accessed 5 May 2013. With reference to Richard L. Wood, see his *Faith in Action: Religion, Race and Democratic Organizing in America* (Chicago: University of Chicago Press, 2002).

37. *New York Times* website, http://www.nytimes.com, accessed 29 January 2010.

38. Website, http://www.huffingtonpost.com/2010/03/22/acorn-disbanding-embattle_n_508893.html, accessed 5 May 2013.

39. Website, http://www.acorn.org/index, accessed 27 January 2010.

40. Robert Fisher, ed. *The People Shall Rule: ACORN, Community Organizing and the Struggle for Economic Justice* (Nashville, TN: Vanderbilt University Press, 2009); and John Atlas, *Seeds of Change: The Story of Acorn, America's Most Controversial Anti-Poverty Community Organizing Group* (Nashville, TN: Vanderbilt University Press, 2010).

41. Website, http://www.thedartcenter.org/mission.html, accessed 27 January 2010.

42. Website, http://www.thedartcenter.org/learn-about-dart/what-makes-us, accessed 5 May 2013

43. Alinsky, *Rules for Radicals,* 63–80.

44. Laurie Green, *Let's Do Theology: A Pastoral Cycle Resource Book* (London: Mowbray, 1990); and Juan Luis Segundo, *The Liberation of Theology* (Maryknoll, NY: Orbis Books, 1976).

45. Peter Reason and Hilary Bradbury, eds. *Handbook of Action Research* (London: Sage, 2006), 1. See also Ernest T. Stringer, *Action Research,* 3rd ed. (London: Sage, 2007).

46. Robert Schreiter, *Constructing Local Theologies* (Maryknoll, NY: Orbis Books, 1985), 18.

47. Dennis A. Jacobsen, *Doing Justice: Congregations and Community Organizing* (Minneapolis: Fortress Press, 2001), 59.

48. Jacobsen, *Doing Justice,* 50ff. See also Dave Beckwith and Christina Lopez, 'Community Organizing: People Power from the Grassroots', Center for Social Change, p. 3, http://www.comm-org.wisc.edu/papers97/beckwith.htm, accessed 24 February 2010.

49. Website, http://www.piconetwork.org/about and http://www.gamaliel.org./Foundation/philosophy, accessed 2 February 2010.

50. Website, http://www.inrc.org/library, accessed 4 February 2010.

51. Henderson and Salmon, *Community Organizing in the UK Context,* 29–30.

52. Website, http://www.midwestacademy.com, and http://www.comm-org.wisc.edu/comm-org, accessed 2 February 2010.

53. Website, http://comm-org.wisc.edu/co/?q=about#history, accessed 5 May 2013.

54. Website, http://www.comm-org.wisc.edu, accessed 2 February 2010.

55. Jurgen Habermas, *The Structural Transformation of the Public Sphere: An Inquiry into a Category of Bourgeois Society,* trans. Thomas Burger and Frederick Lawrence (Cambridge: Polity Press, 1989).

56. Chris Baker and Hannah Skinner, *Faith in Action: The Dynamic Connection between Spiritual and Religious Capital*, final report of the William Temple Foundation's Research Project, 2002–2005.

57. Adam Dinham, Robert Furbey and Vivien Lowndes, eds. *Faith in the Public Realm: Controversies, Policies and Practices* (Bristol: Policy Press, 2009), 5–6.

58. The Gamaliel Foundation Vision Statement, approved November 2005 and revised March 2006, website, http://www.gamaliel.org, accessed 5 February 2010.

59. Beckford, *God and the Gangs,* 115.

60. Jacobsen, *Doing Justice,* 15.

61. Jim Wallis, *God's Politics: Why the American Right Gets It Wrong and the Left Doesn't Get It* (Oxford: Lion Books, 2005), 31. See also the 6 May 2013 interview of Jim Wallis on the 'common good' by journalist Tavis Smiley, website, http://www.pbs.org/wnet/tavissmiley/interviews/sojourners-president-ceo-jim-wallis/?show=17728; accessed 12 May 2013 and Jim Wallis, *On God's Side: What Religion Forgets and Politics Hasn't Learned about Serving the Common Good* (Grand Rapids, MI: Baker Publishing Group, 2013).

62. Wallis, *God's Politics,* 3–4.

63. Wallis, *God's Politics,* 40.

64. Beckford, *God and the Gangs,* 116–121.

65. Website, http://www.gamaliel.org/Platform.htm, accessed 5 February 2010.

66. Website, http://www.gamaliel.org, accessed 5 February 2010.

67. Website, http://www.piconetwork.org/about, accessed 5 February 2010.

68. Website, http://www.thedartcenter.org/mission.html, accessed 27 January 2010.

69. Website, http://www.gamaliel.org, accessed 5 February 2010.

70. Gregory F. Pierce, 'Leaders: Are There Any Volunteers?' in *Activism That Makes Sense: Congregations and Community Organizing* (Chicago, Illinois: ACTA Publications, 1997), 88.

71. Kendall Clark Baker, *Putting Faith into Action: Jesus' Strategic Plan for Mission, a reflection on Congregation, Faith Based Community Organizing* (California: PICO National Clergy Caucus, 1998).

72. Baker, *Putting Faith into Action,* 2.

73. Baker, *Putting Faith into Action,* 6–7.

74. Jacobsen, *Doing Justice,* 81–86.

75. Jill Lawrence, 'Community Organiser Slams Attract Support for Obama', 4 September 2008, website, http://www.usatoday.com, accessed 11 February 2010.

76. Website, http://swampland.blogs.time.com/2008/09/04/what_a_community_organiser_does/, accessed 11 February 2010.

77. Peter Dreier, *Organizing in the Obama Years: A Progressive Moment or a New Progressive Era?* (Comm-Org papers, vol. 15, 2009), website, http://www.comm-org.wisc.edu/papers2009/dreier.htm, accessed 2 February 2010. The Obama for America campaign revolved around the website http://www.barakobama.com, which after his election became Organizing for America.

78. Website, http://www.saddleback.com. Saddleback Church is a conservative evangelical church in California which draws weekly congregations of approximately twenty thousand, making it one of the largest churches in the United States.

79. James Madison, Alexander Hamilton and John Jay, *The Federalist Papers* (London: Penguin Books, 1987).

80. Harvey Mitchell, *America after Tocqueville: Democracy against Difference* (Cambridge: Cambridge University Press, 2002).

81. Edwards, *Civil Society,* 8.
82. At the time of writing, Luke Bretherton is working on a book focusing to a large degree on community organizing provisionally titled *Resurrecting Democracy: Faith, Citizenship and the Politics of the Common Good* (Cambridge University Press).
83. Luke Bretherton, 'The Political Populism of Saul Alinsky and Broad Based Organizing', *The Good Society* 21, no. 2 (2012): 273.
84. Bretherton, 'The Political Populism of Saul Alinsky and Broad Based Organizing', 273.
85. Bretherton, 'The Political Populism of Saul Alinsky and Broad Based Organizing', 273–274.
86. Alinsky, *Rules for Radicals,* xxv.
87. Robert Putnam, *Bowling Alone: The Collapse and Revival of American Community* (New York: Touchstone, 2000), 414.
88. Website, http://www.gallup.com, accessed 12 February 2010. See also the Tearfund report *Churchgoing in the UK,* website, http://www.news.bbc.co.uk, accessed 12 February 2010; and the Pew Forum on Religion and Public Life, *'Nones' on the Rise: One in Five Adults Have No Religious Affiliation* (Washington, DC: The Pew Forum on Religion and Public Life, 2012).
89. Wood, *Faith in Action,* 178.
90. Wood, *Faith in Action,* 184.
91. Grace Davie, *Religion in Britain since 1945: Believing without Belonging* (Oxford: Blackwell, 1994); and *Europe, the Exceptional Case: Parameters of Faith in the Modern World* (London: Darton, Longman and Todd, 2002).

NOTES TO CHAPTER 2

1. Kirk Noden, 'From Olympic People's Guarantees to a Living Wage: Organizing Takes Root in Britain', *Social Policy: Organizing for Social and Economic Justice* 36, no. 2 (2005–2006): 37–38.
2. Henderson and Salmon, *Community Organizing in the UK Context,* 21; MacLeod, *Community Organizing: A Practical and Theological Appraisal,* 5–6; and Mark R. Warren, 'Community Organizing in Britain: The Political Engagement of Faith-Based Social Capital', *City & Community* 8, no. 2 (2009): 118.
3. http://www.londoncitizens.org.uk/pages/members.html, accessed 11 May 2010. This London Citizens' membership directory illustrates its thoroughly multifaith nature.
4. Macleod, *Community Organizing,* 6
5. Henderson and Salmon, *Community Organizing in the UK Context,* 18; and MacLeod, *Community Organizing,* 8.
6. Paul Ballard, ed. *Issues in Church Related Community Work* (Cardiff: University of Wales, 1990), 12.
7. Lina Jamoul and Jane Wills, 'Faith in Politics', *Urban Studies* 45, no. 10 (2008): 10.
8. Jamoul and Wills, *Faith in Politics,* 10. The Matchgirls strike was led by Annie Besant at the Bryant and May factory (East London) in 1888. See website http://www.unionhistory.info/matchworkers/matchworkers.php, accessed 15 March 2010.
9. Paul Bunyan, 'Broad-Based Organizing in the UK: Re-Asserting the Centrality of Political Activity in Community Development', *Community Development*

Journal 45, no. 1 (2010): 123; and Warren, 'Community Organizing in Britain', 105–106.

10. Bunyan, 'Broad-Based Organizing in the UK', 123.
11. http://www.cof.org.uk, accessed 15 March 2010; and the Citizens Organizing Foundation, *Re-Weaving the Fabric of Society: Position Statement of the Citizens Organizing Foundation* (London: the Citizen Organizing Foundation, 2004), 1.
12. Peter Stokes and Barry Knight, *Organizing a Civil Society* (Birmingham: Foundation for a Civil Society, 1997), 20–23.
13. Bunyan, 'Broad-Based Organizing in the UK', 124.
14. Macleod, *Community Organizing,* 8.
15. Macleod, *Community Organizing,* 8.
16. Macleod, *Community Organizing,* 8.
17. Warren, 'Community Organizing in Britain', 107.
18. Warren, 'Community Organizing in Britain', 108.
19. Website, http://www.eastlondonmosque.org.ukk/vision, accessed 19 March 2010.
20. Warren, 'Community Organizing in Britain', 107.
21. Neil Jameson, British Muslims, Influencing UK Public Life: A Case Study', in *British Muslims: Loyalty and Belonging,* edited by Mohammed Siddique Seddon, Dilwar Hussain, and Nadeem Malik. Leicestershire: The Islamic Foundation and the Citizens Organizing Foundation, 2003, 47–48.
22. http://www.londoncitizens.org.uk/pages/training.html, accessed 17 March 2010.
23. http://www.londoncitizens.org.uk/pages/training.html, accessed 2 May 2010.
24. http://www.londoncitizens.org.uk/pages/training.html, accessed 2 May 2010.
25. http://www.progressives.org.uk/articles, accessed 17 March 2010.
26. http://www.guardian.co.uk/politics/2010/feb/19/james-purnell-retrain-community-org, accessed 17 March 2010.
27. Warren, 'Community Organizing in Britain', 108.
28. Website, http://www.geog.qmul.ac.uk/postgraduate/masters/25665.html, accessed 2 May 2010.
29. http://www.citizensuk.org, accessed 3 May 2010.
30. http://www.citizensuk.org, accessed 3 May 2010.
31. http://www.citizensuk.org/telcocitizens (TELCO has sixty-two member groups); http://www.citizensuk.org/shoreditchcitizens (Shoreditch Citizens has twenty-five member groups); http://www.citizensuk.org/southlondoncitizens (South London Citizens has fifty-four members groups); http://www.citizensuk.org/nlcitizens (North London Citizens has forty-two member groups); and http://www.citizensuk.org/chapters/west-london-citizens/wlcitizens (West London Citizens has twenty-three member groups); all accessed 7 May 2013.
32. http://www.citizensuk.org/chapters/citizens-uk-birmingham/birminghamcitizens, http://www.citizensuk.org/chapters/nottingham-citizens/nottscitizens, and http://www.citizensmk.org.uk all, accessed 7 May 2013.
33. Aaron Schutz, 'One-On-Ones', 11 September 2007, p. 1, website, http://www.comm-org, accessed 10 May 2010.
34. Aaron Schutz, 'One-On-Ones', p. 3.
35. Fran Monks, in conversation with Neil Jameson, 'How to Make a Difference', 3 June 2008, p. 1, website, http://howtomakeadifference.net/archives, accessed 11 March 2010.
36. Fran Monks, in conversation with Neil Jameson, 'How to Make a Difference', p. 2.
37. Fran Monks, in conversation with Neil Jameson, 'How to Make a Difference', p. 2.

38. Antonio Gramsci, *Selections from the Prison Notebooks* (London: Lawrence & Wishart, 1971); Edward Said, *Representations of the Intellectual: The 1993 Reith Lectures* (London: Vintage, 1994); and Cornel West, 'Chekhov, Coltrane and Democracy', in Cornel West, ed. *The Cornel West Reader* (New York: Basic Civitas Books, 1999), 554–564.
39. Meet Some of the Leaders of South London Citizens', http://www.south londoncitizens.org.uk, accessed 4 May 2010.
40. http://www.nextleft.org/2009/02/community-organizing-is-answer.html, accessed 11 March 2010. *Next Left* is the blog of the Fabian Society. The Fabian Society is a British socialist forum established in London in 1884. Details at http://www.fabians.org.uk.
41. Jameson, 'British Muslims, Influencing UK Public Policy: A Case Study', 41.
42. The term 'jihad', although often used to refer only to armed struggle, has a far broader and more nuanced definition indicating the duty of all Muslims to struggle for internal holiness and social justice. See, for example, Tariq Ramadan, *Western Muslims and the Future of Islam* (Oxford: Oxford University Press, 2004), 113–114.
43. Citizens Organizing Foundation, *Reweaving the Fabric of Society: Position Statement of the Citizen Organizing Foundation* (London: Citizens Organizing Foundation, 2004), 5–6. In relation to pedagogy, see Paulo Freire, *Pedagogy of the Oppressed* (Middlesex: Penguin Books, 1972).
44. Alinsky, *Rules for Radicals*, 26.
45. http://www.londoncitizens.org.uk home page, accessed 29 May 2010.
46. http://www.citizensuk.org, accessed 29 May 2010.
47. The term 'common good' is widely used to refer to the sharing of social and economic benefits across society in such a way that all people share equally in these benefits. It is a term that has its roots in Judeo-Christian tradition and has been particularly resonant of Roman Catholic social teaching since the publication by Pope Leo XIII in 1891 of *Rerum Novarum*. For an overview of the concept, see David Hollenbach, *The Common Good and Christian Ethics* (Cambridge: Cambridge University Press, 2002). An example of the use of the concept by UK politicians was seen in a speech by the then new Conservative British Prime Minister David Cameron as his Conservative-Liberal Democrat government took power following the May 2010 general election. See website, http://www.catholicherald.co.uk/articles/a0000823.shtml, accessed 1 June 2010.
48. http://www.citizensuk.org, accessed 29 May 2010.
49. Putnam *Bowling Alone*, 2000; John Field, *Social Capital* (London: Routledge, 2003); and Baker and Skinner, *Faith in Action*, 2005.
50. http://www.citizensuk.org, accessed 29 May 2010.
51. http://www.citizensuk.org, accessed 29 May 2010.
52. Jameson, 'British Muslims, Influencing UK Public Life', 46.
53. For further information about the Contextual Theology Centre in East London, see website, http://www.theology-centre.org, accessed 11 May 2010. For information about the Islamic Foundation, see http://www.islamic-foundation.org.uk, accessed 11 May 2010. For information about Luke Bretherton, see http://divinity.duke.edu/academics/faculty/luke-bretherton. It should be noted that Luke Bretherton moved to Duke University in the United States in 2012.
54. http://www.kcl.ac.uk/schools/sspp/education/news/lukebretherton.html, accessed 1 June 2010.
55. Luke Bretherton, *Christianity and Contemporary Politics* (Chichester: Wiley-Blackwell, 2010), 81–88.
56. Bretherton, *Christianity and Contemporary Politics*, 88–89.

57. Macleod, *Community Organizing*, 10.
58. Christopher Baker, *The Hybrid Church in the City: Third Space Thinking* (London: SCM Press, 2009), 70–71 and 77.
59. The Social Gospel emerged primarily amongst liberal Protestants in the United States in the late nineteenth century. The movement arguably declined after World War I but influenced British Anglican theologians such as the Archbishop of Canterbury William Temple and the early work of the US civil rights movement under Martin Luther King, Jr. A key early exponent of the Social Gospel was Walter Rauschenbusch. See Walter Rauschenbusch, *A Theology for the Social Gospel* (New York: Macmillan Co., 1917).
60. Bretherton, *Christianity and Contemporary Politics*, 73–80 and 84–88.
61. 'The Citizens UK General Election Manifesto', 4 May 2010, http://www. citizensukblog.org, accessed 5 May 2010.
62. Ellen Ryan, 'Whatever Happened to Community Organizing?', *Comm-Org Papers* 16 (2010): 8, website, http://www.comm-org.wisc.edu/papers2010/ ryan.htm, accessed 7 May 2010.
63. Jeff Goodwin and James M. Jasper, 'How Are Movements Organized?', in *The Social Movements Reader: Cases and Concepts*, ed. Jeff Goodwin and James M. Jasper (Oxford: Blackwell Publishing, 2003), 166.
64. W. Richard Scott, *Organizations: Rational, Natural and Open Systems*, 5th ed. (Cranbury, New Jersey: Pearson Education International, 2003), 89.
65. Alison Gilchrist, *The Well-Connected Community: A Networking Approach to Community Development*. (Bristol: Policy Press, 2004), 30.
66. Castells, *The Information Age: The Rise of the Network Society*, 1996; and Manuel Castells, ed., *The Network Society: A Cross-Cultural Perspective* (Cheltenham: Edward Elgar, 2004).
67. Zygmunt Bauman, *Liquid Modernity* (Cambridge: Polity Press, 2000); and *Liquid Life* (Cambridge: Polity Press, 2000); Homi Bhabha, *The Location of Culture* (London: Routledge, 1994); and Baker, *The Hybrid Church in the City*, 2009.
68. Gilchrist, *The Well-Connected Community*, 35.
69. Adel M. Abdellatif, 'Good Governance and its Relationship to Democracy and Economic Development', UNDP, The Global Forum III on Fighting Corruption and Safeguarding Integrity, 20–31 May 2003, p. 5, website, http:// www.undp-pogar.org/publications/governance/aa/goodgov.pdf, accessed 13 May 2010.
70. Jamoul and Wills, 'Faith in Politics', 2042.
71. http://www.politics.co.uk/briefings-guides/issue-briefs/employment/national-minimum-wage-$366581.htm. This site offers a useful summary of the background, introduction and level of the national minimum wage. See also website, http://www.hmrc.gov.uk/paye/payroll/day-to-day/nmw.htm, for a UK government summary of the national minimum wage. Both websites accessed 18 May 2010.
72. http://www.buildiaf.org/victories, accessed 18 May 2010. BUILD was affiliated to the Industrial Areas Foundation. The 1994 campaign in Baltimore was followed in 1995 by a similar campaign in Milwaukee and an ACORN-inspired campaign during the same year in Chicago.
73. Margaret Levi, David J. Olson and Erich Steinman, 'Living-Wage Campaigns and Laws', *Working USA* 6, no. 3 (2002–2003): 111 and 112.
74. Sam Hananel, 'Living Wage Could be Factor on Govt Contracts', ABC News, Washington, 26 February 2010, http://abcnews.go.com/Business/ wireStory?id = 9950908, accessed 18 May 2010.
75. http://www.nytimes.com/2013/02/13/us/politics/obama-pushes-for-increase-in-federal-minimum-wage.html, accessed 7 May 2013.

76. http://www.washingtontimes.com/news/2013/mar/15/house-defeats-minimum-wage-increase, accessed 7 May 2013.
77. Jane Wills, 'The Living Wage', *Soundings: A Journal of Politics and Culture* 42, (2009): 33–46.
78. Wills, 'The Living Wage', 34.
79. Thomas N. Corns, Ann Hughes and David Loewenstein, eds., *The Complete Works of Gerrard Winstanley,* vol. 2 (Oxford: Oxford University Press, 2009); and Bradstock and Rowland, *Radical Christian Writings,* 120–137.
80. Wills, 'The Living Wage', 43.
81. Madeleine Bunting, 'It's Time for a Living Wage', *The Guardian,* 26 March 2001, p. 1, http://www.guardian.co.uk/politics/2001/mar/26/workandcareers, accessed 21 May 2010.
82. Jane Wills, *Mapping Low Pay in East London: A Report Written for TELCO's Living Wage Campaign* (London: UNISON and Department of Geography Queen Mary, University of London, 2001). See also http://www.unison.org.uk, accessed 21 May 2010.
83. Wills, *Mapping Low Pay in East London,* 5.
84. Wills, *Mapping Low Pay in East London,* 5.
85. Wills, *Mapping Low Pay in East London,* 3.
86. Catherine Howarth, *Socially Responsible Contracting in London's Financial Districts* (London: The East London Communities Organization, 2003); Yara Evans, Joanna Herbert, Kavita Datta, Jon May, Cathy McIlwaine and Jane Wills, *Making the City Work: Low Paid Employment in London* (London: Queen Mary, University of London, 2005); and Martin Sokol, Jane Wills, Jeremy Anderson, Marg Buckley, Yara Evans, Claire Frew and Paula Hamilton, *The Impact of Improved Pay and Conditions on Low-Paid Urban Workers: The Case of the Royal London Hospital* (London: Queen Mary, University of London, 2006).
87. Alinsky, *Rules for Radicals,* 130.
88. Website, http://www.geog.qmul.ac.uk/livingwage/chronology.html, accessed 17 March 2010, summarizes the timeline of the living wage campaign from 2000 to 2009.
89. Manuel Castells 'City and Culture: The San Francisco Experience', in *The Castells Reader on Cities and Social Theory,* ed. Ida Susser (Oxford: Blackwell Publishers, 2002), 161; and Manuel Castells, *The City and the Grassroots* (Berkeley, CA: University of California Press, 1983).
90. Bretherton, *Christianity and Contemporary Politics,* 74.
91. For details of the London Citizens living wage employer scheme and the 2010 list of living wage employers, see http://www.livingwage.webeden.co.uk, accessed 27 May 2010.
92. Living Wage Unit, *A Fairer London: The 2009 Living Wage in London* (London: Greater London Authority, 2009), 5.
93. http://www.telegraph.co.uk/news/election-2010/7557481/Labour-to-pledge-living-wage-public-sector-pay-rise.html, accessed 27 May 2010.
94. http://www.guardian.co.uk/politics/2010/mar/08/cameron-adviser-backing-living-wage, accessed 27 May 2010.
95. http://www.guardian.co.uk/politics/2013/apr/27/ed-miliband-living-wage, accessed 7 May 2013.
96. Ramadan, *Western Muslims and the Future of Islam,* 192–199.
97. Within the Biblical narrative, see, for example, Exodus 3:7–10, Leviticus 25:1–55, Deuteronomy 15:1–11, Psalm 34:4–7, Psalm 74:19–21, Psalm 146:7–9, Isaiah 1:15–17, Isaiah 58:6–12, Isaiah 61:1–4, Jeremiah 5:27–28, Jeremiah 22:13–17, Amos 2:6–7, Amos 5:10–12, Micah 6:11–16, Matthew 5:3–12, Matthew 25:31–45, Luke 1:46–55, Luke 4:16–21, Luke 6:20–26,

Luke 12:13–21, Luke 16:19–31, Luke 22:24–27, James 2:1–6, James 5:1–6 and 1 John 4:19–21. See also Jorge Pixley and Clodovis Boff, *The Bible, the Church and the Poor* (Tunbridge Well, Kent: Burns & Oates Ltd., 1989), R. S Sugirtharajah, ed., *Voices from the Margin: Interpreting the Bible in the Third World* (London: S.P.C.K, 1991), 227–297; Gustavo, *A Theology of Liberation*, 1974; and Gustavo Gutierrez, *The Power of the Poor in History* (London: SCM Press, 1983), 131–143.

98. Pope Leo XIII, *Rerum Novarum: On the Condition of the Working Classes* (Papal Encyclical, 15 May 1891), especially paragraphs 56, 59, 63, 65 and 66, website, http://www.osjspm.org/majorcod_rerum_novarum_official. aspx, accessed 28 May 2010. See also the Catholic Bishops' Conference of England and Wales, *The Common Good and the Catholic Church's Social Teaching* (Manchester: Gabriel, 1996).

99. Church Action on Poverty, *A Living Wage Church?* (Manchester: Church Action on Poverty, 2002), 5.

100. The Commission on Urban Life and Faith, *Faithful Cities: A Call for Celebration, Vision and Justice* (Peterborough: Methodist Publishing House, 2006).

101. http://www.methodist.org.uk/downloads/coun_layworkers_190107_0726. doc, accessed 28 May 2010.

102. It should be noted that the 2010 General Assembly of the Church of Scotland agreed to help local parishes to pay a living wage to employees, that the 2008 United Reformed Church General Assembly called on all URC Synods and churches to pay a living wage, that one Roman Catholic Diocese has pledged support for the living wage campaign and that all those employed by the Society of Friends in the United Kingdom are paid in excess of the living wage.

103. Jane Wills, *Work, Identity and New Forms of Political Mobilisation: An Assessment of Broad-Based Organizing and London's Living-Wage Campaign* 2008, p. 1–3, website, http://www.identities.org.uk, accessed 28 May 2010.

104. See the agenda for the founding assembly of Birmingham Citizens held on 27 April 2005 in the Great Hall of the University of Birmingham and Sajida Madni, 'Birmingham Citizens Business Plan and Proposal 2009–2010', Birmingham: Birmingham Citizens, 2009 for detail.

105. 'Birmingham Citizens Business Plan and Proposal 2009–2010'. Some of the informal partnerships listed are with Restore, West Midlands Strategic Migration Partnership, Church Action on Poverty, West Midlands Equalities and Human Rights Commission, the Gamaliel Foundation, Faiths for the City, Together Creating Communities Wrexham, Birmingham Roman Catholic Archdiocese, Muslim Aid, Barrow Cadbury Trust, Birmingham City Council, Women's Interfaith Project Birmingham and West Midlands Police Authority. It is important to note that this list encompasses funding bodies and international relationships, as well as more active local and national community organizing partnerships.

106. http://www.changemakersmanchester.org.uk, accessed 10 June 2010.

107. http://www.changemakersmanchester.org.uk home-page, accessed 10 June 2010.

108. http://www.church-poverty.org.uk, accessed 10 June 2010.

109. This conversation took place between myself and Gordon Whitman at the PICO offices in Washington, DC, on 16 April 2010. For reference to Gordon Whitman, see http://www.piconetwork.org, accessed 10 June 2010.

NOTES TO CHAPTER 3

1. See http://www.zapatistarevolution.com; Maria Elena Martinez-Torres, 'Civil Society, the Internet and the Zapatistas', *Peace Review* 13, no. 3 (2001): 347–355, accessed 10 April 2012; and Thomas Olesen, 'Globalising the Zapatistas: From Third World Solidarity to Global Solidarity?', *Third World Quarterly* 25, no. 1 (2004): 255–267.
2. Regarding the Iranian elections in 2009, see *Time* magazine, http://www.time.com/time/world/article/0,8599,1905125,00.html. With reference to protests against the rise in student tuition fees in the United Kingdom in 2011, see http://www.bbc.co.uk/news/magazine-11953186. In relation to the spread of the Arab Spring, see *New Internationalist* magazine http://www.newint.org/books/reference/world-development/case-studies/social-networking-in-the-arab-spring/. Regarding the Occupy movement since October 2011, see http://www.guardian.co.uk/news/blog/2011/oct/14/occupy-england-protests-gather-momentum-via-facebook; http://www.nytimes.com/2011/11/25/business/media/occupy-movement-focuses-on-staying-current-on-social-networks.html. In relation to the sharing of a YouTube video protesting against Joseph Kony, see http://www.youtube.com/watch?v=Y4MnpzG5Sqc.
3. See http://www.presidency.ucsb.edu/data/turnout.php ('2008 US presidential election voter turnout of 57.4%') and http://www.ukpolitical.info/Turnout45.htm (2010 UK general election turnout of 65%). All accessed 12 March 2012.
4. Castells, *The Rise of the Network Society*; *The Power of Identity,* 2nd ed.; and *Communication Power* (Oxford: Oxford University Press, 2011).
5. de Tocqueville, *Democracy in America,Volume I*, 1946
6. Putnam, *Bowling Alone*, 2000. See also Edwards, *Civil Society,* 19.
7. See http://www.teaparty.org/about.php for the movement's description of itself and from the *New York Times,* accessed 13 January 2012; see http://topics.nytimes.com/top/reference/timestopics/subjects/t/tea_party_movement/index.html, accessed 13 January 2012
8. Wallis, *God's Politics,* xxi. Details about Sojourners can be found at http://www.sojo.net; accessed 13 January 2012.
9. Jonathan Birdwell and Mark Littler, *Faithful Citizens: Why Those Who Do God Do Good* (London: Demos, 2012). See also http://www.guardian.co.uk/world/2012/apr/08/religious-people-more-likely-leftwing-demos,   accessed 13 April 2012.
10. Christopher Hitchens, *God Is Not Great: Why Religion Poisons Everything* (London: Allen & Unwin, 2007); and A.C. Grayling, *The Good Book: A Secular Bible* (London: Bloomsbury Publishing, 2011).
11. Robert Furbey, 'Controversies in "Public Faith"', in *Faith in the Public Realm: Controversies, Policies and Practices,* ed. Adam Dinham, Robert Furbey and Vivien Lowndes (Bristol: The Policy Press, 2009), 31.
12. Tariq Modood, 'Civic Recognition and Respect for Religion', in *British Secularism and Religion,* ed. Yahya Birt, Dilwar Hussain and Ataullah Siddiqui (Markfield, Leicestershire: Kube Publishing, 2010), 55.
13. See http://www.tonyblairfaithfoundation.org for information about the Tony Blair Faith Foundation, accessed 10 February 2012.
14. Peter Berger, ed., *The Desecularisation of the World: Resurgent Religion and World Politics* (Grand Rapids, MI: Eerdmans, 1999), 2–4.
15. Steve Bruce, *God Is Dead: Secularisation in the West* (Oxford: Blackwell, 2002).

16. Richard Burgess, Kim Knibbe and Anna Quaas, 'Nigerian-Initiated Pentecostal Churches as a Social Force in Europe: The Case of the Redeemed Christian Church of God', PentecoStudies 9, no. 1 (2010): 97–121. See also website, http://www.telegraph.co.uk/news/religion/8970031/The-return-to-religion.html and http://www.bbc.co.uk/news/uk-22426144, accessed 8 May 2013.
17. Baker and Skinner, *Faith in Action*, 12.
18. John Field, *Social Capital* (London: Routledge, 2003).
19. Adam Dinham and Vivien Lowndes, 'Faith and the Public Realm', in Dinham, Furbey and Lowndes, *Faith in the Public*, 5.
20. Independent Review Team, chaired by Ted Cantle, *Community Cohesion* (London: Home Office, UK Government, 2006).
21. Furbey, 'Controversies in "Public Faith"', 27.
22. Phillip Blond, *Red Tory: How Left and Right Have Broken Britain and How We Can Fix It* (London: Faber & Faber, 2010).
23. Robert Beckford, *God and the Gangs* (London: Darton, Longman & Todd, 2004), 8.
24. Furbey, 'Controversies in "Public Faith"', 31ff.
25. Charles Tilly, *Social Movements, 1768–2004* (London: Paradigm, 2004), 3.
26. Robert Beckford, *Dread and Pentecostal: A Political Theology for the Black Church in Britain* (London: S.P.C.K., 2000), 98ff.
27. Goodwin and Jasper, ed., *The Social Movements Reader*, 3.
28. Anthony Giddens, *Modernity and Self Identity* (Cambridge: Polity Press, 1991), 211–214.
29. Joan Neff Gurney and Kathleen J. Tierney, 'Relative Deprivation and Social Movements: A Critical Look at Twenty Years of Theory and Research', *The Sociological Quarterly* 23, no. 1 (1982): 33.
30. Karl Marx, 'The Communist Manifesto', cited in David McLellan, *Karl Marx: Selected Writings* (Oxford: Oxford University Press, 1977), 227 and 230; and 'Capital: A Critique of Political Economy', cited in McLellan, *Karl Marx: Selected Writings*, 482–483; Emile Durkheim, *The Division of Labour in Society* (New York: The Free Press, 1997), 300–310; and Robert K. Merton, 'Social Structure and Anomie' *American Sociological Review* 3 (October 1938): 672–682.
31. Susan Stall and Randy Stoecker, 'Community Organizing or Organizing Community? Gender and the Crafts of Empowerment', *Gender and Society* 12, no. 6, (1998), 737.
32. Alinsky. *Rules for Radicals,* 53
33. Alinsky, *Rules for Radicals,* 53 and 59.
34. Alinsky, *Rules for Radicals,* 53.
35. Jacobsen, *Doing Justice,* 50ff. See also Dave Beckwith and Christina Lopez, 'Community Organizing: People Power from the Grassroots', Center for Social Change, p. 3, http://www.comm-org.wisc.edu/papers97/beckwith.htm, accessed 17 April 2012.
36. http://www.citizensuk.org/training, accessed 17 April 2012.
37. David McDowell, 'An Organizing Basic: Keep Self-Interest in Mind', 19 November 2010, p. 2, website, http://www.instituteccd.org/library/1693, accessed 17 April 2012.
38. See, for example, http://www.citizensuk.org/campaigns/living-wage-campaign/, http://www.citizensuk.org/campaigns/living-wage-campaign/the-living-wage-foundation/, http://www.livingwage.org.uk/blog and http://www.guardian.co.uk/society/2011/may/01/living-wage-campaign-10-years regarding community organizing campaigns for a living wage in the United Kingdom, and in the United States, see, for example, http://www.universallivingwage.org/,

http://letjusticeroll.org/, http://www.cco.org/issues?id=0002 or http://www.nytimes.com/2006/01/15/magazine/15wage.html?pagewanted=all. All accessed 18 April 2012.

39. Anthony Oberschall, *Social Conflict and Social Movements* (Englewood Cliffs, NJ: Prentice-Hall, 1973), 371ff.
40. Steven Buechler, 'Beyond Resource Mobilization? Emerging Trends in Social Movement Theory', *The Sociological Quarterly* 34, no. 2 (1993).
41. Buechler, 'Beyond Resource Mobilization?', 218.
42. J. Craig Jenkins, 'Resource Mobilization Theory and the Study of Social Movements', *Annual Review of Sociology* 9 (1983): 533.
43. Jacquelien van Stekelenburg and Bert Klandermans, 'Social Movement Theory: Past, Presence & Prospects', in *Movers and Shakers: Social Movements in Africa*, ed. Stephen Ellis and Ineke van Kessel (Leiden: Brill, 2009), 24.
44. Baker and Skinner, *Faith in Action*, 12.
45. van Stekelenburg and Klandermans, 'Social Movement Theory', 25.
46. Buechler, 'Beyond Resource Mobilization?', 222.
47. Buechler, 'Beyond Resource Mobilization?', 225.
48. Doug McAdam, *Political Process and the Development of Black Insurgency, 1930–1970* (Chicago: University of Chicago Press, 1982); Gary Marx and Doug McAdam, *Collective Behavior and Social Movements* (Englewood Cliffs, NJ: Prentice-Hall, 1994); and Doug McAdam, John McCarthy and Mayer Zald, eds., *Comparative Perspectives on Social Movements: Political Opportunities, Mobilizing Structures, and Cultural Framings* (New York: Cambridge University Press, 1996).
49. McAdam, *Comparative Perspectives on Social Movements*, 23.
50. McAdam, *Comparative Perspectives on Social Movements*, 3.
51. van Stekelenburg and Klandermans, 'Social Movement Theory', 28.
52. Freire, *Pedagogy of the Oppressed*, 1972.
53. Castells, *The Power of Identity*, 360.
54. Aldon D. Morris. *Origins of the Civil Rights Movements: Black Communities Organizing for Change* (New York: Free Press, 1986).
55. Aldon Morris, 'Reflections on Social Movements Theory: Criticisms and Proposals', *Contemporary Sociology* 29, no. 3 (2000): 447.
56. Morris, 'Reflections on Social Movements', 447.
57. Andrew Norman, *The Story of George Loveless and the Tolpuddle Martyrs* (Wellington, Somerset: Halsgrove Publishing, 2008). See http://www.tolpuddlemartyrs.org.uk/index.php for information about the Tolpuddle Martyrs.
58. Morris, 'Reflections on Social Movements', 448.
59. Erving Goffman, *Frame Analysis: An Essay on the Organization of Experience* (Cambridge, MA: Harvard University Press, 1974), 21.
60. Robert D. Benford and David A. Snow, 'Framing Process and Social Movements: An Overview and Assessment', *The Annual Review of Sociology* 26 (2000): 614.
61. Marc W. Steinberg, 'Tilting the Frame: Considerations on Collective Action Framing from a Discursive Turn', *Theory and Society* 27, no. 6 (1998): 846.
62. See Beckford, *God and the Gangs*, 90–91; or Margarete Sandelowski and Julie Barroso, 'Reading Qualitative Studies', *International Journal of Qualitative Methods* 1, no. 1 (2002): 76.
63. Schreiter, *Constructing Local Theologies*, 20.
64. Castells, *The Power of Identity*, 61.
65. Goodwin and Jasper, *The Social Movements Reader*, 4.
66. Ron Eyerman and Andrew Jamison. *Social Movement: A Cognitive Approach* (Cambridge: Polity Press, 1991), 367.

67. David F. Aberle, *The Peyote Religion among the Navaho* (Chicago: University of Chicago Press, 1966).

68. See http://www.bringinghope.co.uk/index.asp?idarea=1&idareasub=1 (Bringing Hope) and http://hslda.org (home schooling movement), both accessed 1 March 2012.

69. Paul Gilroy, *There Ain't No Black in the Union Jack* (London: Unwin Hyman, 1987) and http://www.promisekeepers.org (Promise Keepers), accessed 2 March 2012.

70. See http://www.greenpeace.org/international/en (Greenpeace) and http://www.movementforchange.org.uk (Movement for Change), both accessed 10 March 2012.

71. Leonie Sandercock, *Towards Cosmopolis* (Chichester: John Wiley & Sons, 1998), 15ff.

72. Andrew Davey, *Urban Christianity and Global Order* (London: S.P.C.K., 2001), 3.

73. Loretta Winters and Herman DeBosse, *New Faces in a Changing America: Multiracial Identity in the 21st Century* (Thousand Oaks, CA: Sage, 2002); Kimberly McClain DaCosta, *Making Multiracials: State, Family, and Market in the Redrawing of the Color Line* (Palo Alto, CA: Stanford University Press, 2007); and Paul Gilroy, *After Empire: Melancholia or Convivial Culture?* (Abingdon: Routledge, 2004).

74. Steven Vertovec, 'Super-Diversity and Its Implications', *Ethnic and Racial Studies* 30, no. 6 (2007): 1024–1154. The words from Ken Livingstone are cited on 1024.

75. See http://news.bbc.co.uk/1/hi/uk/4266102.stm for an article written in September 2005, just two months after the London bombings and a 2012 YouTube video of a dialogue between Steven Vetovec and Tariq Ramadan in relation to Islam and superdiversity at http://www.youtube.com/watch?v=FESYiuwjetE, accessed 20 March 2012.

76. Castells, *The Power of Identity*, 5–71; and Giddens, *Modernity and Self Identity*, 214–227.

77. Mary Bernstein, 'Identity Politics', *Annual Review of Sociology* 31 (2005): 47–74.

78. Giddens, *Modernity and Self Identity*, chapter 7.

79. Castells, *The Power of Identity*, 6.

80. Castells, *The Power of Identity*, 9.

81. Castells, *The Power of Identity*, 9.

82. Castells, *The Power of Identity*, 421.

83. Castells, *The Power of Identity*, 12.

84. Gilroy, *Against Race: Imagining Political Culture beyond the Colour Line* (Cambridge, MA: Harvard University Press, 2000), 83.

85. Gilroy, *Against Race*, 84.

86. Gaytari Spivak, *In Other Worlds: Essays in Cultural Politics* (New York: Methuen, 1987), 205 and Robert Beckford, *Jesus Dub* (London: Routledge, 2006), 8.

87. Regarding the National Confederation of Dalit Organisations, see http://www.nacdor.org. For information about the Native American Rights Fund, see http://www.narf.org. Both accessed 25 March 2012.

88. See http://www.now.org (National Organization for Women) and http://www.lgcm.org.uk (Lesbian and Gay Christian Movement). Both accessed 25 March 2012.

89. Castells, *The Power of Identity*, 9ff.

90. Gilroy, *Against Race*, 103.

91. Lina Jamoul, *The Art of Politics: Broad Based Organising in Britain*, unpublished PhD thesis. London: Queen Mary University of London, Geography Department, 2006, 21.
92. Jamoul, *The Art of Politics*, 25.
93. Gilroy, *After Empire*, 1.
94. Gilroy, *After Empire*, 161.
95. Independent Review Team, chaired by Ted Cantle, *Community Cohesion*, 2001.
96. See http://www.bbc.co.uk/news/uk-politics-12371994 for a BBC News report of British Prime Minister David Cameron's speech in Munich in 2011 and http://www.bbc.co.uk/news/uk-politics-12376304 for a further BBC report noting criticism that the speech coincided with a large English Defence League demonstration in the United Kingdom in the same week. Accessed 27 March 2012.
97. The birther movement sought to raise questions about the right of Barack Obama to be the president of the United States from 2008 onwards. See http://www.cbsnews.com/8301–503544_162–20057958–503544.html in the United States or http://www.guardian.co.uk/world/2009/jul/28/birther-movement-obama-citizenship in the United Kingdom for a commentary on the issue. Both accessed 27 March 2012.
98. Tariq Modood, *Multiculturalism* (Cambridge: Polity Press, 2007); Iris Marion Young, *Justice and the Politics of Difference* (Princeton, NJ: Princeton University Press, 1990), 163–191; West, *The Cornel West Reader*, 136; and Sandercock, *Towards Cosmopolis*, 76.
99. Young, *Justice and the Politics of Difference*, 157.
100. Young, *Justice and the Politics of Difference*, 59; and Sandercock, *Towards Cosmopolis*, 111.
101. West, *The Cornel West Reader*, 119.
102. Cornel West, *Race Matters: Philosophy and Race in America* (Boston, MA: Beacon Press, 1993), 32
103. See http://www.newsds.org/who-sds for details about Students for a Democratic Society, http://www.glide.org with reference to Glide Memorial Church, San Francisco, http://www.rainbowpush.org for information about Rainbow/PUSH, http://www.tikkun.org in relation to the Tikkun network, http://spiritualprogressives.org/newsite for details about the Network of Spiritual Progressives and http://www.occupytogether.org to find out more about Occupy. All accessed 1 April 2012.
104. See for details about the emergence of Rock against Racism in 1978 http://www.independent.co.uk/arts-entertainment/music/features/rock-against-racism-remembering-that-gig-that-started-it-all-815054.html, accessed 2 April 2012; or Gilroy, *There Ain't No Black in the Union Jack*, 121ff; http://www.respectparty.org regarding Respect; http://www.hopenothate.org.uk for information about Hope Not Hate, accessed 2 April 2012; http://www.cityofsanctuary.org to read about the City of Sanctuary movement, accessed 2 April 2012 and http://stopwar.org.uk for details about the Stop the War coalition accessed 2 April 2012.
105. Richard Phillips and Jamil Iqbal, 'Muslims and the Anti-War Movements', *Muslim Spaces of Hope: Geographies of Possibility in Britain and the West*, ed. Richard Phillips (London: Zed Books, 2009), 163–179; Tahir Abbas, *Islamic Radicalism and Multicultural Politics: The British Experience* (London: Routledge, 2009), 150; and Tariq Modood, 'Muslims and the Politics of Difference', in *Muslims in Britain: Race, Place and Identities*, ed. Peter Hopkins and Richard Gale (Edinburgh: Edinburgh University Press, 2009), 198 and 206.

106. Michael Peter Smith, *Transnational Urbanism* (Oxford: Blackwell, 2001), 4.
107. Saskia Sassen, *Globalisation and its Discontents* (New York: New Press, 1998), xxi.
108. Castells, *The Rise of the Network Society,* 412ff; and Castells, *Communication Power,* 17ff.
109. Castells, *Communication Power,* 21.
110. Castells, *The Rise of the Network Society,* 415; and Castells, *Communication Power,* 36.
111. Manuel Castells, 'Grassrooting the Space of Flows', in *The Global Resistance Reader*, ed. Louise Amoore (New York: Routledge, 2005), 367.
112. See http://www.adbusters.org/ for information about the 'culture jamming' of Ad-Busters, accessed 15 April 2012.
113. Donatella Della Porta, Massimiliano Andreatta, Lorenzo Mosca and Herbert Reiter, *Globalization from Below: Transnational Activists and Protest Networks* (Minneapolis: University of Minneapolis Press, 2006).
114. Goodwin and Jasper, *The Social Movements Reader,* 54.
115. Herbert G. Blumer, 'Collective Behaviour', in *Principles of Sociology,* 3rd ed., ed., Alfred McClung Lee (New York: Barnes and Noble, 1969), 65–121; and Charles Tilly, *From Mobilization to Revolution* (Reading, MA: Addison-Wesley, 1978).
116. Anthony Oberschall, 'Opportunities and Framing in the Eastern European Revolts of 1989', in McAdam, McCarthy and Zald, eds., *Comparative Perspectives on Social Movements,* 93–121; and Gunther Schonleitner, 'World Social Forum: Making Another World Possible?', in *Globalizing Civic Engagement: Civil Society and Transnational Action,* ed. John Clark (London: Earthscan Publications, 2003), 127–150; see http://www.forumsocialmundial.org.br/index.php?cd_language=2, accessed 12 April 2012.
117. Manuel Castells, 'City and Culture: The San Francisco Experience', in *The Castells Reader*, ed. Susser, 161. See further detailed analysis in Manuel Castells, *The City and the Grassroots* (Berkeley CA: University of California Press, 1983).
118. http://www.guardian.co.uk/world/occupy-movement. This website for the *Guardian* newspaper provides an overview of the Occupy movement whose website is found at http://www.occupytogether.org, both accessed 14 April 2012.
119. http://www.citizensuk.org/campaigns/living-wage-campaign/ or http://www.geog.qmul.ac.uk/livingwage/ and http://www.church-poverty.org.uk/living-wage/churches-and-the-living-wage, all accessed 12 April 2012.
120. http://www.tht.org.uk/ (Terence Higgins Trust), http://www.earthday.org (the Earth Day network) and http://www.telegraph.co.uk/news/uknews/1568909/Women-priests-and-their-continuing-battle.html, accessed 12 April 2012.
121. Antonio Gramsci, *Selections from the Prison Notebooks* (London: Lawrence & Wishart, 1971), 10ff.
122. Jane Wills' website is found at http://www.geog.qmul.ac.uk/staff/willsj.html. Her key publications on the living wage include 'The Living Wage', Soundings: A Journal of Politics and Culture (2009): volume 42, 33–46; and 'The London Living Wage', in Global Civil Society Yearbook 2009: Poverty and Activism, ed. A. Kumar, J. A. Scholte, M. Kaldor, M. Glasius, H. Seckinelgin and H. Anheier (London: Sage, 2009). Details about the engagement of current London mayor Boris Johnson with a London living wage first introduced by his predecessor Ken Livingstone in 2005 can be found at http://www.london.gov.uk/media/press_releases_mayoral/mayor-increases-london-living-wage-four-international-employers-sign. Accessed 20 April 2012.

123. Some (mostly London-based) employers that have instituted a living wage between 2005 and 2012 are the London School of Economics, the Institute of Education, Queen Mary College, School of Oriental and African Studies, Birkbeck College, the London School of Hygiene and Tropical Medicine, Goldsmiths College, Barclays Bank, KPMG, HSBC, PriceWaterhouseCoopers and the London boroughs of Ealing, Tower Hamlets and Lewisham.

124. See http://www.citizensuk.org/2010/07/citizens-uk-general-election-assembly-2010/ for a summary of the Citizens UK general election assembly, 3 May 2010.

125. See http://www.ifs.org.uk/pr/poverty_pr_1011.pdf and http://www.ifs.org.uk/comms/comm121.pdf. The Institute for Fiscal Studies reports 'Universal Credit Not Enough to Prevent a Decade of Rising Poverty' (October 2011) and 'Child and Working Age Poverty 2010–2020' (October 2011) noted that in 2010, 2.5 million children and 2.1 million working-age adults in the United Kingdom were living in 'absolute' poverty (defined relatively as 60% or less of the median national annual income) and projected that in 2020 on current trends there are likely to be 4.7 million working-age adults living in 'absolute' poverty. Accessed 2 May 2012.

126. William Gamson, 'Defining Movement "Success"', in Goodwin and Jasper, eds., *The Social Movements Reader*, 350.

NOTES TO CHAPTER 4

1. Henri Lefebvre, *The Production of Space*, trans. Nicholson-Smith, Donald (1974; Oxford: Blackwell, 1991).
2. Lefebvre, *The Production of Space*, 33.
3. Lefebvre, *The Production of Space*, 38.
4. Lefebvre, *The Production of Space*, 42.
5. Edward Soja, *Postmetropolis: Critical Studies of Cities and Regions* (Oxford: Blackwell, 2000).
6. Edward Soja, *Thirdspace: Journeys to Los Angeles and Other Real-and-Imagined Places* (Cambridge, MA: Blackwell, 1996), 65.
7. T. J. Gorringe, *A Theology of the Built Environment: Justice, Empowerment, Redemption* (Cambridge: Cambridge University Press, 2002), 27.
8. Gorringe, *A Theology of the Built Environment*, 7–8.
9. Kim Knott. 'Spatial Theory and Spatial Methodology, Their Relationship and Application: A Transatlantic Engagement', *The Journal of the American Academy of Religion* 77, no. 2 (2009): 77; Sandercock, *Towards Cosmopolis*, 15.
10. Kim Knott, *The Location of Religion: A Spatial Analysis* (London: Equinox, 2005), 11.
11. Eugene M. McCann, 'Race, Protest and Public Space: Contextualizing Lefebvre in the US City', *Antipode* 31 (1999), 181.
12. Bhabha, *The Location of Culture*, 19.
13. Bhabha, *The Location of Culture*, 25.
14. Anthony Pinn, *Why Lord? Suffering and Evil in Black Theology* (New York: Continuum, 1999), 116ff.
15. Bhabha, *The Location of Culture*, 28.
16. Baker, *The Hybrid Church in the City*, 16.
17. Bhabha, *The Location of Culture*, 37.
18. John Ehrenberg, *Civil Society: The Critical History of an Idea* (New York: New York University Press, 1999), 3–19.
19. Ehrenberg, *Civil Society: The Critical History of an Idea*, 41.

20. Ehrenberg, *Civil Society: The Critical History of an Idea*, 85.
21. Michael Edwards, 'Civil Society', *Encyclopaedia of Informal Education*, http://www.infed.org/association/civil_society.htm, p1 of 7, accessed 31 August 2012.
22. Edwards, *Civil Society*, 2.
23. Edwards, *Civil Society*, 7.
24. Edwards, *Civil Society*, 8.
25. Edwards, *Civil Society*, 10.
26. Gramsci, *Selections from the Prison Notebooks*, 10–12; and Anne F. Showstack, *Antonio Gramsci: An Introduction to His Thought* (London: Pluto Press, 1970), 129–204.
27. Simone Chambers and Jeffrey Kopstein, 'Bad Civil Society', *Political Theory* 29, no. 6 (2001): 837–865.
28. http://www.citizensuk.org/, accessed 31 August 2012.
29. Edwards, *Civil Society*, 46.
30. Edwards, *Civil Society*, 47.
31. Edwards, *Civil Society*, 47.
32. Edwards, *Civil Society*, 47.
33. See the website of the Jewish interfaith network Tikkun, for example, http://www.tikkun.org/nextgen, accessed 1 September 2012.
34. Tony Blair, 'The Third Way' (April 1998), quoted in Anthony Giddens, *The Third Way and Its Critics* (Cambridge: Polity Press, 2000), 5.
35. John Kenneth Galbraith, *The Affluent Society* (1958; New York: Houghton Mifflin, 1998); and *The Good Society: The Humane Agenda* (New York: Houghton Mifflin, 1996).
36. Galbraith, *The Good Society*, 4.
37. Joan Rutherford and Hetan Shah, eds., *The Good Society: Compass Programme for Renewal* (London: Lawrence & Wishart, 2006), 15.
38. John Cruddas and Andrea Nahles, *Building the Good Society: The Project of the Democratic Left*, 2012, p. 2, http://clients.squareeye.net/uploads/compass/documents/good%20society%20english%20WEB.pdf, accessed 5 February 2013.
39. Pope Leo XII, *Rerum Novarum*, 1891, paragraph 42, http://www.vatican.va/holy_father/leo_xiii/encyclicals/documents/hf_l-xiii_enc_15051891_rerum-novarum_en.html, accessed 5 September 2012.
40. Archbishop of Canterbury's Commission on Urban Priority Areas, *Faith in the City: A Call for Action by Church and Nation* (London: Church House, 1985); and Commission on Urban Life and Faith, *Faithful Cities: A Call for Celebration, Vision and Justice* (London: Methodist Publishing House, 2006).
41. Bishops Conference of England and Wales, *Choosing the Common Good* (Stoke-on-Trent: Alive Publishing, 2010), 8.
42. Bishops Conference of England and Wales, *Choosing the Common Good*, 8.
43. Edwards, *Civil Society*, 63.
44. Jurgen Habermas, *The Structural Transformation of the Public Sphere: An Inquiry into a Category of Bourgeois Society*, trans. Thomas Burger and Fredrick Lawrence (Cambridge, MA: MIT Press, 1989), 1.
45. Habermas, *The Structural Transformation of the Public Sphere*, 3–14.
46. Habermas, *The Structural Transformation of the Public Sphere*, 54.
47. Craig Calhoun, ed., *Habermas and the Public Sphere* (Cambridge, MA: MIT Press, 1992), 3.
48. Nancy Fraser, 'Rethinking the Public Sphere: A Contribution to the Critique of Actually Existing Democracy' *Social Text* no. 25–26 (1990): 56–80. See also Nancy Fraser, 'Transnationalizing the Public Sphere', March 2007,

http://eipcp.net/transversal/0605/fraser/en, taken from the website of the European Institute for Progressive Cultural Policies, accessed 5 February 2012.

49. Nancy Fraser, 'Rethinking the Public Sphere', in Calhoun, *Habermas and the Public Sphere*, 115.
50. Fraser, 'Rethinking the Public Sphere', 117.
51. Fraser, 'Rethinking the Public Sphere', 118.
52. Fraser, 'Rethinking the Public Sphere', 116.
53. Jamoul, *The Art of Politics*, 21.
54. Jamoul, *The Art of Politics*, 25.
55. Jamoul, *The Art of Politics*, 23.
56. Amin Ash and Nigel Thrift, *Cities: Reimagining the Urban* (Cambridge: Polity Press, 2002), 140; and Sandercock, *Towards Cosmopolis*, 119 and 129.
57. Edwards, *Civil Society*, 68.
58. Steven Vertovec, 'Super-Diversity and Its Implications', 1024–1054; and *Transnationalism* (London: Routledge, 2009).
59. Vertovec, 'Super-Diversity', 1027.
60. Sandercock, *Towards Cosmopolis*, 76.
61. Vertovec, 'Super-Diversity', 10245–1046.
62. Castells, *The Rise of the Network Society*, 412.
63. Smith, *Transnational Urbanism*, 4ff.
64. Gilroy, *There Ain't No Black in the Union Jack*, 247.
65. Websites, The English Defence League, http://englishdefenceleague.org, accessed 7 February 2013; the Ku Klux Klan, http://kkk.bz; accessed 7 February 2013 and The Southern Poverty Law Center, http://www.splcenter.org/get-informed/hate-map, accessed 7 February 2013.
66. Spivak, *In Other Worlds*, 205; and Castells, *The Power of Identity*, 9.
67. Young, *Justice and Politics of Difference*, 157.
68. Young, *Justice and Politics of Difference*, 163.
69. Young, *Justice and Politics of Difference*, 170 and 171.
70. West, *Race Matters*, 32.
71. Tariq Modood, *Multiculturalism* (Cambridge: Polity Press, 2007), 10ff; and *Still Not Easy Being British: Struggles for a Multicultural Citizenship* (London: Trentham Books, 2010).
72. Samuel Huntingdon, 'The Clash of Civilisations?' *Foreign Affairs* 72, no. 3 (Summer 1993): 22–49; and *The Clash of Civilisations and the Remaking of World Order* (New York: Simon & Schuster, 1996).
73. http://www.bbc.co.uk/news/uk-13686586, accessed 9 February 2013 and HM Government, *The Prevent Strategy: A Guide for Local Partners in England*, 2007, https://www.education.gov.uk/publications/eOrderingDownload/Prevent_Strategy.pdf, accessed 9 February 2013.
74. http://www.bbc.co.uk/news/uk-politics-12371994, accessed 9 February 2013.
75. Gilroy, *After Empire*, 26.
76. Office for National Statistics, http://www.ons.gov.uk/ons/rel/census/2011-census/key-statistics-for-local-authorities-in-england-and-wales/rpt-ethnicity.html#tab-Changing-picture-of-ethnicity-over-time, accessed 9 February 2013; website, *The Guardian* newspaper, http://www.guardian.co.uk/uk/blog/2012/dec/11/census-data-released-live-coverage#block-50c71da495cbcfe457e3dbef, accessed 9 February 2013; and website, *Daily Telegraph* newspaper, http://www.telegraph.co.uk/news/uknews/8811861/Britain-more-diverse-than-previously-thought.html, accessed 9 February 2013.
77. Stuart Hall, 'New Ethnicities', in *Stuart Hall: Critical Dialogues in Cultural Studies*, ed. David Morley and Kuan-Hsing Chen (London: Routledge, 1996); and Stuart Hall, 'Cultural Identity and Diaspora', in *Theorising Diaspora*, ed. Jana Evans Braziel and Anita Mannur (Oxford: Blackwell, 2003), 244.

78. Gilroy, *After Empire*, 161.
79. Beckford, *Dread and Pentecostal*,150–151.
80. Nasar Meer and Tariq Modood, 'Interculturalism, Multiculturalism or Both?', in *Political Insight* (Oxford: Wiley-Blackwell, 2012), 30–33.
81. Beckford, *God and the Gangs*, 21.
82. Hans Kung, *Global Responsibility: In Search of a New World Ethic* (London: SCM Press, 1991); and Hans Kung, ed., *Yes to a Global Ethic* (New York: Continuum, 1996).
83. Parliament of the World's Religions, prepared by Hans Kung, *Declaration Toward a Global Ethic* (London: SCM Press, 1993).
84. Jacques Derrida, *The Politics of Friendship*, trans. George Collins (New York: Verso, 1997); or On Cosmopolitanism and Forgiveness (London: Routledge, 2001); and Immanuel Kant, *Perpetual Peace* (Cambridge: Cambridge University Press, 1991).
85. David Held, *Cosmopolitanism: Ideals and Realities* (Cambridge: Polity Press, 2010), 77.
86. Robert Schreiter, *The New Catholicity: Theology between the Global and the Local* (Maryknoll, NY: Orbis, 1997).
87. Gilroy, *After Empire*, 66 and 67.
88. Gilroy, *After Empire*, 80, 83, 89 and 90
89. Gilroy, *After Empire*, 83.
90. Lyda Judson Hanifan, 'The Rural School Community Center', *Annals of the American Academy of Political and Social Science* 67 (1916): 130–138.
91. Pierre Bourdieu, 'Forms of Capital', in *Handbook of Theory and Research for the Sociology of Education*, ed. J.C. Richards (New York: Greenwood Press, 1983), 249.
92. Field, *Social Capital*, 1.
93. Putnam, *Bowling Alone*, 19.
94. Putnam, *Bowling Alone*, 22–23.
95. Baker and Skinner, *Faith in Action*, 2006, 23ff.
96. Baker and Skinner, *Faith in Action*, 23.
97. Baker and Skinner, *Faith in Action*, 26–27, original emphasis.
98. Pew Research Center, *Santorum Voters Disagree: More See 'Too Much' Religious Talk by Politicians*, 21 March 2012, http://www.pewforum.org/uploadedFiles/Topics/Issues/Politics_and_Elections/Religion%20Release.pdf, accessed 11 March 2013.
99. Pew Forum on Religion and Public Life, *Faith-Based Programs Still Popular, Less Visible—Results from the 2009 Annual Religion and Public Life Survey*, 16 November 2009, http://www.pewforum.org/uploadedfiles/Topics/Issues/Church-State_Law/faithbased09.pdf, accessed 11 March 2013.
100. Therese O'Toole 'Faith and the Coalition: A New Confidence to "Do God"?', *Muslim Participation in Contemporary Governance Working Paper*, no. 3, University of Bristol: Centre for the Study of Ethnicity and Citizenship, February 2012, 2.
101. O'Toole, 'Faith and the Coalition', 5.
102. Birdwell and Littler, *Faithful Citizens*, 15.
103. The Commission on Urban Life and Faith, *Faithful Cities*, 3.
104. Antonio Gramsci, *Prison Notebooks*, vol. 3, ed. and trans. Joseph A. Buttigieg (New York: Columbia University Press, 2007), 168.
105. Frantz Fanon, *Black Skin White Masks* (1952; London: Pluto Press, 1986).
106. Paulo Freire, *Pedagogy of the Oppressed* (Middlesex: Penguin Books, 1972) and *Cultural Action for Freedom* (Harmondsworth: Penguin Education, 1972).
107. Paulo Freire, *Pedagogy of Indignation* (Boulder: Paradigm Publishers, 2004), 66.

108. Gramsci, *Selections from the Prison Notebooks,* 12.
109. Gramsci, *Selections from the Prison Notebooks,* 10.
110. Gramsci, *Selections from the Prison Notebooks,* 418.
111. Gutiérrez, *A Theology of Liberation,* 13.
112. Gutiérrez, *The Power of the Poor in History,* 103.
113. West, *The Cornel West Reader,* 551.
114. Said, *Representations of the Intellectual,* 13
115. Tavis Smiley and Cornel West, *The Rich and the Rest of Us: A Poverty Manifesto* (New York Smiley Books, 2012).
116. John Vincent, *Into the City* (London: Epworth Press, 1982), 110–12.
117. Schreiter, *Constructing Local Theologies,* 16–21.
118. Comm-Org can be found at http://comm-org.wisc.edu/co, accessed 12 March 2013.

NOTES TO CHAPTER 5

1. Stephen Bevans, *Models of Contextual Theology* (Maryknoll, NY: Orbis Books, 2002), 70ff.
2. Pinn, *Why Lord?,* 54ff.
3. Gutierrez, *The Power of the Poor in History,* 202.
4. Gutierrez, *The Power of the Poor in History,* 204.
5. Gutierrez, *A Theology of Liberation,* 295.
6. Gutierrez, *A Theology of Liberation,* 176.
7. Leonardo Boff and Clodovis Boff, *Introducing Liberation Theology* (Kent: Burns & Oates, 1987), 55.
8. Gutierrez, *The Power of the Poor in History,* 193.
9. See Marcella Althaus-Reid, *Liberation Theology and Sexuality* (Aldershot: Ashgate, 2006); and Ivan Petrella, *The Future of Liberation Theology: An Argument and a Manifesto* (Aldershot: Ashgate, 2004); or *Beyond Liberation Theology: A Polemic* (London: SCM Press, 2008), for example.
10. Daniel M. Bell, Jr., *Liberation Theology after the End of History: The Refusal to Cease Suffering* (New York: Routledge, 2001).
11. Shannahan, *Voices from the Borderland,* 2010.
12. Gutierrez, *A Theology of Liberation,* 15.
13. Gutierrez, *A Theology of Liberation,* 7.
14. Boff and Boff, *Introducing Liberation Theology,* 39.
15. Gutierrez, *A Theology of Liberation,* 302.
16. Alinsky. *Rules for Radicals,* 53
17. Alinsky, *Rules for Radicals,* 53.
18. Website, http://www.citizensuk.org/training, accessed 17 April 2012.
19. Jacobsen, *Doing Justice,* 50.
20. Jacobsen, *Doing Justice,* 50.
21. Jacobsen, *Doing Justice,* 52 and 53.
22. Jacobsen, *Doing Justice,* 51.
23. Jacobsen, *Doing Justice,* 50.
24. Joseph F. Fletcher, *Situation Ethics: The New Morality* (Louisville, KY: Westminster John Knox Press, 1966), 69.
25. Pope Leo XII, *Rerum Novarum,* 1891, paragraph 42, website, http://www.vatican.va/holy_father/leo_xiii/encyclicals/documents/hf_l-xiii_enc_15051891_rerum-novarum_en.html, accessed 20 February 2013.
26. Baker, *The Hybrid Church in the City,* 71.
27. Baker, *The Hybrid Church in the City,* 71.

28. Catholic Bishops Conference of England and Wales, *The Common Good and the Catholic Church's Social Teaching*, paragraph 13.
29. Catholic Bishops Conference of England and Wales, *The Common Good*, paragraphs 39–40.
30. Bishops Conference of England and Wales, *Choosing the Common Good* (Stoke-on-Trent: Alive Publishing, 2010), 8.
31. Bishops Conference of England and Wales, *Choosing the Common Good*, 8.
32. Shannahan, *Voices from the Borderland*, 224ff.
33. Website, http://www.piconetwork.org/immigration, accessed 23 April 2013.
34. Citizens for Sanctuary, website, http://www.citizensforsanctuary.org.uk, accessed 27 March 2013; and http://www.migrantvoice.org/indx.php?option=com_content&view=article&id=174, accessed 27 March 2013.
35. Citizens for Sanctuary, http://www.citizensuk.org/campaigns/citizens-uk-diaspora-caucus/citizens-for-sanctuary/sanctuary-pledge and Churches Together in Britain and Ireland,, http://www.ctbi.org.uk/pdf_view.php?id=445 (see p8 re sanctuary pledge), accessed 27 March 2013.
36. http://www.citizensukblog.org/category/citizens-for-sanctuary-campaign, accessed 27 March 2013.
37. http://www.guardian.co.uk/commentisfree/2012/oct/23/britain-sill-locking-up-children
38. Beckford, *Jesus Dub*, 1.
39. Beckford, *Jesus Dub*, 67.
40. Shannahan, *Voices from the Borderland*, 85 and 233–236.
41. Beckford, *Jesus Dub*, 91–92.
42. Schreiter. *The New Catholicity*, 2.
43. Schreiter, *The New Catholicity*, 4.
44. Schreiter, *The New Catholicity*, 15.
45. Schreiter, *The New Catholicity*, 26.
46. Schreiter, *The New Catholicity*, 15.
47. Schreiter, *The New Catholicity*, 59.
48. Schreiter, *The New Catholicity*, 12.
49. Schreiter, *The New Catholicity*, 28.
50. Schreiter, *The New Catholicity*, 43.
51. Schreiter, *The New Catholicity*, 54.
52. Schreiter, *The New Catholicity*, 60.
53. Schreiter, *The New Catholicity*, 95.
54. Schreiter, *The New Catholicity*, 95.
55. Schreiter, *The New Catholicity*, 95.
56. Schreiter, *The New Catholicity*, 132.
57. Baker, *The Hybrid Church*, 2
58. Baker, *The Hybrid Church*, 2
59. Baker, *The Hybrid Church*, 3. In the 2001 National Census in the United Kingdom, 677,177 people self-defined as mixed race, up from 228,504 identifying as 'Black—Other' in 1991, the closest category in 1991 to mixed race. In the 2011 National Census, produced after Baker's book was published, this number had doubled—1.2 million people self-defined as mixed race. See http://www.guardian.co.uk/uk/blog/2012/dec/11/census-data-released-live-coverage, accessed 10 May 2013.
60. Jonathan Hearns, *Rethinking Nationalism: A Critical Introduction* (Basingstoke, Hampshire: Palgrave Macmillan, 2006), 20–42.
61. Baker, *The Hybrid Church*, 16.
62. Baker, *The Hybrid Church*, 18. See also John Reader and Christopher R. Baker, eds. *Entering the New Theological Space: Blurred Encounters of Faith, Politics and Community* (Farnham, Surrey: Ashgate, 2009).

63. Bhabha, *The Location of Culture*, 21 and 28.

64. Baker, *The Hybrid Church*, 24.

65. Pete Ward, *Liquid Church* (Carlisle: Paternoster Press, 2002); and Baker, *The Hybrid Church*, 130.

66. Baker, *The Hybrid Church*, 147 and 139.

67. Baker, *The Hybrid Church*, 140.

68. Baker, *The Hybrid Church*, 147.

69. Bretherton, *Christianity and Contemporary* Politics, 17. See also 32–52.

70. Bretherton, *Christianity and Contemporary Politics*, 54.

71. Bretherton, *Christianity and Contemporary Politics*, 50.

72. Bretherton, *Christianity and Contemporary Politics*, 106 and 105.

73. Bretherton, *Christianity and Contemporary Politics*, 147.

74. Bretherton, *Christianity and Contemporary Politics*, 141.

75. Bretherton, *Christianity and Contemporary Politics*, 211.

76. Luke Bretherton, 'A Post-Secular Politics? Inter-Faith Relations as a Civic Practice', *Journal of the American Academy of Religion* 79, no. 2 (2011): 360.

77. Bretherton, *Christianity and Contemporary Politics*, 148.

78. Bretherton, *Christianity and Contemporary Politics*, 152ff and 158.

79. Bretherton, *Christianity and Contemporary Politics*, 212.

80. Bretherton, *Christianity and Contemporary Politics*, 211.

81. Bretherton, *Christianity and Contemporary Politics*, 146.

82. Bretherton, *Christianity and Contemporary Politics*, 145.

83. Bretherton, *Christianity and Contemporary Politics*, 214.

84. Bretherton, *Christianity and Contemporary Politics*, 214.

85. Bretherton, *Christianity and Contemporary Politics*, 215.

86. Bretherton, *Christianity and Contemporary Politics*, 214.

87. Bretherton, *Christianity and Contemporary Politics*, 220.

88. Industrial Areas Foundation, http://www.citizenshandbook.org/iaf.pdf, accessed 27 March 2013; and http://www.industrialareasfoundation.org/organizingtools, accessed 27 March 2013; the Gamaliel Foundation, http://www.gamaliel.org/OurWork/TrainingLeaders.aspx, accessed 27 March 2013; PICO, http://www.piconetwork.org/about, accessed 27 March 2013; and Citizens UK, http://www.citizensuk.org/training, accessed 27 March 2013.

89. http://comm-org.wisc.edu/co, accessed 27 March 2013.

90. Bob Marley, 'Redemption Song', *Uprising* (Kingston, Jamaica: Island/Tuff Gong Records, 1980).

NOTES TO CHAPTER 6

1. Jacques Chéry, 'The Bread-Line of Haiti', 1982. http://www.misereor.org/misereor-org-home.html. Accessed 14 April 2013.

2. Elsa Tamez, *Bible of the Oppressed* (Maryknoll, NY: Orbis Books, 1982), 73

3. Based on Shannahan, *Voices from the Borderland*, 240; see Matthew 13:33 and Luke 13:20–21 [*Yeast*]; Matthew 5:13, Mark 9:50 and Luke 14:34–35 [*Salt*]; Matthew 5:3–12 and Luke 6.20–26 [*Alternative Beatitudes*]; Matthew 18:1–5, Mark 9:33–37 and Luke 9:46–48 [*Children*]; Matthew 19:13–15, Mark 10:32–34 and Luke 18:15–15 [*Blessing Children*]; Matthew 12:15–21 [*Gentle Servant of the Lord*]; Matthew 6:24–24 and Luke 12:22–31 [*Simplicity of Lifestyle*]; Matthew 10:5–10, Mark 6:7–13 and Luke 9:1–6 [*Carry Nothing with You*]; Mark 12:41–44 and Luke 21:1–4 [*the Widow's Mite*]; Luke 17:5–6 [*Faith no Bigger Than a Mustard Seed*]. Regarding 'Liberative Reversals', see Matthew 19:16–30, Mark 10:17–31 and Luke 18:18–30 [*Rich*

Young Ruler]; Matthew 11:4–6 and Luke 7:21–23 [*the Blind See, the Lame Walk*]; Matthew 12:1–14 [*Healing on the Sabbath*]; Matthew 2:13–17 [*Jesus the Refugee Child*]; Luke 4:16–30 [*Good News to the Poor, Release for the Captives*]; Matthew 25:31–46 [*Judgement Based on Liberative Praxis*]; Luke 17:11–19 [*Lepers*]; Luke 7:36–50 [*Prostitutes*]; Luke 10:25–37 and John 4:1–41 [*Samaritans*]; Luke 2:8–20 [*Shepherds*]; Matthew 15:21–28, Luke 8:1–3, Mark 15, Matthew 27:55–56, Luke 23:27–29 and 50–56 [*Women*]; Mark 2:13–17, Matthew 9:9–13 and Luke 19:1–9 [*Tax Collectors*]; Matthew 5:43–48 and Luke 6:27–36 [*Love Your Enemies*]; Matthew 15:10–20 and Mark 7:14–23 [*Purity*]; Luke 14:15–24 [*Hospitality*] and Luke 1:46–55 [*the Magnificat*].

4. Saskia Sassen, *Cities in a World Economy* (CA: Pine Forge Press, 1994), xx

5. http://www.guardian.co.uk/uk/video/2011/aug/11/david-cameron-uk-riots-broken-society-video, accessed 12 May 2013 (see especially 3 minutes, 56 seconds and following).

6. http://www.guardian.co.uk/uk/video/2011/dec/14/ed-miliband-riot-report-video, accessed 12 May 2013. See also, with reference to the London School of Economics and the *Guardian* newspaper report 'Reading the Riots', http://www.guardian.co.uk/uk/series/reading-the-riots, accessed 12 May 2013.

7. Saskia Sassen, *Globalisation and Its Discontents* (New York: New Press, 1998), xxi.

8. Tamez, *Bible of the Oppressed*, 72.

9. Sandercock, *Towards Cosmopolis*, 129.

10. Shannahan, *Voices from the Borderland*, 224ff. See Huntingdon, *The Clash of Civilisations*, 1996.

11. Paul Tillich, *Theology of Culture* (Oxford: Oxford University Press, 1959), 47ff; Don Browning, *A Fundamental Practical Theology* (Minneapolis: Fortress Press, 1991), 46ff; and Gordon Lynch, *Understanding Theology and Popular Culture* (Oxford: Blackwell, 2005), 102–104.

12. The Qur'an, translated by M. A. S Abdel Haleem (Oxford: Oxford University Press, 2010), 518.

13. Website, http://www.piconetwork.org/immigration, accessed 23 April 2013.

14. Tamez, *Bible of the Oppressed*, 70.

15. Kenneth Leech, *The Social God* (London: Sheldon Publishing, 1981), 8.

16. John Vincent, *Into the City* (London: Epworth Press, 1982), 110–12.

17. James Cone, *God of the Oppressed* (San Francisco: Harper Collins, 1975), 134.

18. Cone, *God of the Oppressed*, 135.

19. Shannahan, *Voices from the Borderland*, 243.

20. Bernice Johnson Reagon (Sweet Honey in the Rock), *Chile Your Waters Run Red through Soweto, Good News*. Chicago: Flying Fish Records, 1981.

21. Martin Luther King, 'Letter from Birmingham City Jail' (1963), in *A Testament of Hope: The Essential Writings of Martin Luther King Jr.*, ed. James M. Washington (San Francisco: Harper Row, 1986), 290.

22. Leech, *The Sky Is Red*, 90.

23. http://www.tikkun.org/nextgen, accessed 24 April 2013.

24. http://www.glide.org, accessed 24 April 2013.

25. http://www.glide.org/page.aspx?pid=425, accessed 24 April 2013, for a summary of projects at Glide.

26. Gamaliel Foundation website, http://www.gamaliel.org/OurWork.aspx, accessed 24 April 2013.

27. Ward, *Liquid Church*, 2002.

28. José Marins, Teolide Trevisan and Carolee Chanona, *The Church from the Roots: Basic Ecclesial Communities* (London: The Catholic Fund for Overseas Development, 1983), 11–12 and 10.

29. Marins, Trevisan and Chanona, *The Church from the Roots*, 31.

30. Obama, *Dreams from My Father,* 133ff.
31. Jacobsen, *Doing Justice,* 97.
32. Paul Heelas and Linda Woodhead, *The Spiritual Revolution: Why Religion Is Giving Way to Spirituality* (Oxford: Blackwell, 2005), 5.
33. Gordon Lynch, *The New Spirituality: An Introduction to Progressive Belief in the Twenty-First Century* (London: I. B. Tauris, 2007), 20 and 79.
34. Gutierrez, *A Theology of Liberation,* 204.
35. Christine Dodds, 'Liberating Spirituality and Spirituality of Liberation', in *Liberation Spirituality,* ed. Chris Rowland and John Vincent (Sheffield: The Urban Theology Unit, 1999), 19.
36. Dodds, 'Liberating Spirituality and Spirituality of Liberation', 20.
37. Sandercock, *Towards Cosmopolis,* 213.
38. Sandercock, *Towards Cosmopolis,* 219.
39. Fernando F. Segovia and Mary Ann Tolbert, eds., *Reading from This Place,* vol. 2, *Social Location and Biblical Interpretation in Global Perspective* (Minneapolis: Fortress Press, 1995), 7–15.
40. Robert Fowler, *Let the Reader Understand: Reader-Response Criticism and the Gospel of Mark* (Minneapolis: Fortress Press, 1991), 3.
41. Ernesto Cardenal, *The Gospel in Solentiname* (Maryknoll, NY: Orbis Books, 2010).
42. R. S. Sugirtharajah, *Voices from the Margin: Interpreting the Bible in the Third World* (London: S.P.C.K, 1991), 1–3; Mukti Barton, *Rejection, Resistance and Resurrection: Speaking Out on Racism in the Church* (London: Darton, Longman & Todd, 2005); Michael Jagessar, 'Unending the Bible: The Book of Revelation through the Optics of Anancy and Rastafari', in *Black Theology, Slavery and Contemporary Christianity,* ed. Anthony G. Reddie (Farnham, Surrey: Ashgate, 2010), 81–97; Tamez, *Bible of the Oppressed*; and Robert Beckford, *God and the Gangs,* 96–111; and *Jesus Dub,* 94–100.
43. http://www.ignatianspirituality.com, accessed 30 April 2013.
44. Beckford, *Jesus Dub,* 94.

NOTES TO CONCLUSION

1. 'Remarks for Senator Barack Obama: Remembering Dr Martin Luther King Jr.', Fort Wayne Indiana, 4 April 2008. http://usatoday30.usatoday.com/news/mmemmottpdf/obama-on-mlk-4–4-2008.pdf, accessed 20 May 2013.

Bibliography

Abbas, Tahir. *Islamic Radicalism and Multicultural Politics: The British Experience.* London: Routledge, 2009.

Aberle, David F. *The Peyote Religion among the Navaho.* Chicago: University of Chicago Press, 1966.

Alinsky, Saul D. *Reveille for Radicals.* New York, Vintage Press, 1946.

——. *Rules for Radicals:A Pragmatic Primer for Realistic Radicals.* New York: Vintage Press, 1972.

Althaus-Reid, Marcella. *Liberation Theology and Sexuality.* Aldershot: Ashgate, 2006.

Amoore, Louise, ed. *The Global Resistance Reader.* New York: Routledge, 2005.

Archbishop of Canterbury's Commission on Urban Priority Areas. *Faith in the City: A Call for Action by Church and Nation.* London: Church House, 1985.

Ash, Amin, and Nigel Thrift. *Cities:Reimagining the Urban.* Cambridge: Polity Press, 2002.

Atlas, John. *Seeds of Change: The Story of Acorn, America's Most Controversial Anti-Poverty Community Organizing Group.* Nashville, TN: Vanderbilt University Press, 2010.

Baker, Christopher R. *The Hybrid Church in the City: Third Space Thinking.* London: SCM Press, 2009.

Baker, Christopher R., and Hannah Skinner. *Faith in Action: The Dynamic Connection between Spiritual and Religious Capital.* Final Report of The William Temple Foundation's Research Project, 2002–2005, Manchester, 2006.

Ballard, Paul, ed. *Issues in Church Related Community Work.* Cardiff: University of Wales, 1990.

Baker, Kendall Clark. *Putting Faith into Action: Jesus' Strategic Plan for Mission, a Reflection on Congregation, Faith Based Community Organizing.* California: PICO National Clergy Caucus, 1998.

Barton, Mukti. *Rejection, Resistance and Resurrection: Speaking Out on Racism in the Church.* London: Darton Longman & Todd, 2005.

Bauman, Zygmunt. *Liquid Modernity.* Cambridge: Polity Press, 2000.

——. *Liquid Life.* Cambridge: Polity Press, 2000.

Beckford, Robert. *Dread and Pentecostal: A Political Theology for the Black Church in Britain.* London: S.P.C.K., 2000.

——. *God and the Gangs: An Urban Toolkit for Those Who Won't Be Sold Out, Bought Out or Scared Out.* London: Darton Longmanand Todd, 2004.

——. *Jesus Dub:Music, Theology and Social Change.* London: Routledge, 2006.

Bell, Jr., Daniel, M. *Liberation Theology after the End of History: The Refusal to Cease Suffering.* New York: Routledge, 2001.

Benford, Robert D., and David A. Snow. 'Framing Process and Social Movements: An Overview and Assessment'. *The Annual Review of Sociology* 26 (2000), 611–639.

Berger, Peter, ed. *The Desecularization of the World: Resurgent Religion and World Politics*. Grand Rapids, MI: Eerdmans, 1999.

Bernstein, Mary. 'Identity Politics'. *Annual Review of Sociology* 31 (2005), 47–74.

Bevans, Stephen. *Models of Contextual Theology*. Maryknoll, NY: Orbis Books, 2002.

Bhabha, Homi. *The Location of Culture*. New York: Routledge, 1994.

Bishops Conference of England and Wales. *Choosing the Common Good*. Stoke-on-Trent: Alive Publishing, 2010.

Birdwell, Jonathan, and Mark Littler. *Faithful Citizens: Why Those Who Do God Do Good*. London: Demos, 2012.

Birt, Yahya, Dilwar Hussain and Ataullah Siddiqui, ed. *British Secularism and Religion*. Markfield, UK: Kube Publishing, 2010.

Blond, Phillip. *Red Tory: How Left and Right Have Broken Britain and How We Can Fix It*. London: Faber & Faber, 2010.

Boff, Leonardo, and Clodovis Boff. *Introducing Liberation Theology*. Kent: Burns & Oates, 1987.

Bradstock, Andrew, and Christopher Rowland, eds. *Radical Christian Writings: A Reader*. Oxford: Blackwell Publishing, 2002.

Braziel, Jana Evans, and Mannur Anita, eds. *Theorising Diaspora*. Oxford: Blackwell, 2003.

Bretherton, Luke. *Christianity and Contemporary Politics*. Chichester: Wiley-Blackwell, 2010.

———. 'A Postsecular Politics? Inter-Faith Relations as a Civic Practice'. *Journal of the American Academy of Religion* 79, no. 2 (2011), 347–377.

———. 'The Political Populism of Saul Alinsky and Broad Based Organizing', *The Good Society* 21, no. 2 (2012), 261–278.

Browning, Don. *A Fundamental Practical Theology*. Minneapolis: Fortress Press, 1991.

Bruce, Steve. *God Is Dead: Secularisation in the West*. Oxford: Blackwell, 2002.

Buechler, Steven. 'Beyond Resource Mobilization? Emerging Trends in Social Movement Theory'. *The Sociological Quarterly* 34, no. 2 (1993), 217–235.

Bunyan, Paul. 'Broad-Based Organizing in the UK: Re-Asserting the Centrality of Political Activity in Community Development'. *Community Development Journal* 45, no. 1 (2010), 111–128.

Burgess, Richard, Kim Knibbe, and Anna Quaas. 'Nigerian-Initiated Pentecostal Churches as a Social Force in Europe: The Case of the Redeemed Christian Church of God'. *PentecoStudies* 9, no. 1 (2010), 255–273.

Calhoun, Craig, ed. *Habermas and the Public Sphere*. Cambridge, MA: MIT Press, 1992.

Cardenal, Ernesto. *The Gospel in Solentiname*. Maryknoll, NY: Orbis Books, 2010.

Castells, Manuel. *The City and the Grassroots*. Berkeley: University of California Press, 1983.

———. *The Information Age: Economy, Society and Culture. Vol. 1: The Rise of the Network Society*. Oxford: Blackwell, 1996.

———. ed. *The Network Society: A Cross-Cultural Perspective*. Cheltenham: Edward Elgar, 2004.

———. *The Information Age: Economy, Society and Culture: The Power of Identity* (2nd edition). Oxford: Blackwell, 2010

———. *Communication Power*. Oxford: Oxford University Press, 2011.

Catholic Bishops Conference of England and Wales. *The Common Good and the Catholic Church's Social Teaching*. Manchester: Gabriel, 1996.

Chambers, Edward T., and Michael A. Cowan. *Roots for Radicals: Organizing for Power, Action and Justice*. New York: Continuum, 2003.

Citizens Organizing Foundation. *Re-Weaving the Fabric of Society: Position Statement of the Citizens Organizing Foundation*. London: Citizens Organizing Foundation, 2004.

Chambers, Simone, and Jeffrey Kopstein. 'Bad Civil Society'. *Political Theory* 29, no. 6 (2001), 837–865.

Church Action on Poverty. *A Living Wage Church?* Manchester: Church Action on Poverty, 2002.

Clark, Anna. 'The New Poor Law and the Breadwinner Wage: Contrasting Assumptions'. *The Journal of Social History* 34, no. 2 (2000), 261–281.

Clark, John, ed. *Globalizing Civic Engagement: Civil Society and Transnational Action*. London: Earthscan Publications, 2003.

Commission on Urban Life and Faith. *Faithful Cities: A Call for Celebration, Vision and Justice*. London: Methodist Publishing House, 2006.

Cone, James. *God of the Oppressed*. San Francisco: Harper Collins, 1975.

Corber, Robert, and Stephen Valocchi, eds. *Queer Studies: An Interdisciplinary Reader*. Oxford: Blackwell, 2002.

Corns, Thomas N., Ann Hughes, and David Loewenstein, eds. *The Complete Works of Gerrard Winstanley*. Vol. 2. Oxford: Oxford University Press, 2009.

Davie, Grace. *Religion in Britain since 1945: Believing without Belonging*. Oxford: Blackwell, 1994.

———. *Europe, the Exceptional Case: Parameters of Faith in the Modern World*. London: Darton Longman and Todd, 2002.

Davey, Andrew. *Urban Christianity and Global Order*. London: S.P.C.K., 2001.

DaCosta, Kimberly McClain. *Making Multiracials: State, Family, and Market in the Redrawing of the Color Line*. Palo Alto,CA: Stanford University Press, 2007.

Derrida, Jacques. *The Politics of Friendship*. Trans. George Collins. New York:Verso, 1997.

———. *On Cosmopolitanism and Forgiveness*. London: Routledge, 2001.

Dinham, Adam, Robert Furbey, and Vivien Lowndes, eds. *Faith in the Public Realm: Controversies, Policies and Practices*. Bristol: The Policy Press, 2009.

Durkheim, Emile. *The Division of Labour in Society*. New York: The Free Press, 1997.

Edwards, Michael. *Civil Society*. Cambridge: Polity Books, 2009.

Ehrenberg. John. *Civil Society:The Critical History of an Idea*. New York: New York University Press, 1999.

Ellis, Stephen, and Ineke van Kessel, eds. *Movers and Shakers: Social Movements in Africa*. Leiden: Brill, 2009.

Evans, Yara, Joanna Herbert, Kavita Datta, Jon May, Cathy McIlwaine, and Jane Wills. *Making the City Work: Low Paid Employment in London*. London: University of London, 2005.

Eyerman, Ron, and Andrew Jamison. *Social Movement: A Cognitive Approach*. Cambridge: Polity Press, 1991.

Fanon, Frantz. *Black Skin, White Masks*. London: Pluto Press, 1986.

Field, John. *Social Capital*. London: Routledge, 2003.

Fisher, Robert. ed. *The People Shall Rule: ACORN, Community Organizing and the Struggle for Economic Justice*. Nashville, TN: Vanderbilt University Press, 2009.

Fletcher, Joseph. *Situation Ethics: The New Morality*. Philadelphia: Westminster Press, 1966.

Foucault, Michel. *The Archaeology of Knowledge*. London: Tavistock Publications, 1972.

Foucault, Michel. *The Archaeology of Knowledge*. Abingdon: Routledge Classics, 2002.

Fowler, Robert. *Let the Reader Understand: Reader-Response Criticism and the Gospel of Mark*. Minneapolis: Fortress Press, 1991.

Fraser, Nancy. 'Rethinking the Public Sphere: A Contribution to the Critique of Actually Existing Democracy'. *Social Text* no. 25–26 (1990), 56–80.

Freire, Paulo. *Pedagogy of the Oppressed*. Middlesex: Penguin Books, 1972.

———. *Cultural Action for Freedom*. Harmondsworth: Penguin Education, 1972.

———. *Pedagogy of Indignation*. Boulder: Paradigm Publishers, 2004.

Fryer, Peter. *Staying Power: The History of Black People in Britain*. London: Pluto Press, 1984.

Frost, Jennifer. *An Interracial Movement of the Poor: Community Organizing and the New Left in the 1960s*. New York: New York University Press, 2001.

Galbraith, John Kenneth. *The Affluent Society*.1958. New York: Houghton Mifflin, 1998.

———. *The Good Society: The Humane Agenda*. New York: Houghton Mifflin, 1996

Giddens, Anthony. *Modernity and Self-Identity*. Cambridge: Polity Press, 1991.

Gilchrist, Alison. *The Well-Connected Community: A Networking Approach to Community Development*. Bristol: Policy Press, 2004.

Gilroy, Paul. *There Ain't No Black in the Union Jack*. London: Unwin Hyman, 1987.

———. *Against Race: Imagining Political Culture beyond the Colour Line*. Cambridge, MA: Harvard University Press, 2000.

———. *After Empire: Melancholia or Convivial Culture?* Abingdon: Routledge, 2004.

Goffman, Erving. *Frame Analysis: An Essay on the Organization of Experience*. Cambridge, MA: Harvard University Press, 1974.

Goodwin, Jeff, and James M. Jasper, eds. *The Social Movements Reader:Cases and Concepts*. Oxford: Blackwell Publishing, 2003.

Gorringe, T.J. *A Theology of the Built Environment: Justice, Empowerment, Redemption*. Cambridge: Cambridge University Press, 2002.

Gramsci, Antonio. *Selections from the Prison Notebooks*. London: Lawrence & Wishart, 1971.

———. *Prison Notebooks*. Vol. 3. Ed. and trans. Joseph A. Buttigieg. New York: Columbia University Press, 2007.

Grayling, A.C. *The Good Book: A Secular Bible*. London: Bloomsbury Publishing, 2011.

Green, Laurie. *Let's Do Theology: A Pastoral Cycle Resource Book*. London: Mowbray, 1990.

Gurney, Joan Neff, and Kathleen J. Tierney. 'Relative Deprivation and Social Movements: A Critical Look at Twenty Years of Theory and Research'. *The Sociological Quarterly* 23, no. 1 (1982), 33–47.

Gutiérrez Gustavo. *A Theology of Liberation*. London: SCM Press, 1974.

———.*The Power of the Poor in History*. London: SCM Press, 1983.

Habermas, Jurgen. *The Structural Transformation of the Public Sphere: An Inquiry into a Category of Bourgeois Society*. Trans. Thomas Burgerand Fredrick Lawrence. Cambridge, MA: MIT Press, 1989.

Hanifan, Lyda Judson. 'The Rural School Community Center'. *Annals of the American Academy of Political and Social Science* 67 (1916), 130–138.

Hearns, Jonathan. *Rethinking Nationalism:A Critical Introduction*. Basingstoke, UK: Palgrave Macmillan, 2006.

Heelas, Paul, and Woodhead, Linda. *The Spiritual Revolution: Why Religion Is Giving Way to Spirituality*. Oxford: Blackwell, 2005.

Held, David. *Cosmopolitanism: Ideals and Realities*. Cambridge: Polity Press, 2010.

Henderson, Paul, and Harry Salmon. *Community Organizing: The UK Context*. London: Community Development Foundation Publications, 1995.

Hitchens, Christopher. *God Is Not Great: Why Religion Poisons Everything*. London: Allen & Unwin, 2007.

Hollenbach, David. *The Common Good and Christian Ethics*. Cambridge: Cambridge University Press, 2002.

hooks, bell. *Feminist Theory: From Margin to Center*. Boston: South End Press, 1984.

Hopkins, Peter, and Richard Gale, eds. *Muslims in Britain: Race, Place and Identities*. Edinburgh: Edinburgh University Press, 2009.

Horwitt, Sanford D. *Let Them Call Me Rebel: Saul Alinsky, His Life and Legacy*. New York: Vintage Press, 1992.

Howarth, Catherine. *Socially Responsible Contracting in London's Financial Districts*. London: The East London Communities Organization, 2003.

Huntingdon, Samuel. 'The Clash of Civilisations?' *Foreign Affairs* (1993), 22–49.

———. *The Clash of Civilizations and the Remaking of World Order*. New York: Simon & Schuster, 1996.

Independent Review Team. *Community Cohesion*. London: Home Office, UK Government, 2006.

Jacobsen, Dennis A. *Doing Justice: Congregations and Community Organizing*. Minneapolis: Fortress Press, 2001.

Jameson, Neil. 'British Muslims: Influencing UK Public Policy: A Case Study'. In *British Muslims: Loyalty and Belonging*, edited by Mohammed Siddique Seddon, Dilwar Hussain, and Nadeem Malik. Leicestershire: The Islamic Foundation and the Citizens Organizing Foundation, 2003, 41–51.

Jamoul, Lina. *The Art of Politics: Broad-Based Organising in Britain*. Unpublished PhD thesis. London: Queen Mary University of London, Geography Department, 2006.

Jamoul, Lina and Jane Wills. 'Faith in Politics'. *Urban Studies* 45, no. 10 (2008), 2035–2056.

Jenkins, J. Craig. 'Resource Mobilization Theory and the Study of Social Movements'. *Annual Review of Sociology* 9 (1983), 527–553.

Kant, Immanuel. *Perpetual Peace*. Cambridge: Cambridge University Press, 1991.

Knott. Kim. 'Spatial Theory and Spatial Methodology, Their Relationship and Application: A Transatlantic Engagement'. *The Journal of the American Academy of Religion* 77, no. 2 (2009), 413–424.

———. *The Location of Religion: A Spatial Analysis*. London: Equinox, 2005.

Kumar, A., J. A. Scholte, M. Kaldor, M. Glasius, H. Seckinelgin, and H. Anheier, eds. *Global Civil Society Yearbook 2009: Poverty and Activism*. London: Sage, 2009.

Kung, Hans. *Global Responsibility: In Search of a New World Ethic*. London: SCM Press, 1991.

———. *Yes to a Global Ethic*. New York: Continuum, 1996.

Leech, Kenneth. *The Sky Is Red: Discerning the Signs of the Times*. London: Darton Longman and Todd, 1997.

———. *The Social God*. London: Sheldon Publishing, 1981.

Lefebvre, Henri. *The Production of Space*. Trans. Donald Nicholson-Smith. Oxford: Blackwell, 1991.

Levi, Margaret, David J. Olson, and Erich Steinman. 'Living-Wage Campaigns and Laws'. *Working USA* 6, no. 3 (2002–2003), 111–132.

Living Wage Unit. *A Fairer London: The 2009 Living Wage in London*. London: Greater London Authority, 2009.

Lynch, Gordon. *Understanding Theology and Popular Culture*. Oxford: Blackwell, 2005.

———. *The New Spirituality: An Introduction to Progressive Belief in the Twenty-First Century*. London: I. B. Tauris, 2007.

Macleod, Jay. *Community Organizing: A Practical and Theological Appraisal.* London: Christian Action, 1993.

Madison, James, Alexander Hamilton, and John Jay. *The Federalist Papers.* London: Penguin Books, 1987.

Madni, Sajida. 'Birmingham Citizens Business Plan and Proposal 2009–2010'. Birmingham: Birmingham Citizens, 2009.

Marins, José, Teolide Trevisan, and Carolee Chanona. *The Church from the Roots:Basic Ecclesial Communities.* London: The Catholic Fund for Overseas Development, 1983.

Marley, Bob. 'Redemption Song'. *Uprising.* Kingston, Jamaica: Tuff Gong Records, 1980.

Marlow, Joyce. *The Tolpuddle Martyrs.* London: Deutsch, 1971.

Martinez-Torres, Maria Elena. 'Civil Society, the Internet and the Zapatistas'. *Peace Review* 13, no. 3 (2001), 347–355.

Marx, Gary, and Doug McAdam. *Collective Behavior and Social Movements.* Englewood Cliffs, NJ: Prentice-Hall, 1994.

McCann, Eugene M.'Race, Protest and Public Space: Contextualizing Lefebvre in the US City'. *Antipode* 31.2 (1999), 163–184.

McAdam, Doug.*Political Process and the Development of Black Insurgency, 1930–1970.* Chicago: University of Chicago Press, 1982.

McAdam, Doug, John McCarthy, and Zald Mayer, eds. *Comparative Perspectives on Social Movements: Political Opportunities,Mobilizing Structures, and Cultural Framings.* New York: Cambridge University Press, 1996.

McLellan, David, ed. *Karl Marx: Selected Writings.* Oxford: Oxford University Press, 1977.

McClung Lee, Alfred, ed. *Principles of Sociology,* 3rd ed. New York: Barnes and Noble, 1969.

Merton, Robert K. 'Social Structure and Anomie'. *American Sociological Review* 3 (1938), 672–682.

Mitchell, Harvey. *America after Tocqueville: Democracy against Difference.* Cambridge: Cambridge University Press, 2002.

Modood, Tariq. *Multiculturalism.* Cambridge: Polity Press, 2007.

———. *Still Not Easy Being British: Struggles for a Multicultural Citizenship.* London: Trentham Books, 2010.

Morley, David, and Kuan-Hsing Chen, eds. *Stuart Hall: Critical Dialogues in Cultural Studies.* London: Routledge, 1996.

Morris, Aldon D. *Origins of the Civil Rights Movements: Black Communities Organizing for Change.* New York: Free Press, 1986.

———. 'Reflections on Social Movements Theory: Criticisms and Proposals'. *Contemporary Sociology* 29, no. 3 (2000), 445–454.

Nasar, Meer, and Tariq Modood. 'Interculturalism, Multiculturalism or Both?' *Political Insight,* Volume 3, issue 1 (2012), 30–33.

Noden, Kirk. 'From Olympic People's Guarantees to a Living Wage: Organizing Takes Root in Britain'. *Social Policy: Organizing for Social and Economic Justice* 36, no. 2 (2005–2006), 36–40.

Norman, Andrew. *The Story of George Loveless and the Tolpuddle Martyrs.* Wellington, UK: Halsgrove Publishing, 2008.

Obama, Barack. *Dreams from My Father.* Edinburgh: Cannongate Books, 2007.

Oberschall, Anthony. *Social Conflict and Social Movements.* Englewood Cliffs, NJ: Prentice-Hall, 1973.

Olesen, Thomas. 'Globalising the Zapatistas: From Third World Solidarity to Global Solidarity?' *Third World Quarterly* 25, no. 1 (2004), 255–267.

O'Toole, Therese. 'Faith and the Coalition: A New Confidence to 'Do God'?' *Muslim Participation in Contemporary Governance* working paper no. 3, University of Bristol: Centre for the Study of Ethnicity and Citizenship, (February 2012).

Parliament of the World's Religions. *Declaration toward a Global Ethic*. London: SCM Press, 1993.

Pattison, Stephen. *Pastoral Care and Liberation Theology*. London: S.P.C.K., 1997.

Petrella, Ivan. *The Future of Liberation Theology: An Argument and a Manifesto*. Aldershot: Ashgate, 2004.

———. *Beyond Liberation Theology: A Polemic*. London: SCM Press, 2008.

Phillips, Richard, ed. *Muslim Spaces of Hope: Geographies of Possibility in Britain and the West*. London: Zed Books, 2009.

Pierce, Gregory F. *Activism That Makes Sense: Congregations and Community Organizing*. Chicago: Illinois: ACTA Publications, 1997.

Pinn, Anthony. *Why Lord?: Suffering and Evil in Black Theology*. New York: Continuum, 1999.

Pixley, Jorge, and Clodovis Boff. *The Bible, the Church and the Poor*. Tunbridge Wells, UK: Burns & Oates, 1989.

Porta, Donatella Della, Massimiliano Andreatta, Lorenzo Mosca, and Herbert Reiter. *Globalization from Below: Transnational Activists and Protest Networks*. Minneapolis: University of Minneapolis Press, 2006.

Putnam, Robert. *Bowling Alone: The Collapse and Revival of American Community*. New York: Touchstone, 2000.

Ramadan, Tariq. *Western Muslims and the Future of Islam*. Oxford: Oxford University Press, 2004.

Rauschenbusch, Walter. *A Theology for the Social Gospel*. New York: Macmillan, 1917.

Reader, John, and Christopher R. Baker, eds. *Entering the New Theological Space:Blurred Encounters of Faith, Politics and Community*. Farnham, UK: Ashgate, 2009.

Richards, J.C., ed. *Handbook of Theory and Research for the Sociology of Education*. New York: Greenwood Press, 1983.

Rippin, Andrew. *Muslims: Their Religious Beliefs and Practices*. 3rd ed. London: Routledge, 2005.

Rowland, Chris, and John Vincent, eds. *Liberation Spirituality*. Sheffield: The Urban Theology Unit, 1999.

Rutherford, Joan, and Hetan Shah, eds. *The Good Society: Compass Programme for Renewal*. London: Lawrence & Wishart, 2006.

Said, Edward. *Representations of the Intellectual: The 1993 Reith Lectures*. London: Vintage, 1994.

Sandelowski, Margarete, and Julie Barroso. 'Reading Qualitative Studies'. *International Journal of Qualitative Methods* 1, no. 1 (2002).

Sandercock, Leonie. *Towards Cosmopolis*. Chichester: John Wiley & Sons, 1998.

Sassen, Saskia. *Cities in a World Economy*. Thousand Oaks, California: Pine Forge Press, 1994.

———. *Globalisation and Its Discontents*. New York: New Press, 1998.

Schreiter, Robert. *Constructing Local Theologies*. Maryknoll, NY: Orbis Books, 1985.

———. *The New Catholicity: Theology between the Global and the Local*. Maryknoll, NY: Orbis, 1997.

Scott, W. Richard. *Organizations: Rational, Natural and Open Systems*. 5th ed. Cranbury, New Jersey: Pearson Education International, 2003.

Segovia, Fernando F., and Mary Ann Tolbert, eds. *Reading from This Place. Vol. 2: Social Location and Biblical Interpretation in Global Perspective*. Minneapolis: Fortress Press, 1995.

Segundo, Juan Luis. *The Liberation of Theology*. Maryknoll, NY: Orbis, 1976.

Shannahan, Chris. *Voices from the Borderland: Re-Imagining Cross-Cultural Urban Theology in the Twenty-First Century*. London: Equinox, 2010.

Showstack, Anne F. *Antonio Gramsci: An Introduction to His Thought*. London: Pluto Press, 1970.

Seddon, Mohammed Siddique, Dilwar Hussain, and Nadeem Malik, eds. *British Muslims: Loyalty and Belonging*. Leicestershire: The Islamic Foundation, 2003.

Smith, Michael Peter. *Transnational Urbanism*. Oxford: Blackwell, 2001.

Smiley, Tavis, and Cornel West. *The Rich and the Rest of Us: A Poverty Manifesto*. New York Smiley Books, 2012.

Soja, Edward. *Thirdspace: Journeys to Los Angeles and Other Real-and-Imagined Places*. Cambridge, MA: Blackwell, 1996.

———. *Postmetropolis: Critical Studies of Cities and Regions*. Oxford: Blackwell, 2000.

Sokol, Martin, Jane Wills, Jeremy Anderson, Marg Buckley, Yara Evans, Claire Frew, and Paula Hamilton. *The Impact of Improved Pay and Conditions on Low-Paid Urban Workers: The Case of the Royal London Hospital*. London: University of London, 2006.

Spivak, Gayatri. *In Other Worlds: Essays in Cultural Politics*. New York: Methuen, 1987.

Stall, Susan, and Randy Stoecker. 'Community Organizing or Organizing Community? Gender and the Crafts of Empowerment'. *Gender and Society* 12, no. 6 (1998), 729–756.

Steinberg, Marc, W. 'Tilting the Frame: Considerations on Collective Action Framing from a Discursive Turn'. *Theory and Society* 27, no. 6 (1998), 845–872.

Stokes, Peter, and Barry Knight. *Organizing a Civil Society*. Birmingham: Foundation for a Civil Society, 1997

Stringer, Ernest T. *Action Research*, 3rd ed. London: Sage, 2007.

Sugirtharajah, R. S., ed. *Voices from the Margin: Interpreting the Bible in the Third World*. London: S.P.C.K., 1991.

Susser, Ida, ed. *The Castells Reader on Cities and Social Theory*. Oxford: Blackwell Publishers, 2002.

Tamez, Elsa. *Bible of the Oppressed*. Maryknoll, NY: Orbis, 1982.

Tilly, Charles. *From Mobilization to Revolution*. Reading, MA: Addison-Wesley, 1978.

———. *Social Movements, 1768–2004*. London: Paradigm, 2004.

Tillich, Paul. *Theology of Culture*. Oxford: Oxford University Press, 1959.

Tocqueville, Alexis de. *Democracy in America*. Vols. 1–2. Translated by Henry Reeve. London: Oxford University Press, 1946.

The Commission on Urban Life and Faith. *Faithful Cities: A Call for Celebration, Vision and Justice*. Peterborough: Methodist Publishing House, 2006.

The Bible. New Revised Standard Version. Oxford: Oxford University Press, 1998.

The Qur'an.trans. M. A. S Abdel Haleem. Oxford: Oxford University Press, 2010.

Vertovec, Steven. 'Super-Diversity and Its Implications'. *Ethnic and Racial Studies* 30, no. 6, (2007), 1024–1054.

———. *Transnationalism*. London: Routledge, 2009.

Vincent, John. *Into the City*. London: Epworth Press, 1982.

Wallis, Jim. *God's Politics: Why the American Right Gets It Wrong and the Left Doesn't Get It*. Oxford: Lion Books, 2005.

———. *On God's Side: What Religion Forgets and Politics Hasn't Learned about Serving the Common Good*. Grand Rapids, MI: Baker Publishing Group, 2013.

Ward, Pete. *Liquid Church*. Carlisle: Paternoster Press, 2002.

Warren, Mark R. 'Community Organizing in Britain: The Political Engagement of Faith-Based Social Capital'. *City & Community* 8, no. 2 (2009), 99–127.

Washington, James M., ed. *A Testament of Hope: The Essential Writings of Martin Luther King, Jr.* New York: Harper & Row, 1986.

West, Cornel. *The Cornel West Reader*. New York: Basic Civitas Books, 1999.

———. *Race Matters: Philosophy and Race in America*. Boston, MA: Beacon Press, 1993.

Wood, Richard, L. *Faith in Action: Religion, Race and Democratic Organizing in America*. Chicago: University of Chicago Press, 2002.

Williams, Cecil. *No Hiding Place: Empowerment and Recovery for Our Troubled Communities*. San Francisco: Harper & Row, 1993.

Wills, Jane. *Mapping Low Pay in East London: A Report Written for TELCO's Living Wage Campaign*. London: UNISON and the Department of Geography, Queen Mary, University of London, 2001.

———. 'The Living Wage'. *Soundings: A Journal of Politics and Culture* 4 (2009), 33–46.

Winters, Loretta, and Herman DeBosse. *New Faces in a Changing America: Multiracial Identity in the 21st Century*. Thousand Oaks, CA: Sage, 2002.

Young, Iris Marion. *Justice and the Politics of Difference*. Princeton, NJ: Princeton University Press, 1990.

Index

Abbas, Tahir 79
Aberle, David 73
ACORN 17–18, 32.
action research 20
Alinsky, Saul 2, 10–11, 12–14, 15,
    19–20, 22, 27, 29–30, 39, 43,
    52, 53, 64, 68–9, 91, 119
Althaus-Reid, Marcella 117

Baker, Chris 24, 43–4, 46, 88–9, 123,
    129–32, 136, 153
Baker, Kendall 27
Base Ecclesial Communities 117,
    151–3
Bauman, Zygmunt 46
Beckford, Robert 2, 24–5, 67, 75, 101,
    116, 126, 150, 159
Beckwith, Dave 69
Bell, Daniel 117–8
Benford, Robert 72
Berger, Peter 1, 65
Bevans, Stephen 116
Bhabha, Homi 46, 88–9
bias to the oppressed 1, 3, 4, 25, 41,
    55, 85, 95, 102–3, 107, 117–19,
    122, 124–5, 135, 137–8, 140–1,
    143, 153, 156
big society 2, 66–7, 141
Birmingham Citizens 56–7, 81
Blair, Tony 24, 65, 93, 106, 106
Blond, Philip 66
Boff, Clodovis 55, 117
Boff, Leonardo 117
Bourdieu, Pierre 103
Bretherton, Luke 1, 30, 43–4, 54, 86,
    116, 132–6, 144, 145, 146, 153
Bruce, Steve 65–6
Buechler, Steven 69–70
Burgess, Richard 66

Calhoun, Craig 95–6
Cameron, David 2, 43, 66–7, 77, 81,
    100, 141
Castells, Manuel 9, 45–6, 53, 63, 71,
    73, 74–6, 78–80, 97, 98, 137
catholicity 102, 116, 126–9, 132,
    134–6, 146, 169
Changemakers 58
Christian Realism 43–4, 123
Christology 26–7, 28, 92, 119, 120,
    123, 132, 138–42, 147–8, 156,
    159, 160–2
Church Action on Poverty 55, 80
Citizens Organising Foundation/Citizens
    UK 35–7, 39–43, 56–9, 81, 86,
    89, 92, 119; values 46; and social
    movements 44–5 organizational
    structure 47–8, 49; actions 48–54;
    and political party leaders 43, 81,
    125–6; and training 38–9, 137
civic activism/engagement 10–12, 24,
    27, 29, 30, 78–9
civil society 1, 10, 29–31, 41, 43, 46,
    66–7, 89–93; as associational
    life 44, 90–91; as the good
    society 91–4; and Western
    democracy 91; and Immanuel
    Kant 92; and the golden rule
    93; as the public sphere 95–6;
    and social capital 103–5; and
    liberation theology 117–8
clash of civilizations 125, 130–1, 143
collective action framing 72, 85
COMM-ORG 23, 39–40, 111
common good 1, 85, 88, 91–2, 94–5,
    118, 123–4, 133, 135, 136, 141,
    169; and community organizing
    30, 39, 42, 102–3; and *shalom*
    121, 128, 150

Communities Organized for Greater
      Bristol 35
community cohesion 2, 66, 76–7,
      106–7, 144, 147
community organizers 19–20, 23, 30,
      39, 47, 53–4, 82, 84, 85, 88,
      107, 109–110, 143, 156
community organizing cycle 20–3, 168
community organizing training 23,
      38–9, 137
conscientization 92, 108, 137, 158–9
Cone, James 148
cosmopolitanism 97, 101–3, 133
creation in the image of God 148–7
Cruddas, John 93
cultural politics of difference 74, 77–8,
      84, 88, 96–101, 125–6, 143

DART 13, 19, 20, 26, 27
Davey, Andrew 74
Davie, Grace 32
difference/diversity 66–7, 74, 76–7,
      97–103, 116, 125–8, 143,
      145–6, 147, 154, 169
Dinham, Adam 24, 66
Dodds, Christine 155
dual heritage/mixed race 77, 100–1,
      130
dub practice 126
Durkheim, Emile (anomie) 68

East London Contextual Theology
      Centre 43
Edwards, Michael 10, 29, 64, 90–2,
      95, 96
Ehrenberg, John 90
English Defence League 77, 98
Eyerman, Ron 73

faith and the public sphere 1–2, 24–7,
      64–7, 78, 85, 105–6
faith-based community organizing 3–4,
      15–7, 19, 24, 25–7, 58–9, 95,
      107, 116, 118–9 122, 131, 138,
      141, 143, 144, 145, 152, 153,
      155, 167, 168
Faith in the City 35, 94, 123
Faithful Cities 55, 94, 103–4, 106, 123,
      124
Fanon, Frantz 108
Federalist Papers 29
Fletcher, Joseph 120–1
Foucault, Michel 2–3
Fowler, Robert 158
Fraser, Nancy 95–6

Freire, Paulo 71, 80, 92, 108, 137, 145,
      158
Furbey, Robert 24, 65, 66

Galbraith, J.K 93
Gamaliel Foundation 13, 15–16, 24,
      25–7, 28, 32, 56, 58, 89, 119, 150
Gamson, William 81
Goodwin, Jeff 45, 67–8, 79
Giddens, Anthony 68, 74
Gilchrist, Alison 45, 46
Gilroy, Paul 9, 74, 75–6, 98, 99, 100,
      102–3, 122, 130
Glide Memorial United Methodist
      Church 11, 78, 150
globalization 41, 51, 78–79, 98, 127,
      129
Gorringe, Tim 87–8, 115
Gramsci, Antonio 40; and war of
      position 81, 91, 107–8; and
      hegemony 91; and intellectuals
      53–4, 107–8, 110, 152
Green, Laurie 20
Gurney, Joan 68
Gutiérrez, Gustavo 3, 55, 108–9,
      117–8, 155

Habermas, Jurgen 24, 95
hallow/holy 134–5
Heelas, Paul 155
Held, David 102
hospitality 102, 132–4
human worth 147
hybridity 100–101, 129–31
hybrid social movement 78

identity politics 3, 9, 74–7, 83, 84; and
      essentialism 100–1, 130–1
Ignatian spirituality 159
Incarnation 25, 27, 134, 147–50
Industrial Areas Foundation 13–15,
      20, 24, 32, 50, 56, 57, 58, 64,
      89, 137
intellectuals (organic, public, political)
      53–4, 80, 107–110
Iqbal, Jamil 78
Islamic Foundation 43

Jacobsen, Dennis 21, 25, 26, 119–20, 154
Jameson, Neil 34, 40, 41
Jamison, Andrew 73
Jamoul, Lina 34, 76, 96
Jasper, James 45, 67–8, 79
Jenkins, Craig 69
Jubilee 2000/Jubilee Debt 11–12, 73, 81

King, Martin Luther 10–11, 72, 77, 80, 92, 122, 149
Klandermans, Bert 69–70
Knott, Kim 88–9
Küng, Hans 101, 122
Ku Klux Klan 98

Labour Party/New Labour 66,
langar 147
Leech, Kenneth 4, 148, 150
Lefebvre, Henri 87, 89, 115, 144
Levi, Margaret 50
Liberation 26, 71, 77, 84, 85, 101, 124, 140, 150, 158
liberation theology 3, 4–5, 55, 117–9, 122–3, 145, 159
liberative difference 78, 84, 98, 107, 125, 126, 128, 131, 134, 136, 143–7, 149, 150–1, 153, 154, 156, 158, 161
liberative reversals 140–3, 148, 156, 158, 162, 169, 193–4n
listening 135–6, 155–7
living wage 18, 49–56, 69, 81
London Citizens 38–9, 40–1, 42, 43, 48–54, 80, 106
Lopez, Cristina 69
love 10–11, 92, 94, 124–5, 144–5, 149; *agape*/love 121–2, 133–4, 146, 160–1, 169
Lowndes, Vivien 24, 66

Macleod, Jay 15, 33, 34, 36, 37, 43
Marley, Bob 137
McAdam, Doug 70–1
McCann, Eugene 88
McDowell, David 69
Merseyside Broad-Based Organization 35–6, 56
Merton, Robert (anomie) 68
Modood, Tariq 65, 77, 78, 99, 101
Morris, Aldon 71–2
Moses 26
multiculturalism 4, 42–3, 77–8, 84, 99–102, 125–6, 144, 146–7

Nahles, Andrea 93
new politics 63–4, 68, 168; lessons from 82–5
Niebuhr, Reinhold 43

Obama, Barack 2, 9, 12, 16, 17, 28–9, 32, 50, 64–5, 77, 105–6, 107, 154, 170
Oberschall, Anthony 69, 80

Occupy movement/Occupy Wall Street 63, 65, 71, 73, 78, 79, 80, 88, 96, 109
Olson, David 50
O'Toole, Therese 106

Pastoral cycle 5, 20, 22, 115, 168–9
people's organization 13, 39, 40, 44–5, 47–8, 50, 53, 54, 57, 68, 82, 84, 87, 88, 99, 111, 120, 135–6, 138, 143, 145, 151, 153, 162
Petrella, Ivan 117
Phillips, Richard 78
PICO National Network 13, 16–17, 18, 20–2, 25–6, 27, 31, 32, 57, 58, 89, 125, 137, 147
Pinn, Anthony 89, 116
Pixley, Jorge 55
political intellectual 40, 80, 109, 110, 122
Political Process Theory 70–2, 83
prioritizing insignificance 140–3
public sphere 1, 24–7,42, 64–5, 67, 76, 82, 87–9, 92, 94–6, 124, 131, 133, 142
Purnell, James 38
Putnam, Robert 30–1, 42, 64, 89, 103–4

'race' 77–8, 98–100, 126, 128
Rainbow/PUSH Coalition 11, 32, 78
Ramadan, Tariq 55
reader response Biblical hermeneutics 158, 160–1, 162
reconciliation 128–9, 132
Redeemed Christian Church of God 66
reimagining scripture 157–63
Relative Deprivation Theory 68–9, 83
religious capital 66, 104–5, 106
representational space 87–8, 89, 91, 96, 116, 131–2, 144–5
Rerum Novarum 55, 94, 123
Resource Mobilization Theory 69–70
Respect (political party) 78
Rock Against Racism 78
Rutherford, Joan 93

Said, Edward 40, 109, 130
Sandercock, Leonie 74, 77, 78, 88, 96, 97, 106, 127, 131, 142, 143, 156
Sassen, Saskia 78, 79, 141
Schreiter, Robert 20, 72–3, 84, 102, 109, 110, 126–9, 136, 137, 145
secular/secularization 1, 65–6, 90, 106
Segovia, Fernando 158

Segundo, Juan-Luis 20
self interest 11, 14, 15, 19, 21, 22, 25,
    27, 36, 37, 40, 68–9, 83, 85,
    119–21, 161, 169
Shah, Hetan 93
shalom 121, 128–9, 149–51
Skinner, Hannah 24, 42
Smith, Michael Peter 78
Snow, David 72
social capital 1, 24, 30–1, 42, 64, 66,
    103–7; bonding 66, 76, 83, 98,
    104, 125; bridging 9, 17, 66,
    104, 106, 125; faith groups and
    28, 66, 104–6, 170; linking 9,
    106–7, 125; subversive 141,
    143.
Social Gospel 43–4, 123
social movements 10, 67–73, 74,
    84; history of 67; character of
    68, 76, 120; types of 73; rise
    and fall of 79–82, 83, 85; and
    community organizing 12, 13,
    14, 44–5, 67, 68; faith-based 65,
    70, 75, 78–9, 88, 116, 118, 169;
    and globalization 78–9
social space 86–89, 115–6, 144
Soja, Edward (and social space) 87
spiritual capital 70, 104–5, 116, 138
Spivak, Gayatri 75, 98
spirituality of community organizing
    154–63
Steinberg, Mark 72
Steinman, Erich 50
Stop the War Coalition 11, 68, 73, 78

subversive discipleship 149, 151
superdiversity 74, 77, 78, 97–9, 127–8

Tamez, Elsa 140, 142, 147
The Gospel in Solentiname 159
TELCO 37–9, 41, 50–3, 57
theology of community organizing 2, 3,
    4–5, 44, 59, 115, 116, 120–2,
    124–6, 127, 129, 131–2, 133–7,
    139–54, 158, 162–3, 168
Theology of Community Organizing
    Charter 169
third space 43, 46, 76–7, 87–9, 129,
    131–2, 136, 144–5, 151, 169
Tierney, Kathleen 68
Tikkun 78, 150
Tilly, Charles 67
Tocqueville, Alexis de 9, 29, 64, 89, 91

van Stekelenburg, Jacquelien 69–70
Vertovec, Steven 74, 97–8
Vincent, John 109, 148

Wallis, Jim 25, 64–5
Ward, Pete 132, 151
Warren, Mark 33, 37–8
West Cornel 40, 78, 109, 122, 125,
    130, 158–9
Wills Jane 34–5, 39, 50–2, 56, 81, 86
Woodhead, Linda 155
World Social Forum 79
Young, Iris Marion 77–8, 99, 130

Zakat 55